Disability and the Posthuman: Bodies, Technology, and Cultural Futures

REPRESENTATIONS: HEALTH, DISABILITY, CULTURE AND SOCIETY

Series Editor
Stuart Murray, University of Leeds

This series provides a ground-breaking and innovative selection of titles that showcase the newest interdisciplinary research on the cultural representations of health and disability in the contemporary social world. Bringing together both subjects and working methods from literary studies, film and cultural studies, medicine and sociology, 'Representations' is scholarly and accessible, addressed to researchers across a number of academic disciplines, and practitioners and members of the public with interests in issues of public health.

The key term in the series will be representations. Public interest in questions of health and disability has never been stronger, and as a consequence cultural forms across a range of media currently produce a never-ending stream of narratives and images that both reflect this interest and generate its forms. The crucial value of the series is that it brings the skilled study of cultural narratives and images to bear on such contemporary medical concerns. It offers and responds to new research paradigms that advance understanding at a scholarly level of the interaction between medicine, culture and society; it also has a strong commitment to public concerns surrounding such issues, and maintains a tone and point of address that seek to engage a general audience.

Other books in the series

Disability Studies and Spanish Culture: Films, Novels, the Comic and the Public Exhibition
Benjamin Fraser

Disabled Bodies in Early Modern Spanish Literature: Prostitutes, Aging Women and Saints
Encarnación Juárez-Almendros

Articulating Bodies: The Narrative Form of Disability and Illness in Victorian Fiction
Kylee-Anne Hingston

Disability, Literature, Genre: Representation and Affect in Contemporary Fiction
Ria Cheyne

Disability and the Posthuman

Bodies, Technology, and Cultural Futures

Stuart Murray

LIVERPOOL UNIVERSITY PRESS

First published 2020 by
Liverpool University Press
4 Cambridge Street
Liverpool
L69 7ZU

British Library Cataloguing-in-Publication data
A British Library CIP record is available

ISBN 978-1-78962-164-8 hb
ISBN 978-1-78962-165-5 pbk

Typeset by Carnegie Book Production, Lancaster
Printed and bound in Poland by BooksFactory.co.uk

"What might it mean to welcome the disability
to come? What might it mean to shape worlds capable
of welcoming the disability to come?"
Robert McRuer, *Crip Theory: Cultural Signs of Queerness and Disability*

"There is a little of everything, apparently,
in nature, and freaks are common".
Samuel Beckett, *Molloy*

"The prostheticized body is the rule,
not the exception".
David Mitchell and Sharon Snyder, *Narrative Prosthesis: Disability and the Dependencies of Discourse*

Contents

For Nate and Orla

Acknowledgements

This book took a long time to come together and meandered through many landscapes, both of work and home. I owe much to the patience and care of everyone at Liverpool University Press, particularly Alison Welsby and Jenny Howard, who guided me through the process of publication with real consideration and kindness.

The School of English and Faculty of Arts, Humanities and Cultures at the University of Leeds were generous in providing me with study leave to focus on writing and I am grateful to John Whale and Fiona Becket in particular for all their support as I battled to make a book possible amid the stormy chaos of modern university life. Projects that led, directly or indirectly, to the development of my ideas were funded by the University of Leeds, British Academy, Royal Society, Royal Academy of Engineering and the Wellcome Trust, and I thank all these organisations for their support. I am particularly grateful to the team involved with the Wellcome 'Augmenting the Body' project – Amelia Defalco, Luna Dolezal, Raymond Holt, Sophie Jones, Tony Prescott and Michael Szollosy – all of whom proved just how vital intellectual collaboration is in shaping thought.

I owe a huge debt of gratitude to my son Yann Steunou-Murray who, when he realised the subject of the book I was working on, developed a habit of wandering into my study to suggest texts or topics I might consider as part of the project. It was Yann who drew my attention to the difference between prose and film versions of the Tin Woodman, drew up instructional A4 documents about the history of manga or science fiction, and helped me negotiate the labyrinth that is the Marvel universe.

Many thanks to Becky Chambers, who kindly sent me an advance copy of the third novel in her Wayfarer series so I could incorporate it into my work on her writing. For comments and suggestions about texts, responses to speculative ideas, snatched corridor conversations, and the many other small things that prove vital in the writing of books, I want to thank Neil Badmington, Kirsty Bennett, David Bolt, Ria Cheyne, David Farrier, Dan Goodley, Katrina Longhurst, Donna McCormack, John McLeod, Andy Mudd, Graham Pullin, Margrit Shildrick, Susan Merrill Squier and Liam Wilby. Both Jane Macnaughton and Angela Woods continue to inspire me with their irresistible energy and commitment to thinking about health and the body. My iMac tells me that I listened to Beth Orton's 2002 album *Daybreaker* 613 times while writing, so she clearly bears some responsibility for the book's content.

Like everyone who works in Critical Disability Studies, I have been shaped by the substantial scholarship that has come before, and in relation to this study I want to acknowledge the work of Michael Davidson, Alison Kafer, Robert McRuer, David Mitchell, Tobin Siebers and Sharon Snyder in particular. Their writing often kickstarted ideas when my own thinking lay fallow.

Clare Barker, Amelia Defalco and Sophie Jones read draft sections of chapters and I am grateful for all their suggestions, as well as their support over many years, which made the book better in each instance. I am also indebted to the anonymous readers who reviewed the manuscript. My ideas were developed through talks given in Dublin, Durham, Geneva, Hong Kong, London, Manchester, Newcastle, Ottawa, Oxford, St. Catherines, Stockholm, Swansea, Taipei and York and I want to thank the organisers and audiences at these events.

I would like to thank Clare Brown, Laurence Brown, Jamie Greaves and Fran Kilmurray for their many acts of friendship and especially for not being academics. Special thanks to Marion and Tim McLoughlin, and love to my sister Alison Murray. Thanks and love to Meg, Yann, Lucas, Nate and Orla are, as always, ongoing and everlasting.

A previous draft of part of Chapter 3 was published as 'Disability and memory in posthuman(ist) narrative: reading prosthesis and amnesia in Hollywood's re-membering of the "war on terror"', *Parallax* 23(4) (2017): 439–452. Similarly, an early version of a section of Chapter 4 was published as 'Reading disability in a time of posthuman work: speed and embodiment in Joshua Ferris' *The Unnamed* and Michael Faber's *Under the Skin*', *Disability Studies Quarterly* 34(4) (2017). Thanks to both journals for the right to reproduce material.

Preface: In Search of the Emerald City: Lessons from the Tin Woodman

Near the beginning of L. Frank Baum's *The Wonderful Wizard of Oz* (1900), Dorothy and the Scarecrow, en route to the Emerald City, come across the Tin Woodman, a rusting metallic figure, forgotten and left in a wood. When oiled and liberated from his paralysis, the Woodman explains in an extended anecdote to his rescuers the circumstances behind his transformation from human forest labourer to a figure constructed entirely from tin:

> There was one of the Munchkin girls who was so beautiful that I soon grew to love her with all my heart. She, on her part, promised to marry me as soon as I could earn enough money to build a better house for her; so I set to work harder than ever. But the girl lived with an old woman who did not want her to marry anyone, for she was so lazy that she wished the girl to remain with her and do the cooking and the housework. So the old woman went to the Wicked Witch of the East, and promised her two sheep and a cow if she would prevent the marriage. Thereupon the Wicked Witch enchanted my axe, and when I was chopping away at my best one day, for I was anxious to get the new house and my wife as soon as possible, the axe slipped all at once and cut off my left leg.[1]

Aware of the crisis this posed him, "for I knew a one-legged man could not do very well as a woodchopper", the Woodman visits a tinsmith who manufactures a prosthetic limb to replace the missing leg. Infuriated by this, the Witch of the East continues to enchant the Woodman's axe and, one by one, he chops off his other leg, both arms and finally his head. Each time, however, the tinsmith makes him a more than adequate metal substitute and the relationship with the Munchkin girl remains unthreatened. The Woodman continues his story:

> I thought I had beaten the Wicked Witch then, and I worked harder than ever; but I little knew how cruel my enemy could be. She thought of a new way to kill my love for the beautiful Munchkin maiden, and made my axe slip again, so that it cut right through my body, splitting me into two halves. Once more the tinsmith came to my help and made me a body of tin, fastening my tin arms and legs and head to it, by means of joints, so that I could move around as well as ever. But, alas! I now had no heart, so that I lost all my love for the Munchkin girl, and did not care whether I married her or not.[2]

Finally, caught one day in a sudden rainstorm when out walking, the Woodman's joints rust and he is trapped until Dorothy and the Scarecrow find him. "It was a terrible thing to undergo", he observes, "but during the year I stood there I had time to think that the greatest loss I had known was the loss of my heart. When I was in love I was the happiest man on earth; but no one can love who has not a heart".[3]

The Woodman's protracted transfiguration then, however striking, is in fact a subplot to the main event outlined here, namely his failed romance with the woodland Munchkin girl and the dramatic machinations of the old woman and Witch of the East, intent on ruining their relationship. After all the change he undergoes, the Woodman is finally rendered unrecognisably disabled, and is no longer his former self, not because of his appearance but because ultimately the most central aspect of that self was his capacity to express and receive romantic love. As Dorothy and the Scarecrow find him, the Tin Woodman is devoid of humanity, his metal limbs only the most obvious outward manifestation of an absence in which the real missing element is reciprocated emotion. The complexity of such a state, that the Woodman is all too obviously artificial but that as readers we realise that his major deficiency is clearly *human*, means he can be seen within the terms of the automaton as outlined by Minsoo Kang in his history of that figure. For Kang, the automaton as read through the tradition of the European imagination, is both an object and an idea, a "conceptual chameleon" that promotes complex responses because "they all give the appearance of life [...] but are, to a substantial degree, made of matter that we normally think of as inert or dead".[4] The Tin Woodman's metal body is manifestly inert, particularly when he is seized with rust, but the novel makes clear that his feelings and desires make him recognisably human and 'life-like'. Nothing, it is made clear, can denote a lack of humanity more than not having a heart.

Baum's narrative voice is neutral and appears curiously distant and unconnected to his characters across the book as a whole, but this is deceptive. The details of the events in Oz are often brutal, and none more so than in the proliferation of body parts and the disabilities that ensue, which accompany this particular story of dismemberment. But the anecdote the Woodman recounts, like the accompanying stories of the novel's other central characters, is of course only the prelude to Baum's primary concern: the unwinding of the road to return and restoration in which the Woodman will realise that he has possessed all along that which he believed he lacked. The loss of the body, it emerges, does not mean the absence of those emotional characteristics with which physicality is associated, and the Woodman proves he has a full complement of humanity through his interaction with Dorothy, the Scarecrow, and the Cowardly Lion as their journey progresses.

I focus on the Tin Woodman's narrative because, for all that it is over a hundred years old, I take it ultimately to be a contemporary story. It is representative of a wide cultural belief, one especially prevalent through the twentieth century and into our own, that to be human is to have precisely the kind of embodied wholeness and the capacity to reflect on this cognitively that is manifested in Baum's Woodman; and that, in turn, such wholeness acts as a portal for other characteristics – rationality, autonomy, centred and coherent selfhood – that are equally understood to be central to the articulation of a human state of being. These values are not only philosophical; they are also aesthetic: the Tin Woodman's alignment between the automaton and humanism is notably different from the ways in which the figure was represented for much of the nineteenth century where, in stories such as E.T.A. Hoffman's 'The Sandman' (1816) or Edgar Allen Poe's 'The Man That Was Used Up' (1839), there is a clear sense of terror and the macabre in the revelation (both stories work to reveal characters as automatons) that a human figure is not as he or she seems. But this kind of dread is missing in Baum's story, where the subtext about 'having a heart' speaks more to an idea of integrated wholeness (and the problems attaining it) than a notion of horror that the human body might, in fact, be mechanical. It was not just developments in technology that marked the beginning of the twentieth century as a new era in which automatons were reconfigured in cultural narratives; changes in the perception of the body, and the emotions that it contained, equally altered the manner in which the human/non-human boundary was understood and represented.

The Tin Woodman figuratively reassembles himself, both physically and emotionally, as *The Wonderful Wizard of Oz* progresses: if to be dispersed is to be lost, frozen (as he is when he is found) in time and place and unable to contribute to human life, then to be whole is to have a heart (and vice versa); it is to be mobile and participatory, to be on the yellow brick road travelling to the Emerald City and an understanding of the individual and social self. The Emerald City itself is, of course, not what it seems. The Wizard, a supposedly benign dictator, provides an illusion of control given his use of smoke and mirrors to conjure up expressions of power. Even this status as fake, however, serves what is ultimately a humanist purpose, throwing the responsibility of correction back on to the voyagers themselves. The subsequent realisation that each contains the necessary characteristics 'within' underscores human potential read in terms of wholeness. Though the Wizard, as he admits, is "not much of a magician", the question of an adequate magic is not a problem, for the real 'wonderful' is safely inside each of us, awaiting discovery.[5]

The Tin Woodman's story is a powerful narrative of journey, overcoming and achievement, and has had a considerable afterlife. It manifests itself as a recognisable tale in different guises in contemporary times: multiple Oz novels – some sanctioned by the writer's estate, others less orthodox – have been written following Baum's death in 1919; while in film the overall Oz narrative is rehearsed most famously in the 1939 MGM version directed by Victor Fleming, but also through the prism of race in *The Wiz* (1978) and Walter Murch's darker fantasy, Disney-produced, *Return to Oz* (1985).[6] Specific references to the Woodman's narrative, however, are found in texts as diverse as Brandon McCormick's short 2010 sentimental melodrama, *Heartless: The Story of the Tin Man*, Matthew Perkins' 2013 low-budget, disability-led comedy feature *The Little Tin Man*, and Chris Wedge's and Carlos Saldanha's 2005 animated feature *Robots*, where the character makes a witty cameo at the end of a Baum-inspired narrative of restoration and triumph. In addition, Jon Favreau's *Iron Man* (2008), one of the foundational texts in the explosion of comic-derived superhero films that has marked twenty-first-century Hollywood production and Marvel Studio's first self-produced feature, makes a clear reference to Baum's narrative in the artificial heart and technologically enhanced exoskeleton used by Tony Stark (Robert Downey Jr). In these texts and others, the Tin Woodman signifies his presence, over 100 years since his first appearance.[7] Through this time, he carries the complex ideas of embodiment identified above, as well as the social consequences of this. The lessons of heart and home have powerful resonances and it appears clear that the Emerald City is still a destination many wish to reach.[8]

In what follows, however, I want to ask explicitly *how* the logic and values of Baum's story might still pertain in a specifically contemporary digital age, one in which the physical and the cognitive are not only no longer bound by the ideas of the body that predominated when Baum wrote and during the long period that followed as his story achieved worldwide recognition, but are subject to ever more sophisticated technological developments that advance year upon year. For all that the character features and overcoming narratives that dominate *The Wonderful Wizard of Oz* are still highly visible for example, might we be in a time when our conception of humanity means we need to respond to new stories of what 'wholeness' might mean? Or new ways in which the structures of such a concept might be critiqued? In particular, I want to ask how considerations of disability alter the parameters of such a discussion. Even though the Tin Woodman's story is obviously a disability narrative, for example, with all those amputations and prosthetic limbs, my sense is that reactions to it would not necessarily *immediately* see it such: the possibility of other non-disability readings appear to crowd in before the basic fact of the Woodman's embodiment is registered, and we might ask why that is the case. The answer is, of course, that the metaphors grafted onto disability are still so persuasive that it seems natural to look through a story of dismemberment and ask what it is *really* about; the experience of missing limbs or use of prostheses somehow seeming to naturally signify some other, seemingly more vital, set of concerns. While it can be argued that the fabular and non-realist nature of Baum's text might make such a metaphorical reading seem the most legitimate one, this is only the case if 'legitimate' is seen in terms of notions of wholeness, that fantasy privileges certain forms of coherence, or disability only possesses status and textual power when represented through realist modes. Thought of in such frames, *The Wonderful Wizard of Oz* is only one in a long list of books in which disability is habitually ignored even when it is central to the narrative events being described.[9]

This book asks where ideas of humanity, humanism, wholeness, body and mind might reside when we bring them into dialogue with disability and the various questions of technology, augmentation and the future that cluster around the figure and idea of the posthuman. Working within a frame in which disability is understood to mean difference and not deficit, I want to see *how* that difference is mobilised in the contemporary moment, with its proliferation of technological advancements and the mix of excitement and fear this produces. Looking back to Robert McRuer's epigraph for this book, I want to ask what particular signs of disability might be "to come" when we investigate the stories that cluster around the body and its functions within a technologised future. People with disabilities face (as fantasy images if not literally) what must at times seem like a bewildering range of potential assistive tools and skills, from smart prostheses, exoskeletons, care companions and inclusive design to pharmacological interventions and neurological enhancements. All these reconfigure the spaces in which disabled people experience their lives, whether that is the space of the physical body itself or the environments it inhabits. This new sense of space challenges humanist notions of centred and individualised wholeness, with their associated assertions of rationality and control. In place of such configurations, in a technological and digital age it is more appropriate, I suggest, to look towards the criss-crossing networks, assemblages and collection of multiple possible intersected locations and suggested selves that increasingly define the contemporary moment. It is of course true that networks of difference have always defined social and cultural spaces, particularly in the modern era. Whether through the mobility of capital or the movement of peoples, trajectories of modernity have relied upon webs of affiliation, constantly updated, to write their complex patterns of presence. But I suspect that the assertion that these have accelerated almost beyond recognition, especially in terms of technological change, in this century would not encounter much resistance. And it is this late-modern moment that I want to read as a time (and space) of posthumanism, where the multiple materials of networked cultural processes constitute such profound change that ideas of identity, selfhood and community are being transformed at an extraordinary speed.

The subjects of this study are complex, combining overlapping and intersecting fluidities in attempts to read subjects, aesthetics and discursive formations. I hope, however, that my arguments will be clear. They are that there are exciting, productive possibilities and subversive potentials in the interactions between disability and posthumanism if we read them as generating sustainable yet radical spaces. Such mobilisations push back against those restrictive humanisms that articulate conformist and restrictive powers of containment and aid the practice of discrimination and prejudice. This radical position is more than a rejection of humanism, however; it is also one of new connections and methods of expression, progressive outlines of the place of people in an ever-more technologised future. These connections include ideas not only about the circuits that articulate bodies, affect, temporalities and associated disability presences, but also the modes through which these are imagined, represented, deployed, entangled and enacted within definitional boundaries. It is important (if challenging) to avoid the repetition of existing discourses surrounding the embodiment and critical readings of disabled bodies, especially as situated in related contexts of gender, race and sexuality; equally, it is imperative not to pursue critical thought that proclaims some bodies superior to others because of aggrandised claims about their capacity to be read. The transgressive and resistant technologised disabled body that emerges within the space of posthumanist disability can be an indicator of substantive change (aesthetic, social, political) and not simply the perpetrator of new hierarchies. If at times the future seems impossibly complex, full of global dangers and beyond our capacity to control or even name, the idea of bodies and their relationships with selfhood and community illuminated by this intersectional space provides part of a language of understanding that can challenge acquired modes of thinking as it helps in navigating troubled times.

Both disability and posthumanism can be at times conservative categories, limiting rather than amplifying, but each also contains powerful reverberations – assertive, playful, unsettling, artistic, technical, personal and communal – that are critical and creative. While this book will analyse problematic moments of ignorance and dismissal, it is written in a spirit of a possible (and desired) better future, an associated commitment to change, and a firm belief in the power of the imagination. It is, at heart (to borrow a metaphor), an optimistic study, if not always a study of optimism. My sense of the relationship between disability and the posthuman is not that one somehow explains the other, nor that there is any kind of seamless fit between the two. But putting the two in dialogue results in a productive meeting in which multiple learning spaces are created, and my aim is to map and explore these. Such an exploration is itself maybe a yellow brick road, full of dangers along the way no doubt and suspicious of any simple idea of 'home', but reclaimable as a new type of journey, tin limbs and all.

Notes

1 L. Frank Baum, *The Wonderful Wizard of Oz* (London: Penguin, 1995), p. 38.
2 Baum, *The Wonderful Wizard of Oz*, pp. 38–39.
3 Baum, *The Wonderful Wizard of Oz*, p. 39.

4 Minsoo Kang, *Sublime Dreams of Living Machines: The Automaton in the European Imagination* (Cambridge, MA and London: Harvard University Press, 2011), pp. 5 and 19.
5 Baum, *The Wonderful Wizard of Oz*, p. 114.
6 In 2018, Italian researchers used data obtained from applying four centrality indexes to the IMDb (Internet Movie Database) to establish a rankings list for the greatest 'milestone' films in the history of cinema. The 1939 production of *The Wizard of Oz* emerged at no. 1, as the most influential film in the study (the authors noted that using the IMDb meant that the results obtained prioritised features made in Europe and the US). See Livio Bioglio and Ruggero G. Pensa, 'Identification of key films and personalities in the history of cinema from a Western perspective', *Applied Network Science* 3, no. 50 (2018): https://doi.org/10.1007/s41109-018-0105-0.
7 It is interesting to note in Martin Flanagan, Mike McKenny and Andy Livingston's 2016 study *The Marvel Studios Phenomenon: Inside a Transmedia Universe* that part of Marvel's strategy as it developed its own studio platform was to bring "old and new Hollywood logics together". Certainly, *Iron Man*'s relationship with the Tin Woodman can be read within such a term. *The Marvel Studios Phenomenon: Inside a Transmedia Universe* (New York and London: Bloomsbury, 2016), p. 79.
8 Nathan Filer observes in his 2019 study *The Heartland: Finding and Losing Schizophrenia*, that schizophrenia, arguably the most widely known mental illness condition, came "to be seen as the very heartland of psychiatry; the condition that defines the discipline" as it developed across the twentieth century. That a cognitive condition that is, for some, the very essence of 'madness' can be considered in terms of metaphors of the heart displays just how powerful it is as a term that organises meaning. *The Heartland: Finding and Losing Schizophrenia* (London: Faber & Faber, 2019), p. 9.
9 It is worth noting that disability exists across the Oz books more widely than I have the space to discuss here. In Munchkinland, of course, a 'non-normative' stature *is* in fact the norm, with accompanying society and built environment developed as a consequence of the Munchkin's physical stature, while a number of the other texts feature examples of prosthesis and other disability states. In the 1907 *Ozma of* Oz, there is a classic automaton figure, Tik-Tok, who is mechanical and made out of copper and who needs to be wound with a key. In *The Patchwork Girl of Oz* (1913), the titular character, Scraps, is a 'patchwork' figure who, like the Woodman, is another example of an 'assembled' character. Baum's Patchwork Girl was reworked in Shelley Jackson's 1995 hypertext *Patchwork Girl* (discussed in the notes in the following chapter). Some issues of disability in Baum's first Oz novel are explored in relation to their status as children's literature in Joshua R. Eyler's article 'Disability and prosthesis in L. Frank Baum's *The Wonderful Wizard of Oz*', *Children's Literature Association Quarterly* 38, no. 3 (2013), pp. 319–334.

Introduction: Disabling the Human

What to do with the body?

The Tin Woodman's narratives across L. Frank Baum's Oz books mobilise a core set of humanist values, affirming ideas of heart and home and the normativity of the coherent body and self. But I am claiming that they also anticipate a possible posthuman future and, in doing so, am aware that this is an assertion that requires justification. I will discuss in detail the various debates surrounding the interaction between posthumanism and disability in the next chapter but want to use this introduction to outline the central elements of the connection. Both posthumanism and humanism are notoriously slippery concepts that have different – at times contradictory – meanings in different spaces; from philosophy to global flows of capital, and from political economy to discourse of rights. In using them I have to be alert to the lack of consensus that surrounds them and not to collapse their multiplicities into simplistic single meanings. Likewise, disability cannot be read as a uniform category. As numerous scholars have shown, it also takes multiple (often reductive) forms, including medical categorisation, biocertification and other government/state forms of definition, public perception and the soft power of the media, and processes of individual identity and claim. Ellen Samuels observes shrewdly: "The overwhelming fantasy of modern disability identification is that disability is a knowable, obvious and unchanging category. Such a fantasy permeates all levels of discourse regarding disabled bodies and minds, even as it is repeatedly and routinely disproved by the actual realities of those bodies' and minds' fluctuating abilities".[1] With this in mind, it is clearly impossible to create any distinct or stable signage marked 'disability' that can speak to this spectrum of difference.

In part, it is with these instabilities in mind that I will go on to argue for the value of the processes at work in critical disability and posthumanist methodologies, forms of analysis where it is precisely a critique of wholeness and coherence, a showcase of the unstable, that animates approaches to their subjects. There is a necessity for flexible vocabularies when speaking on topics that are in constant motion and change, and for modes of enquiry that can match the complex intersections inherent in the formations disability and posthumanism take. Equally, bringing together two well-established fields that have their own critical heritages and subject areas has its own set of challenges. Discussions of embodiment and technology, for example (the topic that will form the disability focus of this book), are in no way confined to questions of disability and the body and, even then, they have different emphases viewed through a disability or posthumanist lens. Both optics might display that the body becomes necessarily rethought as a consequence, but there are still substantial differences. As I will show, however, the opportunities for a constructive dialogue between critical disability and posthumanist approaches offer real potential for better understanding the relations between emerging technologies and disability lives, even if there is a wariness within each subject area about the workings of the other. In this study I want to explore the possibility that the tangled uncertainties surrounding technologies of the body can yet produce tangible outcomes in the lives of those with disabilities.

For Pramod Nayar, one of the central critical interventions of critical posthumanist thinking is that it revises and challenges the assumptions of humanism. He expands on this through a precise outline of 'human' and 'humanism':

> The human is traditionally taken to be a subject (one who is conscious of his/her *self*) marked by rational thinking/intelligence, who is able to plot his/her own course of action depending on his/her needs, desires and wishes, and, as a result of his/her actions, produces history. The human has traditionally been treated as male and universal. It is always treated in the singular (*the* human) and as a set of features or conditions: rationality, authority, authority, autonomy and agency.[2]

Humanism, he continues, "is the study of this individual subject and the composite features we now recognise as the human". He goes on:

> It treats the human subject as the centre of the world, which is influenced by the human's thoughts and actions. The freedom of the individual to pursue his choice is treated as central to the human subject. The human's awareness of his self – to recognise himself for what he is – or self-consciousness is also treated as a sign of being human [...] Morality, ethics, and responsibility in the modern era (roughly post-1600) all emerge from this view of the autonomous, self-conscious, coherent and self-determining human. The essence of the human lies in the rational mind, or soul – which is entirely distinct from the body. Change and improvement therefore are deemed to be possible through this power of the rational mind.[3]

Nayar's commentary is sweeping and objections could be raised to a perceived lack of subtlety in his characterisation here. But he writes deliberately to cover a wide critical field and overall his analysis catches the extraordinary force humanism exerts. In his concise study of humanism, Tony Davies agrees with Nayar's assessment regarding the ideological power and reach of this concept of the human: "All Humanisms, until now, have been imperial", he observes, adding: "They speak of the human in the accents and the interests of a class, a sex, a race, a genome. Their embrace suffocates those whom it does not ignore".[4] Humanism has framed the practice of change, both individually and social, over much of past centuries; and its stress on the idea of the coherent and autonomous individual of course has no place for disability. As we have already seen with the Tin Woodman's narrative in the Preface and as Nayar makes clear, humanism's championing of the rational mind means that the body is frequently mistrusted and viewed with disquiet. The body with *disabilities* then, is even more to be feared within classic configurations of 'the human'.

One of the aims of this book is to explore the multiple and various ways that posthumanism challenges humanism's logic of control and capability. For Nayar, posthumanism is especially articulate in the ways in which humans, non-human animals and machines "are now more or less seamlessly articulated, mutually dependent and co-evolving". As a result, "critical posthumanism posits the non-unitary subject" in place of the centred figure of the human that forms the basis of humanism. The result, Nayar argues, is "a more inclusive and therefore ethical understanding of life".[5] Much of what follows in this study will look at these ideas of connections and co-dependencies, and the arguments made for greater inclusivity and better ethics. Central to many posthumanist methods is a rereading of the body seen in terms of the non-unitary self, where the body is no longer sovereign but rather implicated in a host of relationships across boundaries. It is precisely here that humanism's profound fear of the body with disabilities turns into the potential appreciation of the varieties of embodiment that disability presents, both in terms of the human body itself and its interactions with technology. Seeing bodies within networks and connections, and operating across limits, opens up possibilities of understanding subjectivities of all kinds in a space beyond humanism, but allows for an especially profitable focus on those bodies that speak of and to disabilities and their difference.

It is worth stating straight away that while my reading of posthumanism identifies it as inhabiting multiple forms across varied landscapes, I believe that it contains at its core an idea of 'beyond' and 'adaptation' that characterises its extension of, and challenges to, the boundaries of a humanist conception of the subject. Hence the subtitle of this book is (I hope) precise in reading the present in terms of an orientation towards the future, not least because the future is a vital space for disability rights movements as they continue the struggle for services, equality and the affirmation of lives lived with disabilities. In my thinking, then, 'the posthuman', as varied as it is, is predominantly what it sounds like; it is what might come next, after, beyond or outside the human, a set of positions that, in suggesting a trajectory, has obvious appeal for anyone interested in story and narrative, for all that these are not straightforward. I am sympathetic to the idea that posthumanism can be mobilised primarily as a form of *critique*, as one of a number of critical anti-humanisms that seek to de-centre various notions of wholeness. Indeed, my own work functions in this way to a degree, reading the posthuman and its interaction with disability through texts ranged across differing time periods for example (though my focus is very much on the contemporary). There is a considerable body of work that reads posthumanist figures and contexts through cultural history and I am aware that, in starting with a concentration on Baum's story, I am myself reaching back in time.[6] But as I argued in the Preface, I am drawn to the phenomenon as a forward-facing set of moments and practices, and my analysis of the Tin Woodman is not simply the use of posthumanism as a critical tool to unpack an older text; it is rather a process that tries to ask how that text looks forward to outline ideas that are *of the present*, ultimately to ask how we think *now* about bodies, hearts, technology, wholeness and disabled difference. As we shall see, while the claims of posthumanism often appear abstract and vast, assessing the possibilities of grounded future worlds in which they might come to pass is not just exciting, but essential when dynamics of disability are to be considered.

That this is not a simple process goes without saying. Viewing representations of technologised bodies in such a way requires strategies of reading and interpretation that can deal with the slippery complexities of what is entailed. I will discuss, for example, how it is an error to make simplistic assumptions about what constitutes 'technology' and that its relationship with disability embodiment is necessarily progressive, or that it presents an easy fit with definitions of posthumanism itself.[7] But I hope to show that disability studies scholars can work with ideas central to posthumanism, such as replacement and reformatting, adaptation, augmentation and extension, along with the reconfiguration of bodies and their stories that these entail. In his story, the Woodman is certainly adapted, and in ways that are not of his choosing. His physical self is changed beyond recognition, a transformation in keeping with those posthumanist ideas in which the body is superseded by some alternative form, usually one derived from technology. But if the question that then occupies much posthumanist scholarship is whether such a transformation necessarily entails a reconfiguration of all aspects of humanity – including wider questions of ontology, ethics, history and society – Baum's books make it clear that this is not the case with his character. The Woodman's humanity, like those of others in Oz, is in fact brought *more* into focus by the way in which he is changed; his humanism and capacity to act as a self-knowing, rational self are enhanced even as his body loses the skin, bone and tissue that constituted his previous physical self. Here, a technologised transfiguration seemingly fails to speak of any seminal change.

What happens, however, when we refuse the invitation to read the Tin Woodman's story in terms of a redressed absence and, rather than see him in the classic tradition of the automaton or as an (ultimately) emblematic figure of successfully embodied humanness, decide to retain the posthuman possibilities and read him as a cyborg or biohybrid, a *meeting* of material body and technological adaptation?[8] What if we feel that the Woodman is enhanced, rather than diminished, by the transformation he undergoes? To choose one specific factor: how should we read the (presumably positive) fact that he appears to feel no pain at any point in his dismemberment, despite the argument that the experience of pain is central to the human sense of a subjective self?[9] And how might we then expand upon the processes he undergoes, in order to work up ideas of disabled posthumanist subjectivities that articulate new ideas of biopolitics, health, presence or justice? As seen in his own testimony, there is plenty of textual evidence to suggest that the Woodman does not consider his injuries to be traumatic; indeed, there is a pragmatism and ordinariness to the way in which he comes to adapt to his new form. I will stress ideas of the ordinary and the everyday in what follows, as I see them as vital and positive categories for the expression of disability experiences; and though they might appear somewhat mundane when juxtaposed with the excitement that surrounds the posthuman, where discussions of A.I., genetic enhancement and aliens often seem to attract attention for example, I will seek to show how a conception of everyday disability might in fact provide the possibility of grounding posthumanist arguments, turning abstract potential into ordinary, daily activity. This book will return to issues of bodies (and pain), of transformation and memory, of economies (textual and otherwise) and environments, and of the self as I follow the questions the Woodman's story necessarily poses.

The valorising of the Tin Woodman's metal body is continued in his characterisation through the books Baum wrote about Oz following his first, spectacular, bestseller. Aware of the market his story had created, Baum wrote 16 more Oz books, both novels and short stories, before his death in 1919, a powerful franchise that was hugely successful in keeping his imagined land in the public eye.[10] The core characters from the first Oz novel each became the subject of their own tale, while numerous others were invented. *The Tin Woodman of Oz* was one of the last of the series, published in 1918 just before Baum's death. Its opening sees the Tin Woodman as now an emperor – "the Emperor of the Winkies" – who, as the story's first line informs us, "sat on his glittering tin throne in the handsome tin hall of his splendid tin castle in the Winkie Country of the Land of Oz". The Woodman's position and standing, it is made clear, are denoted by the sheer abundance of tin that fills every space in the castle: the corridors are "all lined with ornamental tin" while there are "stately tin archways" and "tin rooms all set with tin furniture"; food appears on a "tin tray", which is "set upon a tin table" with a "tin chair" next to it; the castle's gardens have "tin fountains and beds of curious tin flowers"; and, in an extension of the process by which the natural is usurped by the manufactured, "tin birds perched upon the branches of tin trees and sang songs that sounded like the notes of tin whistles".[11] Tin is a signifier of power and craftmanship, but its proliferation here should also be seen as a legitimating of the Woodman's posthumanist subjectivity. Not only are his prostheses not to be hidden or disowned, the material from which they are made is celebrated throughout the land over which he rules. Artificial here is the new (and beautiful) real.

The scene setting at the start of the novel stresses the value of metal-as-replacement, the technologised non-human standing in for

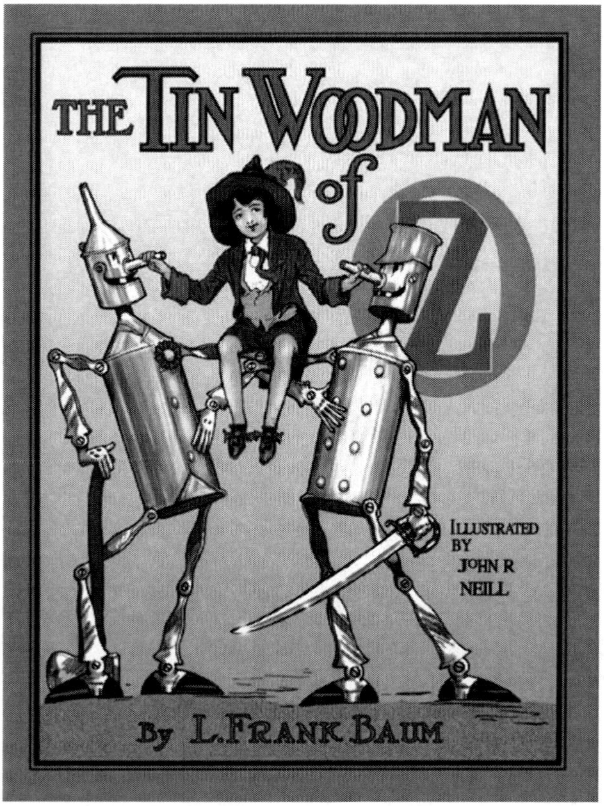

The Tin Woodman of Oz (1918)

a differing conception of 'the whole', and I will develop a number of these ideas about design, engineering and embodiment in the second chapter of this study. But it is in the narrative that follows the opening of *The Tin Woodman of Oz* that we gain the fullest sense of the radical way in which Baum's text can be read to present a contested version of embodiment. The story overall takes the form of a recognisable quest, with the Woodman embarking on a journey to find the Munchkin girl (now given a name: Nimmie Amee), but it is the discussion of love and the specifics of the Woodman's replacement heart that produce the major changes to the novel's transformation narrative. In *The Wonderful Wizard of Oz,* the Woodman notes that his main reason to journey to Oz was to gain a heart and then "go back to the Munchkin maiden and marry her";[12] in the later novel we learn that that even though the meeting with the Wizard in the Emerald City was successful, the Woodman's problem was not alleviated: "the Wizard's stock of hearts was low, and he gave me a Kind Heart instead of a Loving Heart, so that I could not love Nimmie Amee any more than I did when I was heartless".[13] Though told that he had all along the qualities of heart he thought the lacked, it transpires the Woodman received the wrong *type* of heart, a mistake of embodiment and not emotion.

In the second novel, the loveless Woodman frequently articulates a clear preference for the prosthetic self over its human equivalent; "we are", the Woodman notes of the Scarecrow and himself, "somewhat superior to people made in the common way".[14] Indeed, on a very basic level this is conveyed by the Woodman's constant reference to his former corporeal body as mere "meat", which came with all sorts of complications that no longer exist now he is in tin form. There are no difficulties concerning what to wear now he is made of metal, for example, or keeping warm, and when travelling he no longer has to stop and rest at night, or eat, as he is never hungry.[15] In Oz, biomedical complexities and all the notions of a fragile or vulnerable humanity that stem from them appear easy enough to shrug off, and the difference disability brings poses no barriers to individual advancement or fulfilment (and, indeed, might not even be consider disabling as such). And yet it would be wrong to say that overall this constitutes an argument within the novel for any kind of posthumanist sensibility in which human attributes are superseded. The Woodman's rejection of his body as 'meat', for example, is evidence of a heritage of Cartesian thought in which, as Sherryl Vint terms it in her study of science and speculative fiction, "one *is* the mind, effortlessly moving beyond the limitations of the human body".[16] In terms of reading the Cartesian mind/body division in the Tin Woodman, it is clear that, for all that men might be made of tin (or indeed straw), his trajectory across the novels asserts that, ultimately, core human values predominate. Whether it is love, friendship, compassion, fidelity, rationality or truth, humanist concerns drive his actions.

Preferring messiness

For this study, however, the lesson that emerges from a reading of the Tin Woodman is not the clarity of his journey and purpose but rather an apprehension of the *tensions* that clearly exist between his artificial embodiment and the humanism his character espouses and attains. The preference for the tin prostheses and the ease with which they are adapted in his new world sit uneasily with the Tin Woodman's rejection of the corporeality of his biological body, and any reading of either of these possible embodiments never reduces the power that 'heart' or 'home' play in Oz; it is always clear which values are the most important. In the same way that Dorothy's clearly gendered narrative has to be understood with reference *both* to her empowerment as an individual determined to secure her own future *and* in relation to her as a young girl straining to put back together the wholesome, and normative, family unit, the Woodman's prosthetic self is the (constructed) body through which he strives to locate a recognisable humanist world in which he might live. What emerges, then, is a story in which the non-human proliferates in any number of guises that are central to plot development, narrative coherence and overall entertainment, but where ultimately a working idea of heteronormative, rationalist and ableist humanity predominates. In the chapters that follow, this study will highlight this story structure time and again, whether in conversations surrounding the design and engineering of prostheses, issues of embodiment in Hollywood films about the war on terror, or arguments concerning technology and its relationship with work and employment. The Emerald City may be one version of what might lie somewhere over the rainbow (to borrow from the 1939 film version of Oz) when narratives seek the 'beyond' of the human ideal but, as far as disability is concerned, such locations often turn out to be green zones of ableism, fortified spaces of exclusion.

In the remainder of this book, these kinds of messy and contradictory representations will be found to be common. It appears difficult not to want to 'have a heart' in a manner that stresses an association between emotions and ideas of a core humanity, while conversely technological innovation that emphasises artificiality possesses the capacity to seduce us all. As far as disability is concerned, 'heart' can suggest not only biological function, but also compassion and patronising sentiment, while technology can be life-saving, that which is denied to disability communities that lack the resources to access it, or an unwelcome complexity in a life that does not require it.[17] As this study proceeds, it will be necessary to understand that the narrative and ethical conundrums and confusions that mark out these positions are a standard part of the fabric of representation and deployment. Technology, for example, needs to be understood as a set of discourses and manifestations that can be threatening to or unwanted by disability communities. Long-standing debates over the adoption of cochlear implants or prosthetic limbs reveal a deeply rooted ambivalence surrounding the 'value' of technological interventions in disability lives. For many, disabled bodies in and of themselves are whole and sufficient: Tobin Siebers has written of the "potentially meaningful materiality" of such bodies, which can provide "a source of embodied revelation"; while Rosemarie Garland-Thomson has developed a similar idea of 'disability gain', where the disability life *lived as is* provides not only a full individual existence but also examples of subjectivity that have resonance in the contemplation of all lived experience.[18] The exploration of technology in the chapters that follow will carry these positions forward and will not be swayed by posthumanist assertions that it can only be considered progressive when thought of as human enhancement. As we shall see, the technological augmentation of the non-disabled body (in military contexts for example) can function to stress fragility and vulnerability in ways that create complex equations around embodied precariousness.

The challenge is, then, for an engaged criticism to attempt to tease out the variants and consequences of disabled posthumanism/posthumanist disability. In outlining the ways in which I aim to do this, my choice of texts and approaches requires explanation and justification, as does the structuring of the book as a whole. As a core concern, I have sought out textual moments where representations and deployments of disability and of the posthuman (as I understand those terms) combine and inform one another. This is not as straightforward as it might seem: are all depictions of non-human bodies or every character who manifests physical or cognitive difference in science or speculative fiction, for example, posthumanist or disabled? The answer to this question must be 'no' and I am wary that sweeping claims about how 'different' bodies might *always* constitute disability states run a clear risk of making critical perspectives featureless. To take a set of examples from science fiction: the work of Octavia Butler (especially the *Xenogensis* trilogy [1987–1989]) has proved seminal to an emerging literary/cultural/disability strand of posthumanist criticism because of its representation of co-evolution, modified biology and species blurring, among other topics; but while the multiple robots that feature in the stories of Isaac Asimov also signal complex conceptions of bodies, technological developments and non-human futures, these features are not automatically evidence of disability presence.[19] Likewise, the variety of aliens that populate Butler's writing often inscribe highly subtle ideas of race through the ways in which they are removed from any sense of biological origins and embodied norms; but in Iain M. Banks' science fiction, where the proliferation of species also indicates a literal sense of a post/beyond human, alien status does not act as a metaphor for this kind of posthuman*ist* racial difference. Asimov and Banks' writings do not constitute de facto disability or posthumanist narratives simply because they contain representations of technology or bodies that appear to differ so much from those found in the present. Even while the difference represented in their works might serve to highlight for readers a contemporary plurality of states of embodiment, disability is not somehow to be found *inherently* in such depictions. Ideas of inherence are unproductive in reading either disability or posthumanism, where it is rather formations of the multiple and contradictory that better tell of the various states that the terms manifest, and aesthetic and intellectual conceptions of the subject matter that drive what alternative bodies and cultures/societies mean. An advanced robot or alien body can be the site of conservative ableism (this is in fact true of many of Asimov's stories) as much as it might, as in Butler, signify radical posthumanist or disability possibilities.[20]

My selection, therefore, necessarily involves a teasing out of depictions and deployments of bodies, textual contexts and subject matters that suggest the value of such critical readings and exemplify the arguments the book wishes to make. I have chosen to focus on contemporary texts, mainly made in the last 15 years, because it is these narratives that are most suggestive of the intersections of bodies and technologies in ways that *do* portray a critical disability/poshumanist nexus. It is, however, worth again stressing the messy and often contradictory nature of these portrayals. So, for example, the films I analyse in Chapter 3 view the wars in Iraq and Afghanistan through optics in which the uneasy relationship between technology and the body produces specific disability stories about the present. The intersections, however, are also true of speculative and science fiction, such as the work of Becky Chambers that ends Chapter 2's investigation of engineering, disability and gender. In Chambers' novels, imagined futures are spaces in which bodies and technology come together in suggestive possibilities of agency and community. There is no one way in which disability and posthumanist stories take form and the material in this study operates as a series of encounters with the fictions in all their variety.[21]

Disability present and futures

The topics on which the book focuses across its chapters – respectively, contemporary cultural theory and aesthetics, design/engineering and gender, the visualisation of prosthetic technologies in the representation of war and conflict, and depictions of work, time and sleep – illustrate the subjects in which I found the most sophisticated narratives of disability in a posthumanist present. The introduction to each chapter will outline why this is the case, but the focus deserve to be glossed here and I hope that it indicates a matrix in which a critical disability story might be told. Work, prosthetics and cultural theory are familiar spaces where disability and technology are discussed and analysed, though I aim to do so in new ways, while engineering and representations of war are possibly new areas to explore. For each topic I sought out texts that have, for the most part, received little critical attention. In part, this is because the books, films and events I analyse have been published, screened or happened very recently; but it is also because I want to build on and extend scholarship that already exists. Critical disability studies has an exciting momentum and real sense of engaged commitment to the issues of the present, and I want this book to be part of that process.

Chapter 1 concentrates on recent theoretical writings on disability and posthumanism because these provide a frame for the study as a whole. It also explores the intellectual spaces in which the subjects take shape and moves to a discussion of how these come together in select science fiction films. Disability studies and critical posthumanism have much in common: a critique of humanist norms; a recognition of complex embodiment; and a commitment to intersectionality and inclusive practice among them. But they also harbour suspicions of one another. For the most part, disability studies has argued for a need to ground theoretical reflection in an understanding of the lived experience of people with disabilities, while much scholarship on posthumanism is wary of the identity politics that might result from such politics of location. Posthumanism outlines sophisticated interactions between bodies and technology and the networks these produce, but disability theorists frequently critique this as a set of abstract processes that refuse to engage with the material consequences of such connections. Certainly, as I will argue, scholarship on posthumanism has had little to say about disabled bodies until very recently. The most important divergence between the two subject areas comes in arguments surrounding transhumanism. Transhumanist assertions that the application of future technology will allow for bodily and neurological enhancement, and the 'improvement' of humans as a result, are met with hostility by many with disabilities who see in them suggestions that disability is a condition that might, and indeed should, be eradicated in a science-led drive towards 'perfection'. The chapter will explore these and other debates, especially as they form around cultural representations and the ways stories are told about the bodies and technologies of the future.

In Chapter 2, I look at the ways technologised bodies are designed and engineered, and especially how these processes are gendered.

Cultural theory and critical disability studies have much to say about how bodies are produced in narratives and through social discourses, but rarely do so through any interaction with the engineering practice through which, in a literal way, such production take place. The Tin Woodman's body is, of course, engineered, but in what I claim is a typical silence this work is an aspect of the Oz books that passes almost totally without comment. The chapter argues that it is vital to understand the logic and techniques of design and engineering given that many disability experiences are produced through the intersection between body and technology. Such an intersection is also a prime space in which posthumanism explores the possibility of cyborg subjectivities, the meeting of 'man and machine' that provides contemporary culture's excitement about technologies of the future. It is here, we are often told, that 'science fiction becomes reality' and the chapter analyses science and speculative fiction and film in which artificial, robotic and cyborg bodies are designed and produced, outlining how this production needs to be understood through a disability lens. There are, of course, no reasons why robots or cyborgs need a gender, but as the ubiquity of the 'man and machine' comment above indicates, it is frequently the case that these production processes are saturated with claims about gender. The chapter will focus on texts where women are engineered, but also where they undertake the engineering. There is a long heritage of assumptions about 'natural' links between engineering science and male authority, and I am interested in the ways in which disability readings can align with feminist and posthumanist critique to unpack such presumptions. The chapter also asserts that a disability-inflected conception of female engineering animates contemporary cultural production, highlighting the ideas of subject and community this produces.

Chapter 3 focuses specifically on film and visualising depictions of the connections between disability and posthumanism as they are manifest in a set of contemporary narratives about war and conflict. The development of military weaponry is a high-profile space in which the interaction between human and non-human technology takes place, particularly given the extraordinary amounts of funding available to state defence institutions. Body armour, vehicles, ordnance, drones and other examples of military technology create multiple instances of posthumanist assemblage, and I use a broad conception of prosthetics to read these intersections, claiming that their articulations of embodiment are disability stories even as they appear to be narratives of hyperability, scientific strength and male authority. The chapter juxtaposes a series of Hollywood features exploring the wars in Iraq and Afghanistan with films made in Iraq and Iran that narrate the conflict from alternative points of view, ones that often lack the kinds of sophisticated technology that so marks American storytelling. In each, the power of the visual, of *seeing* disabled bodies, is paramount. Theorising about technologised bodies and cyborg futures is vital, but it is through visualising and encountering such bodies that the future will be experienced. Seeing the weaponised soldier, as well as the disabilities such technologies *produce* through the disasters they create, creates a powerful identification that reaches across many aspects of contemporary life, from media images of refugees to stories of disabled veterans. The chapter will claim that fiction film, again often full of the messy contradictions that define the meeting of disability and posthumanism, offers opportunities to unpick the terms of this power and the reach of its meanings.

Chapter 4 looks at the place of disability in what I term the time of posthumanist work. Work and employment are categories in which there are many public narratives about the 'problems' of people with disabilities. In a contemporary late-capitalist world that privileges ideas of work productivity and efficiency, those with disability are frequently deemed 'slow', inefficient and often the recipients of benefits understood to be by rights the property of those who *can* work. For its part, posthumanism and work is less overtly a space of visible technology and more an excitement about the possibilities digital worlds offer for the development of the hyper-efficient worker, and so the chapter explores claims made about 24/7 work cultures, seen through ideas of speed and time. I explore narratives of embodied work, in which disability is a central driver of depictions of subjectivity; and of sleep, a state deemed to be highly 'unproductive' and, as such, problematically wasteful. Sleep is not usually read through a disability lens, but its resistance to narratives of the productive superhuman makes it an ally of a disability-led critique of contemporary obsessions with work and efficiency and the chapter argues for its place evaluating the damage created when *not being able to keep up* is deemed a personal failure and communal liability.

Grounded posthumanisms

Disability takes multiple forms, of course, and as we will see there are many ways of articulating current trajectories of contemporary posthumanism. While macro arguments will help us see questions more clearly, case studies and specific readings will always revise exactly what we think we are asking. So, as both subjects continue to develop in complexity the question to be asked is how it is best possible to chart their various points of intersection. The language of the posthuman is one full of discussions of prostheses and body adaptation, of cognitive variation and neurological difference, and of ethics, technologies and societies developed through recognition of the consequences of such change. While for some it might appear that this is a debate that is abstract and theoretical, we can observe that in very real ways the interface between bodies, minds and technology central to posthumanist thinking *already exist*: it is manifest in those with disabilities. To note this is not to make a simplistic move that collapses the person with disability into some kind of cyborg state, only recognising them as having disabilities if they interact with technology; but whether through the engineered modification of limbs, the use of wheelchairs and other assistive technologies, or an understanding of neurodiversity in (for example) those on the autistic spectrum, lives lived with disability provide everyday examples of the philosophical speculation and biopolitical contexts with which much writing on posthumanism engages. In an opinion piece written for the *New York Times* in May 2018, disabled designer Liz Jackson noted that people with disabilities are the "original lifehackers". "Disabled people have long been integral to design processes", Jackson writes, citing the development of kitchen utensils or new touchscreen technologies as examples; but the stories that might articulate this, she stresses, "often go untold... our contributions are often overshadowed or misrepresented, favoring instead a story with a savior as its protagonist". 'Lifehacking' is, as Jackson recognises, a posthumanist idea (and will be explored in Chapter 4 in relation to notions of work and 'efficiency'), but the claim for disability originality she makes is provocative in orienting both a 'disability first' design perspective, and the novelty central to the daily interactions between people with disabilities and the worlds in which they live.[22]

This study seeks to articulate these complexities. I want to remain cognisant of Jackson's intervention and avoid an over-analytic (or indulgent) immersion into the intersections between posthumanist and disability *theoretical* standpoints, simply because there are so many other important topics and questions to be covered. An initial draft of this introduction devoted several pages, many of them articulating much frustration, about the absence of disability from the foundational texts that outline and analyse the posthuman. Suffice to say that the history of disability in posthumanist thought is mixed to say the least. To differing degrees, writings by many scholars working on the posthuman for the most part either ignore disability or contain one or two sentences in which is it mentioned, to then be largely ignored or, in some cases, dismissed. But, in the spirit of critical optimism mentioned in the Preface, it is better to work with the emerging trajectories of engagement that *can* be used, to focus on new thinking about bodies, minds and selves that offer potential to bring disability and posthumanism together, even if it is necessary to note these absences as yet another example of the excision of disability experiences from areas where they are, in fact, seminal.

The insularity of much scholarship on posthumanism, especially the elevation of the critic/theorist as visionary (ironically, given its decentring focus, theories of the posthuman often champion the *singular* figure of the hyper-perceptive critic),[23] sets up a tension between the insights it can deliver and the more recognisable narratives of rights and activism that typify many critical accounts of disability. Anyone with experience of thinking about, or working with, questions of disability cannot dismiss the notion of rights or agency, to give the most powerful examples, as easily as a number of writers on posthumanism might imply we should.[24] Can the very existence of 'rights', and an associated idea of justice, be a smokescreen for the practice of a coercive politics? Can it create hierarchies of 'needs' and promote discrimination as a result? Is it open to abuse? The answer to all these questions, as many have shown, is an obvious yes. 'Rights' is, for example, obviously speciesist in its formation as a theory of 'human rights', arguably accelerating environmental damage as a consequence of promoting the human as the foundational, and most important, class of life on the planet. On a smaller scale, 'rights' can create social and economic divisions through their enactment of a politics of preference in which certain communities are privileged at the expense of others. Yet knowing this does not disqualify an appropriately reflective and nuanced argument for the acknowledgement that those with disabilities, like other groups subject to marginalisation, have been contained within histories of prejudice that leave their present (and future) as a space where rights and justice are meaningful and beneficial (if too frequently absent) terms, where indeed they may well save lives.

As an example, the terms of both the United Nations Convention on the Rights of People with Disabilities (UNCRPD), adopted in 2006, and the World Health Organisation's 2011 *World Report on Disability* frame disability within fundamental humanist terms of personhood and equal rights. The 'Disability and Human Rights' section of the WHO report reiterates the need to respect the "difference and acceptance of persons with disabilities as part of human diversity and humanity" and to recognise the "inherent dignity [and] individual autonomy" of people with disabilities, "including the freedom to make one's own choices" as well as the central "independence of persons".[25] Both documents are hugely important and substantive interventions into the global nature of, and challenges to, disability and it is a particularly obdurate and uncompromising critical/theoretical approach that ignores the importance of the UN and WHO in fighting the prejudices and harm experienced by peoples with disabilities globally on a daily basis, even knowing that the recommendations of each are routinely ignored, including (though unsurprisingly) by those who are signatories or contributors to them. With this in mind, it should be noted that, within the fundamentally social, economic and political logic articulated by both organisations, posthumanism is seen (if it is considered at all) as a distracting and reductive critical position, one that evades the real needs of real people as they live the experiences of their disabled lives. For all that there is a pressing need to critique the exclusionary terms of humanism and its problematic concepts of bodies and selves, it would be a profound mistake to turn away from those instances where humanism aligns with and advocates a desire for disability justice; and that this frequently means a distrust of posthumanist thinking is a fact that disability scholarship on technology needs to bear in mind.

Martha Nussbaum explores these complex spaces in detail in her 2007 study *Frontiers of Justice: Disability, Nationality, Species Membership*, noting that "the problem of doing justice to people with physical and mental impairments" is one of the major issues facing the practice of social justice. People with disabilities, she continues, "have not as yet been included, in existing societies, as citizens on a basis of equality with other citizens".[26] As befitting a writer on law and ethics, Nussbaum is interested in disability's (non)place in the wider social contract that outlines human interrelationships and she is erudite on questions of dignity, flourishing, functioning and capability that arise as a consequence of this. The fact that (as her book's subtitle indicates) she also discusses questions of species membership shows that Nussbaum's investigations are not static in their comprehension of personhood, however, and her scholarship displays how justice and rights can be worked through discussions of disability that still recognise the flexibilities inherent in the lives of disabled people.

Conversely, given her stress on transgressing boundaries and dedication to critiquing notions of a unified self, Donna Haraway might not immediately appear as a critic invested in the discourses of rights.

Haraway's commitment to deconstructing selfhood, autonomy and the privileged position of grounded selfhood is thorough and extensive, but her call for "a finally amodern, reinvented desire for justice", which is the product of making "situated knowledges possible in order to be able to make consequential claims about the world", aligns techniques of reinvention with the pursuit of justice. It not only gestures towards complex theories that might outline the present, but also suggests the real, consequential, possibilities produced by the new posthumanist complexities that make up our world. I will discuss Haraway's work, and responses to it, in detail in the next chapter, but it is worth noting that writers as diverse as Nussbaum and Haraway (though it should be noted that they have affinities in their stress on the need to further the frontiers of women's experiences) illustrate how experiences of the body can be aligned with 'situated knowledge' in a time of flexible identity positions.

Appreciating and inviting a post-identity theory of subjectivity, as many critics writing on posthumanism do, does not necessarily mean that concepts such as rights, autonomy and agency cannot equally be conceived of in post-identity formations. As I hope the examples in this book will show, 'identity', though often a highly problematic appellation, is not such a wrecking ball of a subject positioning that its removal requires the concomitant destruction and erasure of all the multiple ideas with which it is associated. Indeed, as the following chapter will explore, recent years have seen the emergence from within disability studies of important critiques of identity-centred cultural locations that nevertheless remain committed to disability justice. I agree with Margrit Shildrick's observation that there needs to be a commitment to theoretical openness in our configuration of disability, a range of what she terms "postconventional theories" that refuse "to settle on a singular perspective", but rather "continue a process of intersectional exploration". However, the assumption that, as she puts it, "the meaning of disability [...] cannot be contained in a single constellation" should mean that theories resulting from such logic should open, rather than close, doors to more sophisticated formations.[27]

In fact, the revisions a consideration of disability is now making to theories of posthumanism suggest a capacity to produce considerable change to the subject's intellectual parameters. This book will suggest productive processes of disability critique that extend from a consideration of cultural texts, but the question goes beyond issues of representation, narrative and deployment. Take, for example, the place of animals in contemporary writing on posthumanism.

For many, the 'post-anthropological' or 'non-human' turn and unpacking of the idea of 'the human' have necessitated a revision of human–animal relations in thinking about the present, and a number of scholars discuss such relations as being central to current understandings of posthumanity.[28] But the relationship between disability and animals introduces a complexity to such debates. On the one hand, disability positions suggest unique affinities between humans and animals: Temple Grandin's autism, for example, has led not only to her being able to articulate profound connections to animal identities, but famously also to new methods of designing cattle slaughterhouses as a consequence; while Dawn Prince-Hughes has shown in *Songs of the Gorilla Nation* how her autism is likewise central to the ways in which she feels linked to the subjectivities of fellow primates.[29] On the other hand, comparisons with animals have been one of the foundational ways in which those with disabilities have been claimed to be 'subnormal' – 'freaks' and 'monsters' – throughout history. Thinking this through, it is entirely possible that admitting to the centrality of disability perspectives in conceptualising the posthuman might allow us to give clearer detail to the differentiation between modern/eugenic thought and contemporary questions of species relations, and that the *specific* forms of disability–animal connections can provide insights into the topic of human–animal interfaces that other subjects simply cannot. When this admission is made, other examples come to mind: the methods by which questions of environment, disaster and financial economies interact, to cite one possible global/biocapital/posthumanist network, are illuminated in distinct ways when conceived as disability enquiries, precisely because 'environment', 'disaster' and 'economy' all carry specific inflections when understood as disability concerns.[30] The difference that disability carries can be a vital factor in helping us see the choices faced in a posthumanist present by disabled *and* non-disabled communities alike.

Optimism and the value of stories

Excited by the material I was using and the ideas that were emerging, I began writing this book in a mood of optimism. In an early draft, I wrote at this point of the introduction that "it is possible to feel that we are now in a time when a welcome to a disability future might be extended" by disabled and non-disabled alike. I registered the increasing incorporation of positive disability values and role models into language and society, and what felt like a commitment to the continuation of this. Because of the successes of the various disability rights movements and through processes of education, disability issues and people with disabilities arguably now have a profile unimaginable even ten or 15 years ago, and critical work being undertaken in disability studies is moving from the necessary deconstruction of the old modes of representation to highlight newer, and more productive, forms of portrayal. While I still believe much of this to be true, recent developments in global politics have made such a position seem naive at best. There is more than enough evidence to suggest that the latest political, economic and health configurations of the contemporary world, understood in a global sense across societies and cultures, place new and increasingly impossible demands on those with disabilities, and that the prejudice and exclusion that has marked the history of disability not only will continue but will take more systemic and therefore insidious forms. This book will, therefore, discuss features of the emerging technologised world that threaten the validity of disabled lives: biocapitalism and the consumerisation of health; technoscience and the question of 'damage'; work, labour and the idea of 'benefit'; and biology and citizenry; all the contested questions of becoming that Nikolas Rose has eloquently termed "the politics of life itself".[31] As mentioned previously and as we will see, the assumption (made by many involved in the development of disability technologies) that scientific advances constitute 'progress' is debateable. While it would be foolish to deny the value of many assistive technologies, the contexts in which they are often framed – particularly issues of access and economic costs – frequently challenge and even prohibit the advantages that they can deliver.

I find, however, that I still want to retain a positive sense of the value of scholarly intervention and to continue to subscribe to that version of disability studies that values critique precisely because, having worked to show the details of the worlds in which we all (variously) live, it then gestures towards choices that can be made that allow for a more ethical participation in culture and society. Any book that takes ideas of the future as its subject should be suitably circumspect, and the claims I make are put forward with this knowledge in mind. There is a need to speak of (and to) continuity as well as change, but this can be done with an emphasis on the positives that change might bring. In no way do I wish to distance myself from critical work that highlights the discrimination practised by the forms of neoliberalism that increasingly dominate all aspects of our societies and threaten all kinds of communities, those with disabilities included; I have learned much from such studies, agree with many of the observations they make and will use them in this book. But I am a believer in the power of advocacy in the same way that I value the processes of critique, and one of the first lessons of practising disability studies is to acknowledge that those who live with disabilities are active, not passive, participants in the narratives that surround them, and shape their lives, on their own terms, on a daily basis. I want to continue and extend such activities here.

This book is also one that is passionate about the productive potential of fiction and the imagination. In a time when critical insight is frequently gauged by the way it crosses and transgresses disciplinary boundaries, it is easy to forget the core values of stories and imagination. I believe that the best scholarship needs to range widely, and that to understand disability in the contemporary moment and its projected futures requires more than a simple unpacking of how it might be represented in a novel or film; and I have learned a huge amount from colleagues in other, often far-flung, disciplines: engineering, robotics and the health and social sciences especially. But I am not interested in making literature a form of sociology or anthropology, or seeing films as an adjunct to the telling of 'health stories'. For all that the chapters that follow roam across a variety of critical and disciplinary landscapes, I am more convinced than ever of the power and insight that comes from reading or watching creative imaginings.

Fiction's ability to articulate disability in an increasingly posthumanist world is, I believe, a vital part of the way in which we comprehend its presence. I will discuss Michael Bérubé's work on disability and literature in the next chapter, but it is worth here noting his observation about the specific complexities of literary practice. "Narrative *deployments* of disability", he writes, "do not confine themselves to representation. They can also be narrative strategies, devices for exploring". Bérubé's use of 'deployment' suggests a particular sophistication; he notes: "I say 'deployments' [...] rather than 'depictions' or 'representations', because I will argue [...] that disability and ideas about disability can be and have been put to use in fictional narratives in ways that go far beyond any specific rendering of any disabled character or characters".[32] In what follows, I want to pick up on these ideas of fiction's aesthetics, strategy, exploration and deployment, and to stress that imaginative portrayals possess a capacity to inform our understanding of disability that other forms of enquiry cannot replicate. In economies that favour only certain forms of production, it has become too easy to question not only the power of creative imaginings but also the value of humanities (and especially literary/cultural) scholarship. By way of response, I want this book to be a belligerent response to such attitudes and a championing of the creative, and critical, aesthetic.

Notes

1 Ellen Samuels, *Fantasies of Identification: Disability, Gender, Race* (New York and London: New York University Press, 2014), p. 121. See also pp. 121–212 for more on what she terms "Fantasies of Measurement".

2 Pramod Nayar, *Posthumanism* (Cambridge: Polity, 2014), p. 5.

3 Nayar, *Posthumanism* (Cambridge: Polity, 2014), pp. 5–6.

4 Tony Davies, *Humanism* (London: Routledge, 2008), p. 15. The literature outlining humanism is of course vast and impossible to cover here. Davies' book acts as a useful introduction. Equally, Yuval Noah Harari's *Homo Deus: A Brief History of Tomorrow* provides an accessible and eloquent account of what he terms "the humanist revolution" and how it is challenged in a digital, data-driven future. *Homo Deus: A Brief History of Tomorrow* (London: Vintage, 2017), see especially pp. 258–323 and 411–462.

5 Nayar, *Posthumanism*, p. 8.

6 See, for example, the contents of *The Cambridge Companion to Literature and the Posthuman*, in which the various contributions range across literary periods, modes and themes precisely in this manner. Bruce Clarke and Manuela Rossini (eds), *The Cambridge Companion to Literature and the Posthuman* (Cambridge: Cambridge University Press, 2017).

7 See Don Ihde, *Bodies in Technology* (Minneapolis and London: Minnesota University Press, 2002).

8 Alex Goody raises the possibility of recognising the Woodman in such a fashion by addressing the topic in the first paragraph of a chapter entitled 'Robots, Cyborgs and the Technological Body' in his 2011 book *Technology. Literature and Culture*, though he only explores the topic in a single paragraph and his observations, which are more descriptive than analytical, stress a political reading. Baum "raised particular political questions about the effect of technology on humanity" he writes, observing that the "Tin Woodman and his prosthetic body have been created by ruthless injustice and he needs to have his heart/humanity restored to him". Goody also discusses Baum's 1913 novel *The Patchwork Girl of Oz*, and its reworking by Shelley Jackson in her 1995 hypertext *Patchwork Girl*, later in the chapter. See Goody, *Technology. Literature and Culture* (Cambridge: Polity 2011), pp. 136 and 163–166. *Patchwork Girl* is also discussed by Katherine Hayles in *My Mother Was a Computer: Digital Subjects and Literary Texts* (Chicago, IL: The University of Chicago Press, 2005), p. 143.

9 See Elaine Scarry's seminal *The Body in Pain: The Making and Unmaking of the World* (Oxford: Oxford University Press, 1988); David B. Morris, *The Culture of Pain* (Berkeley and Los Angeles: University of California Press, 1991) and *Illness and Culture in the Postmodern Age* (Berkeley and London: University of California Press, 1998), pp. 107–134; and Sara Ahmed's discussion of "The Contingency of Pain" in *The Cultural Politics of Emotion*, 2nd ed. (Edinburgh:

Edinburgh University Press, 2014), pp. 20–41. Ronald Schleifer's *Pain and Suffering* (New York and London: Routledge, 2014) offers a good overall survey of both scientific and cultural narratives of pain. There is also a long tradition of covering questions of pain in work that stems from anthropological and sociological work in narrative medicine. See especially Mary-Jo DelVecchio et al. (eds), *Pain as Human Experience: An Anthropological Perspective* (Berkeley: University of California Press, 1994), as well as the literary/cultural scholarship that engages with this, such as Ann Jurecic's *Illness as Narrative* (Pittsburgh, PA: University of Pittsburgh Press, 2012), pp. 43–66.

10 Following the immediate success of the first Oz novel, Baum also adapted it for a musical that played in Chicago and on Broadway between 1902 and 1904 before touring the US. Following Baum's death, the franchise continued with subsequent books being published by other writers, notably Ruth Thompson and John R. Neill (the illustrator for the majority of Baum's own Oz novels), all recognised as part of the Oz 'canon'. The last such novels, written by Sherwood Smith, were published in 2005 and 2006, while non-estate publications were released in 2014 and 2015.

11 L. Frank Baum, *Oz: The Complete Collection*, vol. 4 (London: Simon and Schuster, 2013), pp. 441–445.

12 L. Frank Baum, *The Wonderful Wizard of Oz* (London: Penguin, 1995), p. 39.

13 Baum, *Oz: The Complete Collection*, p. 453. Early on in *The Tin Woodman of Oz*, the Woodman repeats the story of his transformation to Woot, a young wanderer travelling through Oz, but this time in considerably more detail than in *The Wonderful Wizard of Oz*. Now, we learn, the witch not only enchanted the axe to sever the Woodman's limbs, she herself "seized the axe and chopped [his] body into several small pieces, after which, thinking that at last she had destroyed [him], she ran away laughing in wicked glee" (p. 450). With each attack, however, the Woodman comes to see his replacement tin prostheses as superior to the body parts he has lost: "I was a much better man than ever, for my body could not ache or pain me, and I was so beautiful and bright that I had no need of clothing", and the Munchkin girl – now named as Nimmie Amee – equally only finds reason to love the Woodman more: "the girl agreed with me that a man all made of tin was far more perfect than one formed of different materials" (pp. 450–451).

Challenged by Woot that he deserted Nimmie, and so that his heart cannot be deemed especially 'kind', the Tin Woodman resolves to find his lost love, and the remainder of the novel takes the form of a quest. On their journey, the Woodman, Scarecrow and Woot come across Captain Fyter, a soldier whose story is identical to that of the Woodman: engaged to Nimmie Amee after she knew the Woodman, he was likewise dismembered by the Witch, restored by the tinsmith, and ultimately reduced to a rusting hulk on a forest path (the only difference with the Woodman is that Fyter carries a sword and not an axe; otherwise they are almost literal doubles). Amazed by the similarity in their histories, the Woodman and Soldier resolve to find Nimmie and let her marry which of the two she chooses. When they do locate her, however, they find Nimmie already married, to a man the tinsmith has constructed from all the human body parts taken from the Woodman and Soldier (apart from, in a nice touch, one missing arm, lost and therefore necessitating a single tin limb). The standoff that ensues, between three figures, all more or less formed from the same materials, has a surrealism that breaks free from Baum's habitually spare prose, creating a textual excess reminiscent more of Lewis Carroll.

Though nominally human, Nimmie's husband has few of the characteristics that pass for humanity in Oz. He is rude and petulant, not "a husband to be proud of" as Nimmie admits, "because he has a mixed nature and isn't always an agreeable companion" (p. 628). Yet she rejects the overtures of both the Tin Woodman and Soldier, preferring her current arrangement in part because, in a strange echo of her own previous relationship with the old woman for whom she worked, she has trained her husband in a number of domestic tasks and has no wish to have to repeat the process. "You two gentlemen threw him away when you became tin", she tells her visitors, "so you cannot justly claim him now. I advise you to go back to your own homes and forget me, as I have forgotten you" (p. 629). Both the Tin Woodman and Solider are happy to accede to this, seeing nothing of value in their former human selves and thankful that they escaped becoming Nimmie's servant: "we have much to be thankful for", as the Soldier puts it (p. 630). And while each is now tin, Baum asserts that they "are still themselves", still carry the full humanity of their individuality, and rather it is the new husband who is a "Nobody", a "mix-up", and who "must be someone else" (pp. 627–628).

14 Baum, *Oz: The Complete Collection*, p. 461.

15 Baum, *Oz: The Complete Collection*, p. 461.

16 Sherryl Vint, *Bodies of Tomorrow: Technology, Subjectivity, Science Fiction* (Toronto: University of Toronto Press, 2007), p. 103 (emphasis in original). Vint's observation comes in the context of her reading cyberpunk fiction of the 1980s, especially that of William Gibson, where the word 'meat' is used to describe the body left behind as characters immerse themselves of the virtual reality of cyberspace, a process Vint describes as "the (impossible) desire to escape the vicissitudes of the body and occupy the place of self-mastery" (p. 104). It is worth noting that in Gibson's hugely influential and boundary-breaking 1984 novel *Neuromancer* a process is described that appears to be the complete opposite of the Tin Woodman's transformation. Instead of the human body replaced by artificial additions, as with the Woodman's narrative, in Gibson's post-punk universe, saturated by collections of abstract data with which his protagonists negotiate, a character performs a stage show in which a human body appears limb by limb in a kind of download-as-theatre. Seemingly from nowhere, a woman's hand appears, to be followed by another, then "[t]he act progressed with a surreal internal logic of its own. The arms were next. Feet. Legs [...] Then the torso formed... caressed into being, white, headless and perfect [...] Now limbs and torso had merged... The head was there, the image complete" (pp. 167–168). The last clause here gives the game away however; though seemingly human, the body created on stage is, in fact, just another of the novel's data manifestations. But rather than this image being an example of a lack of humanity, Gibson's story makes it clear that the very idea of the human body is just one competitor in the battle for self and presence, jostling with any number of virtual adversaries. In *Neuromancer*, the enhanced body, whether the product of plastic surgery, pharmaceutical intervention, or – as in the above example – visual illusion, is an everyday part of the landscape the characters inhabit. Here, the transgression of the human is

ordinary, and, as a result, the very idea of disability and what it might mean is challenged.

17 In *Exits to the Posthuman Future*, Arthur Kroker discusses a patent application for an iPhone app "that involves synching your heart to the smartphone" in a process that transmits biological date from body to phone that creates a "mobile heart monitor". For Kroker, this suggests "the first tentative steps in a greater migration from body to code, a data archive housing the biorhythms of the remotely scanned heart". Kroker, *Exits to the Posthuman Future* (Cambridge: Polity, 2014), pp. 7–8.

18 Tobin Siebers, *Disability Theory* (Ann Arbor: University of Michigan Press, 2008), p. 25; Rosemarie Garland-Thomson, 'Disability gain', paper presented at 'Avoidance in/and the Academy: The International Conference on Disability, Culture and Education', Liverpool Hope University, September 11, 2013. I am grateful to Clare Barker for bringing these references to my attention.

19 Nayar, *Posthumanism*, pp. 127–128 and 134–135.

20 Elaine L. Graham's analysis of science fiction in her 2002 study *Representations of the post/human* points to the degree to which much of such fiction (her focus is on *Star Trek* and its various spin offs) functions conservatively. She writes that such narratives depict "the relationships and boundaries between humans and machines, the natural and the artificial, while strenuously maintaining the integrity of the modern Western humanist subject at the heart of their broadly technophilic visions". *Representations of the post/human: Monsters, Aliens and Others in Popular Culture* (Manchester: Manchester University Press, 2002), pp. 176 and 132–153.

21 It should not be presumed that stories of posthumanist technologised embodiment are always primarily concerned with the present and future alone. Lidia Yuknavitch's 2017 novel *The Book of Joan*, set in an off-world suborbital complex where human sexuality and gender distinctions have all but disappeared, is recognisably posthuman, especially in its focus on embodiment; but it is also a reworking (and not simply a retelling) of Joan of Arc's narrative of resistance in which ideas of the mystical are preserved.

22 Liz Jackson, 'We are the original lifehackers', *New York Times*, May 30, 2018, www.nytimes.com/2018/05/30/opinion/disability-design-lifehacks.html. Accessed September 17, 2018.

23 See, for example, Carey Wolfe's continual return to the work of Jacques Derrida and Bruno Latour, or Rosi Braidotti's focus on Gilles Deleuze.

24 Wolfe is especially scathing here. *What is Posthumanism?* is animated by a sustained opposition to what, at one point, he terms "some form of authenticity or presence typically associated with analog media". Such associations/dismissals of identity with an outdated technological past are not untypical of scholarship on posthumanism. See *What is Posthumanism?* (Minneapolis and London: University of Minnesota Press, 2010), p. xxxiv.

25 World Health Organisation, *World Report on Disability*, 2011, p. 9. For details of the UNCRPD, see www.un.org/development/desa/disabilities/convention-on-the-rights-of-persons-with-disabilities.html. Accessed July 24, 2018.

26 Martha C. Nussbaum, *Frontiers of Justice: Disability, Nationality, Species Membership* (Cambridge, MA: Belknap/Harvard University Press, 2007), n.p.

27 Margrit Shildrick, *Dangerous Discourses of Disability, Subjectivity and Sexuality* (Basingstoke: Palgrave Macmillan, 2009), pp. 170 and 172.

28 See, for example: Wolfe, *What is Posthumanism?* pp. 99–126; Nayar, *Posthumanism*, pp. 77–99; Rosi Braidotti, *The Posthuman* (Cambridge: Polity, 2013), pp. 55–104; Patricia MacCormack, *Posthuman Ethics: Embodiment and Cultural Theory* (Abingdon: Routledge, 2012), pp. 57–78; Richard Grusin (ed.), *The Nonhuman Turn* (Minneapolis: Minnesota University Press, 2015); and Mel Chen, *Animacies: Biopolitics, Racial Mattering, and Queer Affect* (Durham, NC: Duke University Press, 2012).

29 See Temple Grandin's *Animals in Translation: Using the Mysteries of Autism to Decode Animal Behavior* (New York: Scribner, 2005) and *Animals Make Us Human: Creating the Best Life for Animals* (Boston, MA: Houghton Mifflin Harcourt, 2009); and Dawn Prince-Hughes, *Songs of the Gorilla Nation: My Journey Through Autism* (London: Souvenir Press, 2004).

30 Anthony Carrigan discusses this nexus in relation to the fallout from nuclear testing in the Pacific. See 'Postcolonial disaster, Pacific nuclearization, and disabling environments', *Journal of Cultural and Literary Disability Studies* 4, no. 3 (2010), pp. 255–272. As I completed the final reading of the proofs for this book prior to its publication, much of the world was either practising isolation or experiencing lockdown as a result of the Covid-19 pandemic. The ways in which this moment in history will come to be understood through disability experiences will come to be written, but there is no doubt that the disability versions of this particular disaster will be profound and long-lasting.

31 Nikolas Rose, *The Politics of Life Itself: Biomedicine, Power and Subjectivity in the Twenty-First Century* (Princeton, NJ: Princeton University Press, 2007).

32 Michael Bérubé, *The Secret Life of Stories: From Don Quixote to Harry Potter, How Understanding Intellectual Disability Transforms the Way We Read* (New York: New York University Press, 2016), p. 2.

CHAPTER ONE

(Post)human Subjects, Disability Deployments

Introduction: getting carried away

Thinking about posthumanism can be an exciting business. In the initial wave of critical writing on the explicit idea of the posthuman produced in the late 1980s and 1990s, signs of exhilaration and anticipation proliferated. The heady mix of possibilities that came from considering a space beyond the human, one full of technological advancement and individual freedoms, prompted a series of breathless questions: what might it mean to leave the human, and humanism, behind? How might we, as a species, move *beyond* the body, or indeed what *types* of bodies might be generated as a result of these interactions? What kinds of thresholds and transgressions would be involved in any such moves? What will our relationship to technology, or other non-human forms, be in a posthuman future? And what might we learn about embodiment, ethics, society, gender, race and culture in such formations? The tone was possibly best captured by Judith Halberstam and Ira Livingston in the introduction to their 1995 collection, *Posthuman Bodies*, in which the posthuman appeared full of an almost revolutionary potential to collapse or eradicate categories and boundaries:

> Queer, cyborg, metametazoan, hybrid. PWA; bodies-without-organs, bodies-in-process, virtual bodies: in unvisualizable amniotic indeterminacy, and unfazed by the hype of their always premature and redundant annunciation, posthuman bodies thrive in the mutual deformations of totem and taxonomy. We have rehearsed the claim that the posthuman

> condition is upon us and that lingering nostalgia for a modernist or humanist philosophy of self and other, human and alien, normal and queer is merely the echo of a discursive battle that has already taken place – and the tinny futurism that often answers such nostalgia is the echo of an echo. We stake our claim between these echoes and their answers.[1]

This is critical thinking as the leading edge of a giddy prophecy. Halberstam and Livingston's 'claim' is for nothing less than a complete reordering of the ways in we know and express ourselves, and the essays in their volume focused on subjects – class identities and machines, posthuman feminism, pregnant men, deviant subjectivities, monstrous becomings – that explore how such thinking might affect a wide range of subject positions: personal, political, social and fictional.

In a similar vein, Hans Moravec – a seminal figure in the development of thinking about the future of robotics and A.I., and in post- and tranhumanist discourses more widely – begins his 1988 study *Mind Children: The Future of Robot and Human Intelligence* with the vision of "a world in which the human race has been swept away by the tide of cultural change, usurped by its own artificial progeny". If, Moravec notes, robots and A.I. appear crude and simplistic at the time in which he was writing, "within the next century they will mature into entities as complex as ourselves, and eventually into something transcending everything we know – in whom we can take pride when they refer to themselves as our descendants". Freed from "the plodding pace of biological evolution", he continues, "the children of our minds will be free to grow to confront immense and fundamental challenges in the larger universe".[2] Eleven years later, in 1999, appropriately on the cusp of the new millennium, Moravec would restate his thesis in *Robot: Mere Machine to Transcendent Mind,* observing that "the development of intelligent machines" is "a near term inevitability" and asserting that "each advance will provide intellectual rewards, competitive advantages, and increased wealth and options of all kinds". If Halberstam and Livingston were driven by the critical and theoretical possibilities of the posthuman horizon, Moravec stressed what he understood to be the evolutionary inescapability (he termed it "escape velocity") of the transition from human to robot: "I consider these future machines our progeny [...] Like biological children of previous generations, they will embody humanity's best chance for a long-term future".[3] Each of these visions appeared to be as far as, if not further than, one can imagine.

Other scholars writing on the emergence of the posthuman and the potential for change it pre-figured were more cautious. "These are strange times", Rosi Braidotti begins her 2002 study *Metamorphoses: Towards a Materialist Theory of Becoming,* "and strange things are happening". She continues:

> Living at such times of fast changes may be exhilarating, yet the task of representing these changes to ourselves and engaging productively with the contradictions, paradoxes and injustices they engender is a perennial challenge. Accounting for fast-changing conditions is hard work; escaping the velocity of change is even harder. Unless one likes complexity one cannot feel at home in the twenty-first century. Transformations, metamorphoses, mutations and processes of change have in fact become familiar in the lives of most contemporary subjects.[4]

The result, Braidotti observes, is "that the challenge lies in thinking about processes, rather than concepts", and "the point is not to know who we are, but rather what, at last we want to become, how to represent mutations, changes and transformations". Braidotti's circumspection demands that the excitement found in pronouncements such as those from Halberstam and Livingston, or the inevitability inherent in Moravec's visions of the future, must be held up to scrutiny, its details examined and understood. In the end, as she notes, such changes are not just about the possibilities of new selfhoods, but also "vital concerns [...] for the scientific, social and political institutions that surround such selves".[5] The posthuman condition, she asserts, is one in which "the human is now displaced in the direction of a glittering range of [...] technological variables" that can be considered "both exhilarating and painful".[6] But for all the glitter, it is a position that needs to be analysed in its grounded and located practices. For Braidotti, who would develop a complex set of theories of the posthuman, especially around embodiment, in work spanning more than a decade following the publication of *Metamorphoses,* the variability of the future demands processes of continual questioning rather than mere celebration.[7]

In *How We Became Posthuman: Virtual Bodies in Cybernetics, Literature and Informatics,* her visionary study published – like Moravec's *Robot* – in 1999 just as a century of incredible technological transformation ended, Katherine Hayles offered an equally alert account of the promise of the posthuman. Hayles explores the challenges of posthumanist futures, articulating a moment of liberation in anticipation of progressive change that nevertheless has real-world consequences:

> [T]he posthuman does not really mean the end of humanity. It signals instead the end of a certain conception of the human, a conception that may have applied, at best, to that fraction of humanity who had the wealth, power and leisure to conceptualize as autonomous beings exercising their will through individual agency and choice [...] Yet the posthuman needs not be recuperated back into liberal humanism, nor need it be construed as anti-human. Located within the dialectic of pattern/randomness and grounded in embodied rather than disembodied information, the posthuman offers resources for rethinking the articulations of humans with intelligent machines.[8]

For Hayles, as the end of the millennium drew near the liberal humanist subject had come to dominate the perception of what 'humanity' was. The progression of that subject through modernity was one of a projected totalising power, producing the exclusion and trauma that has characterised much of the modern and contemporary periods. But perception is not the same as actuality, and in place of a humanity that Hayles now felt was vanishing a posthumanist subjectivity was emerging, one that will enact a more democratic idea of citizenship, informed (as opposed to restricted) by embodied engagement with information and the virtual, and especially enabled by interactions with technology. Such a reading is the antithesis of that narrative of modernity that saw the developments of the industrial revolution spiral into the horrors of war, totalitarianism and genocide. Hayles' posthuman is not without its dangers, and her tone is cautionary, but is overwhelmingly an opportunity for a better future.[9]

Though Hayles is explicit in advocating that her sense of the posthuman is not entirely anti-human, its parameters clearly overlap with the attacks on humanism found in the work of theorists such as Michel Foucault and Louis Althusser, those who, in Foucault's own memorable phrase, had posited the "death" of the "recent invention" that is man.[10] Indeed, part of the energy behind critical work on posthumanism in the 1990s was precisely that it appeared as a new frontier for anti-humanist cultural theory, extending the writing of a previous generation of scholars. Addressing precisely this idea of a critical genealogy, Neil Badmington included Foucault and Althusser, along with a range of other thinkers stretching from Frantz Fanon to Jean-Francois Lyotard, in his *Posthumanism* reader, published in 2000. This gave the subject a number of possible jumping-off points even as the volume sought to define the subject's breadth by stressing its central figures. In seeking to outline the concerns of the field, Badmington also caught that sense of promise in the 1990s' configuration of the posthuman and anticipation of the future: "Wherever they look", he said of the writers collected in his reader, expressing the excitement of the moment, "they witness Man breathing 'himself' to death, raising himself to ruins. Posthumanism is out there".[11] More prosaically (but in greater detail), Pramod Nayar also locates the origins of posthumanism in a variety of anti-humanist critical disciplines – poststructuralism, feminism, technoscience studies and critical race studies – that flourished at the end of the twentieth century. Such work, Nayar asserts, "demolished the myth of the unified, coherent, autonomous, self-identical human subject", and subsequently "posited the subject, and biology, as a construct of discourses, of enmeshed and co-evolved species and technologies". While Nayar is not as overtly exhilarated about the 'out there' qualities of the posthuman figure as some other writers on the subject, he nevertheless makes grand claims for its possibilities: "By demonstrating the end of the sovereign human subject, critical humanism prepares the ground for the new form of the human, the posthuman".[12]

For her part, Hayles made it clear that debating the timing of any transition to a posthumanist state was a pointless exercise, as the posthuman was nearer than Badmington suggested: "Increasingly, the question is not whether we will become posthuman, for posthumanity is already here. Rather, the question is what kind of posthumans we will be".[13] It appeared that the door was open to a future in which science fiction could become 'fact', knowledge thresholds would be crossed, and where the only limits we might place on ourselves were those produced by technology and our own imaginations.[14] As Robert Pepperell put it in his 1995 book *The Post-Human Condition*, employing a dramatic metaphor to suggest the coming change, "we are approaching the *electrification of existence* – there is a tangible sense of a storm in the air".[15]

By way of contrast, traditionally disability is rarely thought to be exciting. Based on ideas that circulate in the public imaginary, few would advocate that being disabled puts one on the threshold of a future in which 'the human' was about to be productively supplanted. The converse is more likely to be true: many perceive disability to involve a state that precisely falls short of being fully human, and that is best described in terms of an absence, lack or loss. Lennard J. Davis notes that, "most constructions of disability assume that the person with disabilities is in some sense damaged while the observer is undamaged. Furthermore, there is an assumption that society at large is intact, normal, setting a norm, undamaged".[16] Such assumptions are to be found everywhere, from employers believing that staff with disabilities are naturally less productive than their non-disabled counterparts, to the effects of the soft power embedded in the objects and images that stress hyperability and pervade our (especially popular) culture. Disability *futures* are almost never thought to be desirable and appear rather as fraught spaces of struggle. In *The Biopolitics of Disability,* their 2015 analysis of disability read within frames of neoliberalism and ablenationalism, David Mitchell and Sharon Snyder observe how disabled subjectivities become trapped in neoliberal ideas of the future, whether medical, financial or aspirational, that mean "the unchallenged desirability of normative lives" characterises disabled futures as continuously lacking. A result, they assert, is that disability embodiment is always rendered peripheral.[17] Extending this idea of exclusion, Alison Kafer notes in her 2013 study *Feminist, Queer, Crip* (a text I will use in detail in the next chapter), that majority cultures frequently "assume that a 'good' future naturally and obviously depends upon the eradication of disability" and this constitutes an "assumption that this kind of 'elsewhere', one without disability, is one 'we' all want".[18] A disabled future, it appears, is not in any way to be desired.

To give one relevant (and another turn-of-the-millennium) example, the October 2000 issue of the US magazine *Backpacker* carried an advert for Nike's new trail running shoe the Air Dri-Goat. Next to an image of the shoe, a paragraph stressed its technical features that helped prevent injury:

> Fortunately the Air Dri-Goat features a patented goat-like outer sole for increased traction so you can taunt mortal injury without actually experiencing it. Right about now you're probably asking yourself "How can a trail running shoe with an outer sole designed like a goat's hoof help me avoid compressing my spinal cord into a Slinky on the side of some unsuspecting conifer, thereby rendering me a drooling, misshapen non-extreme-trail-running husk of my former self, forced to roam the earth in a motorized wheelchair with my name embossed on one of those cute little license plates you get at carnivals or state fairs, fastened to the back?" To that we answer, hey, have you ever seen a mountain goat (even an extreme mountain goat) careen out of control into the side of a tree? Didn't think so.[19]

Following numerous complaints, Nike issued an apology, but the point being made is clear: physical disability – "drooling, misshapen", "husk" – is the antithesis of fitness and the body that is whole. Using a motorised wheelchair is a version of being human, Nike clearly suggests, that

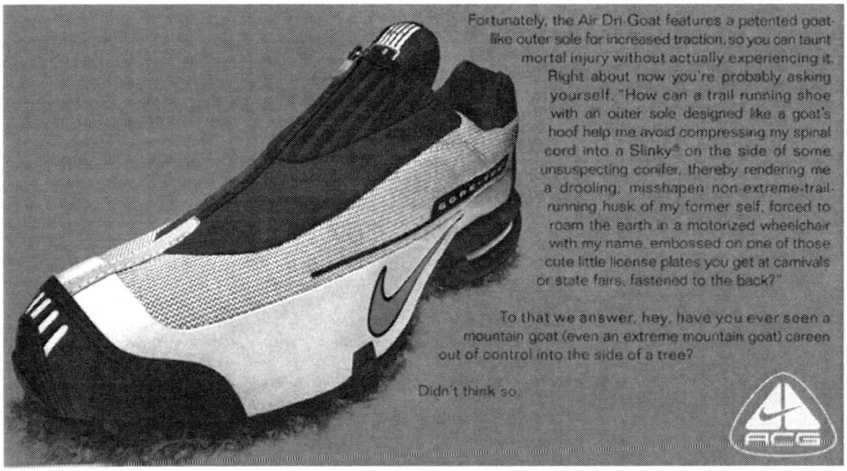

"a drooling, misshapen husk" *Backpacker* (October 2000)

no one would want. In its combination of a global corporatism with a promotion of 'active' embodiment, the advert creates a version of wholeness and health open to, as Kaushik Sunder Rajan puts it in an illuminating phrase, "everyone with purchasing power". Sunder Rajan's wide-ranging 2006 study *Biocapital: The Constitution of Postgenomic Life* unpacks the idea of what he terms "life as a business plan", where a global biocapitalism commodifies health in terms of "venture science", a meeting of bodies and markets where "the tension between the 'lie' of corporate PR and the 'truth' of science" results in the formation of a certain kind of contemporary subjectivity.[20] This insight into global economics of health and the incorporation of individual subjects into corporate networks reminds us that the combination of biological material and information is one way in which posthumanism, in its neoliberal form as an assemblage of capital, extends to all aspects of world health. I will return to these ideas in Chapter 3, but it is worth saying here that it is clear such structures are going to exclude most people with disabilities: they have restricted 'purchasing power' due to the exclusionary practices of capitalist systems; and the situated workings of biocapitalism will always find the difference of disability bodies largely abhorrent (as the advert itself makes clear). That the Nike copywriters seemed unable to imagine that their description might connect to the lives of real people, or that there would be any problem with this, only reinforces the status of disability here as a subject position thought to be outside of any standard norm. As with so much to do with disability lives, they were simply not considered.

The above observations carry clear weight, but in our very contemporary moment the picture is more complicated than this outline might appear. Both the breathless excitement of posthumanist possibilities and the assumed 'natural' negative of disabled subjectivity assume different proportions when considered 20 years after the above end-of-millennium examples. If it is still true that, for a broad public consciousness, posthumans are most frequently thought of as robots or dynamic cyborgs, and people with disabilities as lacking some core element of humanity, the actual terrain in which each set of topics functions is rather criss-crossed with ambiguity and doubt. Looking back on her late 1990s work in her subsequent study *My Mother Was A Computer,* Hayles noted that "the interplay between the liberal humanist subject and the posthuman that I used to launch my analysis in *How We Became Posthuman* has already begun to fade into the history of the twentieth century", and that "new and more sophisticated versions of the posthuman have evolved", citing in particular the development of "computational technologies" that mean we have all increasingly become "integrated into globally mediated networks" as a consequence.[21] Such integration continues at an often bewildering pace: posthumanism's focus on systems and subjects is always being updated by new forms of technological assemblages that increasingly encompass the entire planet with ever more complex webs, evolving ideas of function and 'worth' in which the meaning of bodies is ever-shifting.

Partly this evolution stems from changing relationships between the present and ideas of the future. Sunder Rajan observes that the politics of the biocapital are "a game played in the future" because of the elements of risk involved, and this future is forever written and rewritten as the vagaries of markets and biopolitics continually reposition ideas of health and wholeness.[22] Similarly, Melinda Cooper in *Life as Surplus: Biotechnology and Capitalism in the Neoliberal Era,* her 2008 study of the relationship between the life sciences and economics, explores what she terms "the promise of the bioeconomy" in the context of a contested neoliberal landscape that is "essentially speculative".[23] This speculation adumbrates a culture of surplus lives, including health lives, across the globe. Citing what we might recognise as a variety of posthumanist (though she does not use the term) contexts – tissue engineering, stem cell research, and the biological dimensions of the US war on terror – Cooper outlines ideas of "life beyond the limits" as biotechnology and capitalism shape the science at work in our contemporary world.[24] The new empires, she asserts, are biotechnological and biocapitalistic, founded on the "catastrophism" integral to the workings of neoliberalism.[25] In the chapters that follow, I will explore the ways in which disability is implicated in these global networks, but it is worth noting here that, disabled or non-disabled, we all inhabit murky new worlds of political power and market forces and the precarious health futures they envisage.

Precarious posthumanisms

A consequence of these kinds of ambiguity is that twenty-first-century writing on what Francis Fukuyama has termed, in his book of the same title, "our posthuman future" is noticeably less celebratory in exploring what might lie in the space outside or beyond the human than the scholarship of the 1990s. For his own part, Fukuyama, a conservative humanist with a firm belief in what he calls the "stable continuity" of human nature, finds reason to worry about the potential consequences in the development of scientific systems, where "the most significant threat posed by contemporary biotechnology is the possibility that it will alter human nature and thereby move us into a 'posthuman' stage of history".[26] Here, posthumanism denotes a subjectivity you would not want to have if, like Fukuyama, you feel that "we share a common humanity that allows every human being to potentially communicate with and enter into a moral relationship with every other human being on the planet".[27] In such arguments, 'common humanity' becomes aligned with agreed morality and other core concepts, such as a belief in the power of liberal democracy and capitalist markets (especially as practised by US governments). Set against this, the posthuman is a space that, for Fukuyama, is full of a fear of designer babies, genetic engineering and other affronts to the very idea of humanity.

Writers more sophisticated than Fukuyama and more sympathetic to posthumanist ideas nevertheless also pause when seeking to name the ways in which they might alter our present. "There is an undeniably gloomy connotation to the posthuman condition", Braidotti writes at the start of her 2013 book *The Posthuman*, "especially in relation to genealogies of critical thought". She argues that productive forces of critical and cultural theory animated the 1970s and 1980s, but that the present is rather defined by "theory fatigue" and "a zombified landscape of repetition without difference and lingering melancholia". In the face of this, however, Braidotti wants to return to posthumanism's positive possibilities and remobilise its theorising to "explore ways of engaging affirmatively with the present, accounting for some of its features in a manner that is empirically grounded without being reductive and remains critical while avoiding negativity".[28] For Braidotti, a grounded and located posthumanism avoids the open-endedness and sometime fanciful opinionising found in earlier writing. Spaces of the posthuman, she contends, can and should be political. This argument is possibly one that still needs to be won, given the continued philosophical fascinations with extending human life or creating biohybrid cyborgs, but it helps contextualise ways in which disability, as a lived and located experience, can be read through critical posthumanist methods.

In another study of the subject that seeks to maintain an engaged complexity, Bruce Clarke stresses that the productive potential of posthumanism needs to be understood as just one feature in a landscape where complex environments make it impossible for any single idea of the individual or social to supersede others. Drawing on narrative and systems theory, Clarke's 2008 book *Posthuman Metamorphosis* asserts that: "Posthumanism cognizes the human as one among numberless other situations of complexity – a productive disunity tasked with the quest, different for every psychic and social system, of working out a viable coordination of its systemic and environmental multiplicities".[29] While Clarke's analysis makes less room for politics than Braidotti's, his stress on systems and environments here certainly allows for an extension of his arguments into social and cultural settings, Both writers, while convinced of the potential and merits of posthumanism are nevertheless wary of oversimplifying its effects and manifestations. Conscious of the many variables in which the posthuman may be implicated they, like other current theorists, plot its coordinates with care.

That plotting, and indeed that care, takes the subject in different directions. Cary Wolfe's 2010 study *What is Posthumanism?* is a theory-driven meditation on "what thought has to become in the face of those challenges" produced by confronting a posthumanist present.[30] For Wolfe, posthuman*ist* thought (he draws careful distinctions between 'posthuman', 'posthumanist' and their various other linguistic formations) is to be valued because it "opposes the fantasies of disembodiment and autonomy, inherited from humanism itself".[31] But Wolfe's attention to care is such that his study, committed to not falling into what he sees as a humanist-style trap of declaring 'knowledge', becomes an exercise in academic looping in which 'thought' and the thinkers that practise it become the heroes of his argument. The regular citing of Jacques Derrida, Niklas Luhmann, Bruno Latour and other theorists as the continual, and only seemingly important, points of reference works to create a reified and, ultimately, banal version of his subject. For Wolfe, posthumanism is "always already post-". "Posthumanism" he asserts, articulating the point further, "in my sense isn't posthuman at all – in the sense of being 'after' our embodiment has been transcended".[32] Relativism of this kind, in which the posthuman is to be found in a variety of carefully constructed and theoretically informed reading practices that can name and critique the problematically embedded nature of humanist thinking, might be seen as a method of keeping a flexible and curious critical system always engaged with knowledge effects and their excesses. In contrast with a figure such as Braidotti, however, Wolfe's writing works to evacuate the space of what the posthuman might be, relegating it to specific academic concerns (such as in Wolfe's book: disciplinarity; the place of deconstruction; a 'proper' appreciation of Derrida, and the role of the humanities). For Wolfe, the conclusion that "'we' are not 'we'" is sufficient to articulate a number of complexities around the future; for me it rather speaks of the problem writing on posthumanism exhibits when it chooses to inhabit the subject's complexities – and to *over*-emphasise caution – without seeking to extend any thesis about its grounded, material consequences. In truth, it is clear that Wolfe very much is working with a 'we' in mind, and that is the cohort of scholars who make up his academic peer group.[33]

By way of contrast, and as I noted in the introduction, my sense of the posthuman is oriented foremostly, though not exclusively, around an idea of the 'after'. This focus on the future, and the present seen through the lens of the future, does not, I would stress, imply any necessary complicity with a reductive humanist positioning. Looking hard at the after and beyond means that the category of 'the future' becomes meaningful in literal ways, something essential to what I understand an ethical consideration of disability to be.[34] The genuine promise in posthumanist critical thinking here, whether evident in finding value in technological development or rethinking social and cultural categories that outline inclusion and agency, can be judged to be efficacious through the ways in which it impacts upon the lives of those with disabilities. If the subject continues to develop the kind of theoretical blind alleys we see in the work of Wolfe and others, it runs the risk of becoming an Emerald City of its own – all curtains, colours and mirrors – and potentially unable to find a language with which it can address the located conditions of personhood it seeks to inform.[35] As Hayles says: "For some people, including me, the posthuman evokes the exhilarating prospect of getting out of some of the old boxes and opening up new ways of thinking about what being human means", and for all that some canonical poststructuralist thinking might seem radical, it too can surely be found in the 'old boxes'.[36] Nikolas Rose agrees with this emphasis on change, observing in *The Politics of Life Itself* that changes around core questions of existence in the early twenty-first century mean that "a threshold has been crossed" and that, as a consequence, "we are inhabiting an emergent form of life".[37] The challenge for contemporary critical work in posthumanism then is to extend beyond the exhilaration of thinking alone, and for the emergent to find forms in which we might locate ourselves. It is precisely in relation to this that mapping the ways in which such work intersects with disability could prove to be such a valuable exploration of what a material posthumanism might be.

Critical disability futures: intersections and aesthetics

If writing on the posthuman is increasingly displaying complex interactions with notions of systems and processes, then the work of critical disability studies as it has developed over the last two decades is equally becoming attuned to a need to create more sophisticated contexts for the spaces in which disability functions. Validating identity, for example, is no longer the primary goal of a criticism that has embraced what Alison Kafer and Eunjung Kim have termed the "edges of intersectionality"; spaces that "shift, extend and reorient" patterns of disability theory.[38] Alignments with feminism, queer studies and critical race studies have created new possibilities for understanding how disability is lived and deployed, especially in terms of an interconnectedness that engages with the variety of contemporary subject positions.[39]

One noticeable necessary revision to the stereotypical idea of disability 'loss' has been a positive shift in much public perception of disability conditions. While this could rightly be termed gradual, only applies in some geocultural locations and is by no means global, it is probable that the waves of protest that would accompany Nike's advert, were it to be published now, would far exceed those made in 2000. While it is still the case that many governments continue to produce legislation that discriminates against those with disabilities, as explored in the UK context by Frances Ryan in *Crippled: Austerity and the Demonisation of Disabled People* (2019) for example, and that the kinds of disability hate crimes discussed by Katharine Quarmby in her excoriating study *Scapegoat: How We Are Failing Disabled People*

(2011) are all too common, and while the austerity that has followed in the worldwide recession sparked by the financial crisis of 2008 has affected disabled people more than other sections of the population, it is still the case that the education of the non-disabled majority about disability issues is now taking place at a pace not seen before.[40] Articulating this balance of discrimination and understanding is a precarious and difficult process, but activists and scholars (with disabilities and without) committed to better disability futures, used to having to point to *mis*representations and *mis*understanding and to having to fight for basic civil rights, now negotiate such campaigning in an environment where, despite injustices, at least more people are prepared to listen. So, for example, in *Dangerous Discourse of Disability, Subjectivity and Sexuality,* her examination of the theoretical positions surrounding disability subjectivities, Margrit Shildrick is cautiously positive about the ways in which recent change offers the possibility for more productive disability narratives: "Given, however, the apparent pace at which the certainties of the modernist world-view are being transformed both globally, where narratives of national progress and social order are challenged both theoretically and materially, and at the level of the individual where identity is destabilised, there is every opportunity to take a relatively optimistic approach".[41] That Shildrick can be optimistic when "identity is destabilised" indicates the way in which disability studies has negotiated a move from a narrow focus on social formations of disability to wider conceptions of subjectivity that speak of complex embodiment in the contemporary world. Shildrick's work has explored "leaky bodies" and the boundaries of embodiment, arguing that neither the body or the subject can be seen to be secure categories, but that it is precisely this insecurity that can form the basis of materialist criticism.[42]

In disciplinary terms, this means that critical disability studies has sought to respond to the multiplicities of current disability locations by stressing a need for methods that work by bridging different theoretical approaches. In his 2008 study *Disability Theory,* Tobin Siebers argues that the complex embodiment central to disability experience is most appropriately explored through ideas of intersectional identity, for example, while similar intercategorical analyses have worked to highlight the various structural contexts through which questions of disability can be seen to overlap with those of class, race, gender and sexuality.[43] These explorations of the criss-crossing ideological forces that shape contemporary disability attempt to respond to the kinds of sophisticated embedded networks that currently form disability knowledge or produce disability deployments.

So, to cite some specific contexts: in thinking about the production of disability in literary/cultural narratives, critics now think differently about discourse and metaphor than in 2000 when David Mitchell and Sharon Snyder published *Narrative Prosthesis: Disability and the Dependencies of Discourse,* their ground-breaking analysis of the role disability plays in literature.[44] As we saw with the reading of the L. Frank Baum's Tin Woodman in the Preface to this book, metaphorical accounts of disability work to render disability conditions transparent in the work they do to highlight non-disabled stories, and it was Mitchell and Snyder's work that helped most in the articulation of how this is a practice that occurs across literatures and across time. Disability in fiction frequently functions, in their words, as "a stock feature of characterization [and] an opportunistic metaphorical device", as well as a "pervasive category of narrative interest" that animates textual discourses in the production of disability as a perceived 'problem'. As they observe: "Nearly every culture views disability as a problem in need of a solution".[45] Yet, as we also saw in the Introduction, not only can such readings be resisted (and, indeed, are *more likely* to be resisted by a disability literate readership), metaphors can now be used in productive ways to tell disability stories. Amy Vidali has noted that re-evaluating the metaphors that carry disability offers a potential for "creative and historic reinterpretations" of the narratives in which they are contained.[46] It is precisely the possibilities inherent in the metaphorisation of markers of disability that mean they can become grounding points for the articulation of complex arguments of cultural distinction and difference. As Clare Barker asserts using a similar logic, representations of disability wounding in postcolonial literatures create metaphors that are "physical and mental, literal and allegorical, and allegorical, human and ecological [...] drawing attention to the embodied nature" of situated disability histories.[47]

Part of the ongoing reflection around disability and cultural production has been a renewed concentration on disability aesthetics. In the work of Tobin Siebers, Michael Davidson and others, disability is shown to be central to a formation of the aesthetic, particularly from the modern period onwards. In *Disability Aesthetics,* his 2010 study of the representation of disability in visual art in particular, Siebers discusses how the "underlying corporeality of aesthetics" has often been replaced with "idealist and disembodied conceptions of art", resulting in "a nonmaterialist aesthetics that devalues the role of the body and limits the definition of art".[48] By way of contrast, Siebers articulates a position that "conceives of the disabled body and mind as playing significant roles in the evolution of modern aesthetics, theorizing disability as a unique resource discovered by modern art and then embraced by it as one of its defining concepts". He goes on:

> My claim is that the acceptance of disability enriches and complicates notions of the aesthetic, while the rejection of disability limits definitions of artistic ideas and objects. In the modern period, disability acquires aesthetic value because it represents for makers of art a critical resource for thinking about what a human being is [...] Disability does not express defect, degeneration, or deviancy in modern art. Rather, disability enlarges our vision of human variation and difference, and puts forwards perspectives that test presuppositions dear to the history of aesthetics.[49]

Siebers' argument that disability is *integral* to the workings of modern art echoes my assertion that the bodies, minds and experiences of those with disabilities are central manifestations of a posthumanist present. The core issue here, as Davidson explains, is the necessary rethinking that comes from such an observation. "Disability aesthetics", he observes, "foregrounds the extent to which the body becomes thinkable when its totality can no longer be taken for granted, when the social meanings attached to sensory and cognitive values cannot be assumed".[50] As both Davidson and Siebers show, it is not that disability has been excluded in the history of art, but rather that it is, as Siebers says, "rarely recognized" as being seminal to modern cultural production.[51] Similarly, the questions raised by bodily adaptation and transformation, cognitive difference, genetic research and the newly networked subject that emerges from them are, as I will show, all topics that are suffused with disability concerns, but are rarely discussed as such. It is when, in Davidson's elegant phrasing, we "shift the emphasis from the private appreciation of a beautiful object to the social consent it produces", or turn "our attention from the insular act of perception to the constituencies enlisted in its validation", that we can grasp the extent to which disability functions as such a constant presence in forms of cultural production.[52] What working with Siebers and Davidson's insights allows is that transition from thinking about theoretical and ideological conceptions of the relationship between disability and culture, to the specific aesthetic and textual iterations of that linkage.

The mainly contemporary texts discussed in this book, then, are explored with a number of Siebers' concerns in mind, particularly in terms of the productive power disability can bring to cultural representation. Where any account of the posthuman must necessarily diverge from his thinking, however, comes in assessing the status of the 'modern' as a category through which a critical enquiry might be framed. *Disability Aesthetics* does not detail exactly what Siebers means by 'modern'; whether it is resolutely modern*ist*, for example, though his examples are predominantly from the twentieth and twenty-first centuries, many of them avant garde. He also uses the word to distinguish modern art from its 'classical' counterpart, a differentiation that suggests more questions around temporality than of any specific cultural movement. But, as we have seen, many scholars of posthumanism equate 'the modern' with the advance of liberal humanism, and the subsequent codification of bodies and minds that resulted as a consequence. Certainly, we can read modern*sim* as a set of contradictory texts on this topic: the potentially progressive aesthetics of cubism's twisted bodies, say, as set against the prejudices about disability seen in the diaries and letters of D.H. Lawrence, Virginia Woolf and other titans of modernist cultural production.[53] There is no doubt that the critique of the modern practised by many theorists of posthumanism – unpacking its connections to eugenics, speciesism and a restricted notion of the 'human' for example – is valid; but equally Siebers' valorisation of the power of modern and avant-garde aesthetics to undo the logics of dominant social and cultural discourses has a long history of its own.

Possibly a way to break out of the reductive looping that might result from such a position is to remember Rose's comments earlier about thresholds, and to recognise that the 'emergent form of life' he identifies posits posthumanism, like the modern, as a genuine moment of systemic rupture. The forms of capital that now govern biomedical personhood, and the technologies that circumscribe human/non-human interaction, constitute trajectories of emergence not seen before. Seen in this light the 'modern', whether understood as time period or artistic approach, belongs to the past, and the contemporaneous nature of posthumanist culture requires forms of critique that are specific to its multiple manifestations. It is, to borrow from Davidson, disability's 'left-handedness' and its potential to 'resituate' relations through its particular difference that can intersect and critique our posthuman present.[54]

Crip, disarticulate and secret futurities

As Robert McRuer has observed, we live in what he terms "crip times", a period when "unruly bodies" occupy both public and imaginative spaces.[55] McRuer's work outlines the position of disability within contemporary political and artistic processes. It is a vital consideration for this study because it names (in particular) the socio-economic contexts that frame posthumanism, serving to remind that the term does not only exists in philosophical and cultural imaginaries. McRuer's argument demands a recognition of "the absolute centrality of disability to now-global politics of austerity", a position that, as he notes, has "rarely been theorised explicitly or comprehensively".[56] In another example of the kind of threshold mentioned above, twenty-first century global austerity produces new shapes of disability experiences. Through practices of commercialisation and commodification, the reduction of public services and the deliberate erosion of community, material products of economic decision-making create disabled bodies that are forced into positions of precarity. As I will explore further in Chapter 4, market demands for greater 'flexibility' and 'personal responsibility' work to characterise disabled lives as inefficient; and the development of technology that is heralded by many champions of posthumanism needs to be understood as part of this marketisation. The possibility of the contemporary cyborg and the materials of the latest prostheses or exoskeletons, all elements suggesting the promise of assistive technologies in articulations of disability futures, operate within a ruthless market logic that exacerbates the binary between abled and dis/abled subjectivities.

But McRuer's emphasis on the 'unruly' is not only a comment on the actions of borderless capitalism. It also signals an identification of disability resistance. His use of the term crip, which has been part of his own work for over ten years, names those moments of artistic and social disability response to austerity.[57] Cripping contemporary capitalist globalisation involves "asking how cultural formations and movements circulate round, emerge from, and resist the hegemonic global political economy of neoliberal capitalism". What McRuer terms the "edgy and powerful valences" of crip insight work as both social resistance and critical methodology.[58] Crip times, then, are not simply moments of the hateful suppression of disability possibilities; they are equally part of what McRuer notes is the "fabulous potential" of "actively collective or coalitional" cultural disability politics.[59] McRuer's work is important because it navigates the balance between socio-economic modes of production and the power of disability expression. Though he does not use the term to focus on posthumanism, crip times clearly articulates posthuman moments, seen as *both* the coming together of a set of global material constructions that are often punitive and discriminatory, and productive philosophical/theoretical contemplation and artistic production that critique this. This study will follow his work in attempting to crip the politics and texts of a disability/posthumanist present, as well as its suggested futures. Cripping is especially important because, as a critical method, its unruliness is excessive and, therefore, is in line with the commitment to messiness and contradiction that I want to stress as one of the core subjects of this study. Crip possesses the capacity both to enter and critique the logic of market commodification control and then to vocalise (often to shout) what McRuer terms the "flamboyantly anti-identitarian" advocacy central to the art, culture and politics made by people with disabilities.

To vocalise is to articulate, and the articulation of contemporary disability bodies and subjectivities in a time of a posthumanist technologised present is, as we have seen, a difficult process. It also involves a recognition of what James Berger identifies as the "*dis*articulate" (emphasis mine), a cultural expression "which cannot be accounted for and which thus has some undetermined subversive power".[60] Berger's focus in his 2014 book *The Disarticulate: Language, Disability and the Narratives of Modernity* is on cognitively and/or linguistically impaired characters in modern fiction, but his observation works more broadly. It serves to remind that disability does not always shout out; indeed, part of the interaction between disabled presence and contemporary assistive technologies concerns the *amplification* of the vocal, through new forms of (for example) voice recognition software or neurological sonification communication systems. But Berger's point is that the dis/inarticulate is a site of disability power, and at different instances this study will analyse how textual representations of perceived 'voicelessness' (and, concomitantly, an absence of embodiment) function rather as capacities and moments of subversion. They are what Michael Bérubé – like Berger, writing on intellectual disability – terms the "secret life of stories"; often instances where narratives are productively disabled through prevention or contestation.[61] Bérubé identifies this secrecy not only in the ways that texts deploy (to use his key term) disability but also because it is a "social relation, involving beliefs and social practices that structure the apprehension of disability".[62] McRuer's crip advocacy, then, is also Berger's disarticulate and Bérubé's secret. It is the noise and the quiet of disability presence, a productive pairing this book will embrace.[63]

As noted previously, contemporary critical disability studies is increasingly adept at naming and negotiating a post-identity landscape of disabled experiences, but it needs to be stressed that disability *is still also* often identity and identification. The history of disabled people is, as Rosemarie Garland-Thomson, David Mitchell, Sharon Snyder, Ellen Samuels and many others have shown, is one of being displayed and named, while McRuer's crip practices map the reclamation of identities made by people with disabilities as a response to this. Identity remains vital when analysing the relationships that run through disability presence. In *Disability Theory* Tobin Siebers articulates a powerful "defense of identity politics and a counterargument to the idea [...] that identity politics cannot be justified because it is linked to pain and suffering" (or, we might add, a declared simplistic apprehension of the body). He goes on: "Identities, narratives and experiences based on disability have the status of theory because they represent locations and forms of embodiment from which the dominant ideologies of society become visible and open to criticism". Properly defined, Siebers asserts, identity is "an epistemological construction that contains a broad array of theories about navigating social environments".[64] In considering posthumanism, we can extend Siebers' "broad array of theories" beyond the purely social. The modes of embodiment the posthumanist body produces through interactions of human and technology create particular contemporary forms of identity, social but also imagined. Likewise, I am drawn towards Samuels' articulation of the "fantasies of identification" that have accompanied the attempted naming of those with disabilities, because what she rightly sees as the "inevitable" historical failure of "neatly categorizing all bodies and identities" in previous centuries continues into our own age.[65] More than with most disability narratives, those shaped by technologies create fantasies – of rehabilitation, restitution, cure and (in a posthumanist age) of the superhuman. In what follows, stories of fantasy and the fantastic will be common, and I share with Samuels the need to look for what she terms "future identifications" and the exploration of "alternatives to scientific knowledge models for authenticating identities". As she goes on to observe: "Representation is not the only step towards material change, but neither is it a passive reflector of such change".[66] As with the arguments made by McRuer, Berger and Bérubé, Samuels acknowledges disability's capacity to be both metaphor and materiality, to function as abstract and grounded, and she asserts the power of cultural narratives in the telling of disability experience.

Charting the subtle, complex and often difficult intersections between disability and posthumanism is a challenge, but the best recent work in disability theory makes it clear that disability itself contains the kinds of located, subversive and potent power that makes such a process possible. David Mitchell, Susan Antebi and Sharon Snyder's careful unpicking of the relationship between materiality, biopolitics and crip affect outlines the beginnings of a theory attuned to the value of critical posthumanist methodologies in reading the materiality of the disabled body. They note that: "Posthumanist disability theory offers an opportunity to provide a substantive theoretical reworking of the repetitive employment of impaired – read: socially marked and biologically determined as undesirable – bodies as diagnostic tools of things gone awry in their social and environmental contexts". Such theory, they continue, "recognize[s] that matter itself exerts influence and agency that ultimately outstrips any human ability to deterministically channel its substantiality into false discursive singularities". One result of this apprehension of matter is that it "returns disability to its proper place as an ongoing historical process of materiality's dynamic interactionism. It situates disability not as deviant, but rather as evidence of the 'excess' that marks materiality agency and reaches beyond the realm of the cultural while shaping its formulations".[67] Whether in the plasticity of stories and aesthetics charted in McRuer, Berger and Bérubé, or through the productively excessive material agency identified by Mitchell, Antebi and Snyder, critical disability and posthumanist insight is increasingly being understood to find common cause.

To bring these perspectives together, then, and to think of posthumanist subjects as they interact with disability deployments (to return to this chapter's title) is to stress this book's desire to participate in the ongoing evolution of critical disability studies. It is to signal a commitment to the development of disability aesthetics and critique within global political and economic systems, and to assert the power of cultural texts to throw into relief the ideological forces that shape contemporary worlds. If discussions of the posthuman have been transformed by ongoing developments in global biotechnologies within the space of the last decade, then those transformations have also brought an unparalleled rate of change to the lives of those with disabilities. Because of this, thinking about posthumanism and disability, whether in terms of technology, bioethics, material locations or public understanding, go hand in hand, the shadow of the one inevitably falling on the other. The challenge, however, is to outline and work with critical systems that do justice to the complexities and pace of change the relationship displays; returning to Rosi Braidotti's observation stated at the start of this chapter, to engage "productively with the contradictions, paradoxes and injustices they engender". Braidotti herself, in her most recent work *Posthuman Knowledge* (2019), notes how disability can provide exactly this kind of production. She observes:

> Critical disability studies are perfectly at ease with the posthuman subject, because disability has always contravened the classical humanist conception of what it means to be human. The converse is also true as disability invites a critical analysis to the posthuman, to the extent that disability epitomizes a posthuman enhancement of the self while simultaneously demanding recognition of the self in the humanist register.[68]

For me, the kind of invitation Braidotti see here lies in the conversations that are taking place around the future of the body, and especially the stories that those conversations tell.

Face off

A central debate in thinking about the relationship between disability and technology surrounds what exactly technologised bodies are supposed to *be*, and equally what they are *for*. How they enact and make meaning of the multiple and varied discourses that run through them tells a story of the way futures of the body are imagined. Biotechnology has the improvement of lives as a central purpose, while medical intervention is tasked with saving and prolonging life. The excitement and promise of technology set out a future landscape of body augmentation and enhancement that appears to offer unlimited possibilities for better human health. Those possibilities are, however, paralleled with counter statements of the need for caution in celebrating technological development. As seen earlier with Francis Fukuyama's fears of an emerging posthuman future, for many the changes that will come with A.I. or genetic modification are a profound threat to current concepts of humanity.

These issues of promise and threat are central to philosophical and technofantasist transhumanist approaches to the relationship between technology and the body. In the work of high-profile figures such as Nick Bostrom, Julian Savulescu, Anders Sandberg and others, transhumanism ultimately celebrates the possible "reinvention" of the human self, what Bostrom and Savulescu call the "enormous potential benefits" of "the opportunity fundamentally to change the human condition".[69] Similarly, metaphysician Andy Clark asserts "that human bodies and minds are essentially open to episodes of deep and transformative restructuring" through the use of technology.[70] Such thinking and language suffuse writing on transhumanism, where ideas of life enhancement, uploaded consciousnesses and transcendent engineering all jostle in what Gregory Stock, discussing germline manipulation in his 2003 book *Redesigning Humans: Choosing Our Genes, Changing Our Future,* calls "the battle for the future".[71] Clark's essay and an extract from Stock's book both feature in *The Transhumanist Reader,* a seminal collection of writings on the topic published in 2013. The *Reader* outlines a comprehensive set of transhumanist thinking, including a 'Transhumanist Declaration', a working document first announced by 23 scholars and scientists in 1998 and modified over the years that followed, that calls for "morphological freedom – the right to modify and enhance one's body, cognition and emotions".[72] While transhumanism is not a unified field (Stock calls transhumanists "a hodgepodge of individuals loosely united by a desire to transcend human limitations"[73]), this assertion of the right to technological change sits as a core argument across much of the spectrum of transhumanist thinking, for all that there is much discussion of the ethical caution that needs to be exercised in the pursuit of such 'freedom'.

In his essay in *The Transhumanist Reader,* Anders Sandberg places transhumanism in direct dialogue with disability. Discussing morphological freedom, Sandberg notes how many people with disabilities "over time have become used to" their personal forms of embodiment and have "integrated them into their self-image". Any suggestion of using technology as a cure for this population, he continues, "quite often is experienced as an attack on their human dignity". One result of this, he observes, is that "the disability movement has been a strong supporter of the right to determine one's body" and that, as a consequence, there "seems to be a natural point of agreement between transhumanists and the disability movement which might prove fruitful in future debate".[74] On the face of it, Sandberg is here identifying points of interaction that align disabled difference with trans/posthumanist theory, but such connections feel uneasy in an essay that also makes reference to "handicapped people" and "deranged persons".[75] His characterisation of 'the disability movement', with its sense of a singular purpose, suggests that for Sandberg 'disability' is more a category through which to discuss abstract ethics than a recognition of a varied set of lived experiences, a common critical practice in analytic philosophical accounts of the relationship between technology and disabled bodies. Possibly the contradiction is best summed up in his use of the phrase 'human dignity'; if dignity can be considered a state essential for people with disabilities (though one often denied), its juxtaposition with 'human' suggests the kind of coherent humanist self that both disability and posthumanism challenge. For many scholars of disability, it is transhumanism's avowed desire to extend the human through a recourse to humanist conceptions of the subject that is the problem. To move 'beyond' in this way is both to seek an idea of perfection (a state that always has had the supposedly 'broken' body of disability as its antithesis), and a commitment to technological research that chases a future while ignoring the everyday situations of peoples with disabilities (and others who lack access to resources) in the here and now.[76]

"Transhumanists philosophies", Russell Blackford writes, "are philosophies of self-transformation and self-overcoming", terms that echo precisely the neoliberal fixation on the ever-expanding capabilities of the self and evoke one of the major contemporary demands – 'overcoming' – that society demands of those with disabilities. Blackford expands this outline of transhumanist philosophies with a clearer focus on the nexus between technology and the body:

> Ultimately, transhumanists argue, technological intervention in the capacities of the human body and mind will lead to alterations so dramatic that it will make intuitive sense to call the deeply altered people of the near and not-so-near future *posthuman*: they will be continuous with us but unlike us in many ways. Optimistically, they might *be* us, greatly changed. On the transhumanist picture, we are not posthuman yet, but we are a bridge, or a rope, between historical humans and beings with posthuman capacities. And what do we plan to transcend? Not the order of nature, but merely our own limitations.[77]

Disabled bodies have always been those considered to have 'limitations', while it is clear that Blackford's characterisation of a common 'we' and 'us' here articulates a generalised norm of humanity that, in fact, functions through its exclusion of those with disabilities. It is this logic that, in the end, exemplifies transhumanist conceptions of the future, and not Sanders' sketch of a potentially more tolerant characterisation of different bodies.

In order to see how such ideas function in cultural narratives, I want here to explore the tensions between transhumanist ideas of the transcendence of limitations, posthumanist notions of non-unitary subjects, and disability accounts of complex embodiment through a reading of the X-Men films, one of the most popular and financially successful superhero franchises of the twenty-first century. As stressed throughout this book, it is in the competing contradictions of imagined narratives that crucial formations of the relationship between technology and future bodies are played out, and certainly the cultural reach of the X-Men films means that their conception and deployment of differently visualised bodies provide powerful images of variation to a global audience. The characters of the X-verse are both hyperable and precariously vulnerable; they embody strength and fragility and enact narratives of humanist restitution even as they suggest networks of posthuman affiliation. Reading their stories provides a way to show how the complexities of cultural theory and aesthetics discussed in this chapter are animated in textual forms.

The X-Men films, particularly the first three in the franchise – *X-Men* (2000), *X2* (2003; also known as *X Men 2* and *X-Men United*) and *X-Men: The Last Stand* (2006) – use the central idea of the 'mutant' to promote a broad narrative of social acceptance and integration, inviting identification from a range of non-majority communities. They can be read in terms of teenage estrangement, racial and sexual equality (the sexism of the titles notwithstanding), abuses of political power, and post-9/11 debates surrounding immigration and security.[78] The ways the films function when seen through a disability optic, however, makes a compelling case for the validity of reading their depiction of the complexities of embodied disabled difference.[79] The mutation common to all the X-characters ("the key to our evolution" as the voiceover at the start of the first film puts it) is genetic, and the films' deployment of human variation, social prejudice and medical/technological interventions occur in a specific posthumanist context where ideas of mutants having evolved 'beyond' humanity are central to each feature. More specifically, disability politics figure recurrently, from the advocacy, indeed superiority, of difference espoused by the Brotherhood of Evil Mutants to the highly disability-specific debate around the idea of 'curing' at the start of *X-Men: The Last Stand*. Possibly most tellingly, disability is central to major character Charles Xavier (Patrick Stewart) through the constant presence of his iconic wheelchair, marked with an X on each wheel and always the focus of the shots in each film in which Xavier is introduced. Seemingly well aware of the questions of bodies and minds they are raising, the first X-Men films were the most complex global popular representations of disability in the first decade of the twenty-first century.[80]

X2 poses a set of intriguing connections between ideas of disabled difference and posthumanist technologies and ethics. It has two characters in wheelchairs. First, and most obviously, there is Xavier, the leader of the X-Men and a figure blessed with cognitive powers that allow him telepathic access to the thoughts of others. Xavier is a teacher, strategist and diplomat, and an example of leadership for those at the school ('for gifted youngsters') he heads. He is also an eloquent defender of mutant difference in the face of powerful government opposition, but one committed to brokering a peaceful relationship with the human majority. In the film's fictional universe, he is, to employ the kind of racial/cultural reading the narrative invites, the Martin Luther King figure, as against the Malcolm X style separatist tendencies of Eric Lensherr/Magneto (Ian McKellen) and his Brotherhood, a grouping determined to destroy those non-mutants who oppose difference. But if the Xavier/Magneto relationship is the most dramatic in the film (and indeed across the other features in the series), it is arguably not where the most interesting face-off in this particular narrative takes place. The second character in a wheelchair is Jason Stryker (Michael Reid MacKay), a mutant and the son of Colonel William Stryker (Brian Cox), the film's principle villain and a figure dedicated to eradicating the X-Men because of a hatred of their difference. Like Xavier, Jason has significant powers (both are 'level 5' mutants, the 'highest' ranking possible), but if Xavier represents a (more than) capable characterisation of disability, Jason enacts traditional associations of disabled difference. Hated and rejected by his father, Jason had been a student at Xavier's school, but when it becomes clear that Xavier's intention was to attempt to respect and develop, rather than cure, his son's exceptionality, Stryker chooses to turn Jason into a weapon through which he can enact genocide against all mutants.[81]

The confrontation between the two characters comes as a result of this weaponisation of Jason and, specifically, his disability/exceptionality. Xavier has developed Cerebro, a machine that channels telepathy and through which he can identify and connect to all mutants on Earth, a process that allows for the dissemination of his version of liberalism and tolerance against a backdrop of worsening human–mutant relations. Stryker, however, recognises the value of Cerebro as a vehicle for his genocidal impulses and develops a second version of the machine that not only identifies Earth's total non-mutant population, but has the power to destroy it. Because of his cognitive powers, Jason is able to manipulate the system to threaten mass slaughter. As a result, the two characters in wheelchairs face off against one another, inside Cerebro, in a battle of minds over the future of the planet's population. As Petra Kuppers has observed, Xavier's various wheelchairs in the film denote an intriguing intersection between technology, style and disability; they "are sometimes made of hard glistening steel, sometimes made of clear, clean, lightweight, unbreakable glass or plastic" and overall form "part of a stylish and stylized world into which the cinema viewer is inducted". The glass wheelchair Xavier uses, Kuppers notes, is "gorgeous", while the "geometry and balance" he achieves when in his wheelchairs "are indicators of Xavier's modesty, calm and balanced approach", signifying "an orderly man/machine hybrid, a being who creates his own environment as an extension of his telepathic mind".[82] His wheelchairs are, we might say, full of a technologised posthumanist confidence and convey a highly aestheticised acceptance of difference (something that extends to the wider use of visuals in conveying the attractiveness of all the X characters). Jason, on the other hand, lacks all such visual markers. Hunched in a hospital-style smock in what appears to be a rudimentary (basic, inexpensive, unglamorous) wheelchair, connected to machinery and scarred from operations that link *his* disability to the murderous practices of Holocaust-like, experimental, medicine, Jason is a 'monstrous' figure produced by his father's pathology. His monstrosity is only heightened by the fact that, in order to confuse Xavier during their conversation, he morphs his appearance to become a young girl, a figure whose innocence is set firmly against his own manipulated degradation.

Where, then, is the posthuman and where is the disability in this scene? Which wheelchair (and which incumbent) invites the stronger claim in any consideration of narrative meaning or ethics in this fiction? Xavier's disabled difference is represented as a powerful positive force, one marshalled for the benefit of all in his desire to maintain peace; whereas it appears that Jason – through no fault of his own (he is after all not in control of his actions) – is best understood as exemplifying a force of destruction. In such a reading, Xavier is a paradigmatically benevolent and progressive example of the posthuman, blending cognitive diversity with technology and a philosophical ability to see 'beyond' to a future in which human and mutant can co-inhabit and co-evolve. In the character of Xavier, the X-Men films appear to welcome the disability to come in any posthumanist future. He becomes the transhumanists' cyborg, a hybrid not only in terms of physical and cognitive capabilities, but also of judgement and morality, convinced that the evolution that has produced the X mutation has also created moral and ethical clarity in recognising what is good and right.[83] The enthusiasm noted earlier for a holistic trans/posthumanist subjectivity that might contain the best virtues of corporeal existence

Disability, technology and the human. Jason (Michael Reid MacKay) and Charles Xavier (Patrick Stewart) in *X2*

and informational/technological expertise finds its hero in Xavier and the enacting of his benevolent mutant self.

It is precisely because Xavier is such a transhumanist icon that, when we pause to consider his place within the wider fabric of the film, he makes for an unconvincing example of any disability subjectivity or politics. He is, for example, clearly the most *humanist* character in the entire story, his inclusive values set against not only Magneto's separatism, but arguably more importantly Stryker's warped and delusional vision of what humanity might be, and the unenlightened, limited conception of society conceived of by government and expressed by President McKenna (Cotter Smith). Xavier's teachings, the film makes clear, should apply to everyone he encounters, mutant or human. It is also obvious that Xavier is a particular and peculiar exemplar of a certain biocapitalistic version of disability tolerance; visually his school contains all the trappings (ivy-covered walls and wood-panelled corridors) of an exclusive private establishment, while the film's ideas of education and inclusivity, its notion of a future *community*, cannot suppress a specifically American idea of individual advancement and neoliberal capability.[84] *X-2*'s visual style also oozes a glamorous capitalism, particularly through its casting of supermodels (Rebecca Romijn as Mystique) and use of clothing and gadgetry; the school's jet, for example, exhibits technological capabilities beyond anything the US government can muster.

As we saw earlier in the theorising of Siebers, Davidson, McRuer, Berger and Bérubé however, disability representation and deployment enacts not only morality tales of restitution and overcoming but carries within these a capacity for critique and revision. The different bodies involved in the face off between Xavier and Jason remind us of Davidson's observation of "the extent to which the body becomes thinkable when its totality can no longer be taken for granted". Such newly thinkable bodies are, as McRuer noted, 'unruly' and they carry within them the 'disarticulate' subversive power identified by Berger as well as the 'secrets' Bérubé locates within disability stories. Jason portrays all these things. Set against the shining transhumanist capability of Xavier, Jason's disability appears less the example of pathology it is possibly intended to be, and more, because the meaning of his body and its interaction with technology can no longer be taken for granted, a corrective to the excesses of Xavier's stylish tolerance. If the X-Men films work to continually stress the necessary acceptance of otherness and diversity, especially as they relate to disability, Jason reminds us that they only do so within certain frames of reference. Misshapen and broken, Jason is the version of disability that the film works so hard to oppose and erase, but the place he occupies in the narrative – his central importance to the story, as evidence in the scene with Xavier – works to undermine the power of this argument. In all its ordinariness, Jason's wheelchair cannot help but remind us that Xavier's wheelchair is less about disability than it might seem and is rather the vision of a certain form of *desire*, a wish that the future will be inclusive. But, as we might expect from a Hollywood A-list feature, it appears to be a desire in which the costs (here maybe literal costs) of such inclusivity are hidden. Jason's monstrosity – his scars and the various cords and leads that connect him to (unknown) machines – speak to the physical damage societies do to disabled bodies, in opposition to the perfect physical integration between man and machine we see in Xavier, or the stylised difference on display in other characters in the film, such as Mystique or Nightcrawler (Alan Cummings), whose bodies are marked (blue tattoos or scales) with their mutant identities.

Xavier wins the face-off between the two characters; ultimately his power and the value for which he stands are the stronger, though he needs to be aided by Magneto. What then happens to Jason is highly problematic: as the film gathers pace towards its climax and the complex in which Stryker has established his version of Cerebro is about to be destroyed in a flood following the breaking of a dam, Jason is simply left (unrepresented, unfilmed), presumably to perish. We see Stryker's demise in some detail, as it is the necessary closure to the film's main antagonistic relationship, but the story simply forgets about Jason. He is afforded no kind of ending, not even a straightforward narrative one in which he is killed. He simply disappears. In the ways in which Jason is overlooked, we can see parallels with those communities of the disabled who find themselves excluded: whether from majority power structures and decision-making processes, or from social representation and cultural stories; left behind as interest focuses elsewhere. His unruliness, however, and the presence of his disarticulate, forgotten body, allows for the critical insight that unpicks the politics of disability in the film.

Structurally, the narrative complexity in *X2* is similar to that of Baum's Tin Woodman discussed earlier. In the Oz stories, the posthumanist embodiment of the Woodman and experience of his physical self are in tension with his emotional and moral desires, the former suggesting a way of living in the world that is challenged by the latter's conception of 'heart and home'. With *X2*, the underpinning ideas of tolerance and a progressive politics create a matrix of ethical inclusion, but the terms of such inclusion become destabilised when we pause to consider the film's actual detail of disability. Such a contradiction is recognisable in many of the contemporary Hollywood features that represent embodied difference in clearly posthumanist contexts, particularly narratives of superhuman abilities. To give but one example, the 2017 film version of *Ghost in the Shell*, starring Scarlett Johansson and directed by Rupert Sanders, is an adaptation/remake of the manga narrative of the same name by Masamune Shirow first serialised in 1989, and subsequently made into an animated film in 1995 by Mamoru Oshii.[85] Like its Japanese predecessors, the US feature depicts a cyberpunk world in which technological body adaptations are common and characters sport a variety of augmentations and enhancements, from limited skin grafts to the insertion of human brains into full-body prostheses. But whereas the Japanese versions of the narrative explore the kinds of networked ideas of body, self and community that arise from this, the US film accentuates the search for origins of central character police Major (Johansson). Major has a human brain inside a full manufactured body, but in a search for a resolution of this interaction the story enacts a set of questions around her selfhood that produces a flatly humanist story of a protagonist coming to terms with change.

The reduction of the original *Ghost in the Shell* story to the humanist trajectory of the 2017 film centres on the simplification of the overall script and especially the narrative's end. In both the manga and the 1995 film, Major merges her 'ghost' with that of the Puppet Master, the embodied A.I. criminal figure she has been hunting for the bulk of the story, to create a networked/combined body and self. In the 2017 production, the Puppet Master figure, Kuze (Michael Carmen Pitt), turns out to be a childhood friend of Major who (in an echo of the Wolverine narrative in the X-Men films) was a test subject in a government experiment programme into the creation of cyborgs, one that included Major and which wiped both characters' memories.

When Kuze offers to merge with Major, she refuses and returns to her mother, from whom she was taken as a child and whom she has rediscovered.[86] In place of the complex future-facing assemblages of the Japanese narrative(s), the US *Ghost in the Shell* reconstitutes personal selfhood within the context of a reactivated family dynamic. The film is visually stunning, evoking a posthumanist, cyberpunk-inflected urban environment in great detail, but in its own way it is still an account of Dorothy trying to find her way home from Oz. Even with the most sophisticated technologised prosthetic body available, Major decides that "humanity is our virtue" (as she says in the voiceover that closes the film) in a deliberate choice of the human over the "manufactured". In pursuing justice through her role as a police officer, Major will be guided by the 'real' self she has rediscovered.[87]

Conclusion: on not resolving

As noted earlier, Rosi Braidotti claims that in a time of posthumanism, "the point is not to know who we are, but rather what, at last, we want to become, how to represent mutations, changes and transformations". As we have seen, the mutations of the X-Men films display the conditions to be complex: high-profile deployments of disability often working towards humanist conclusions but carrying within them the unruliness of the disabled body that unsettles both the aesthetics and cultural politics of the films' representations. Braidotti does not disaggregate the 'we' in her assertion, but within the context of her writing it does not come across as the standard humanist plural as noted earlier in Blackford's work, assuming continuity across all humans on the planet. It appears rather as the possibility of other choices and associations, an invitation to choose the positions 'we' might wish to occupy: disabled, crip, multiple, liminal.

Here, then, we might make a critical choice similar to that suggested in the preface in relation to Baum's Tin Woodman, one that embraces a posthumanist complex embodiment and sees technology aligned with disability possibilities as opposed to humanist conceptions of self. In terms of the different versions of *Ghost in the Shell*, this means rejecting the fanfare of Hollywood and learning from the possible selves and worlds found in Shirow's and Oshii's imaginings. Manga and anime resound with what Hajime Nakatami calls "thematics of order and disorder, self and other, and humans and nonhumans", though neither form sees these as problematic boundaries that require solving.[88] So, for example, the various puppet, doll, cyborg or automata figures that recur through the different Japanese *Ghost in the Shell* narratives work to explore the uncanniness of ningyō ('human-shaped figure') in the representations of interactions between humans and non-humans.[89] It is precisely the coming together of these different possibilities, and not their resolution, that drives meaning in Shirow's manga and Oshii's film, where the networks of body/self/other/biology/human/machine point towards the shape of cultural futures.

The stories disability tells open up the contexts and relationships in which bodies and technologies come together. As I have tried to show in this chapter, these combinations result in a matrix of aesthetics, theory and politics, as well as the complex heritage of comprehending disability and crip subjects. Appreciating disabled bodies helps unveil the humanism central to much transhumanist thinking, but also posits alternative affinities with those strands of critical posthumanist thinking that champion non-unitary selves and a grounded, material technological space in which those selves might exist. It also allows for critical rereadings of those texts in which technologised bodies create powerful images and narratives of embodied difference, a process I will continue in the chapters that follow. And, as many disability scholars observe, it reminds us that all these processes are political, whether the politics of identity and location, questions of access to developing technology, or aesthetic and representational practice. It is this wide sense of politics that I want to carry forward into the chapters that follow.

Notes

1 Judith Halberstam and Ira Livingston, 'Introduction: posthuman bodies' in Halberstam and Livingston (eds), *Posthuman Bodies* (Bloomington and Indianapolis: Indiana University Press, 1995), p. 19.
2 Hans Moravec, *Mind Children: The Future of Robot and Human Intelligence* (Cambridge, MA and London: Harvard University Press, 1988), p. 1.
3 Hans Moravec, *Robot: Mere Machine to Transcendent Mind* (Oxford: Oxford University Press, 1999), p. 13.
4 Rosi Braidotti, *Metamorphoses: Towards a Materialist Theory of Becoming* (Oxford: Wiley-Blackwell, 2002), p. 1.
5 Braidotti, *Metamorphoses*, pp. 1–2.
6 Braidotti, *Metamorphoses*, p. 213.
7 Braidotti's work on the posthuman has been explored in relation to sociological approaches to disability studies. See Dan Goodley, Rebecca Lawthom and Katherine Runswick Cole, 'Posthuman disability studies', *Subjectivity* 7, no. 4 (December 2014), pp. 342–361.

8 N. Katherine Hayles, *How We Became Posthuman: Virtual Bodies in Cybernetics, Literature, and Informatics* (Chicago, IL and London: The University of Chicago Press, 1999), pp. 286–287.

9 Subsequent work on posthumanism, technology and the body has not always agreed with Hayles' account of the value of embodiment. In *Cyborgs and Barbie Dolls*, Kim Toffoletti concludes her engagement with Hayles' work by remaining "unconvinced that we can speak unproblematically about material existence, especially in a context where real and virtual worlds are no longer clear" (Toffoletti, *Cyborgs and Barbie Dolls: Feminism, Popular Culture and the Posthuman Body* (London and New York: I.B. Tauris, 2007), pp. 16–17). Despina Kakoudaki, writing in 2014, critiques Hayles for producing a paradigm of the posthuman that is "both the precondition of human embodiment [and] the precondition of our seamless merger with computer networks and virtual technologies". Kakoudaki notes that, while this "concept of the posthuman refers to contemporary modes of subjectivity, highlighting the constructed and embedded nature of the self within technological, social, and political contexts", it "may also express vague, apocalyptic, and transcendental aspirations for moving beyond the limits of the body or beyond matter altogether" (Kakoudaki, *Anatomy of a Robot: Literature, Cinema, and the Cultural Work of Artificial People* (New Brunswick, NJ, and London: Rutgers University Press, 2014), pp. 16–17).

10 Michel Foucault, *The Order of Things* (New York: Vintage, 1973), p. 387.

11 Neil Badmington, 'Introduction: approaching posthumanism' in Badmington (ed.), *Posthumanism* (Basingstoke: Palgrave, 2000), pp. 9–10.

12 Pramod K. Nayar, *Posthumanism* (Cambridge: Polity, 2014), p. 29.

13 Hayles, *How We Became Posthuman*, p. 246.

14 The idea of 'science fiction becoming fact' is a common refrain when discussing the status and promise of contemporary technology, especially from those figures involved in the production of such technologies. But this perspective can only see fiction as content and, in asserting that future humans will merge with machines, or construct spaceships that can travel across the galaxy (and many other classic tropes of the genre), it completely misses the messiness and contradictions that in fact are central to the way fiction works. If science fiction *could indeed* become fact it would create all manner of productive uncertainties, far beyond mere questions of utility.

15 Robert Pepperell, *The Post-Human Condition* (Exeter: Intellect, 1995), p. i (emphasis in original).

16 Lennard J. Davis, *Enforcing Normalcy: Disability, Deafness and the Body* (London and New York: Verso, 1995), p. 14.

17 David T. Mitchell with Sharon S. Snyder, *The Biopolitics of Disability: Neoliberalism, Ablenationalism, and Peripheral Embodiment* (Ann Arbor: University of Michigan Press, 2015), p. 6. See also chapter 1, 'From Liberal to Neoliberal Futures of Disability', pp. 35–62.

18 Alison Kafer, *Feminist, Queer, Crip* (Bloomington and Indianapolis: Indiana University Press, 2013), p. 20.

19 *Backpacker*, October 2000, p. 3. I consider it no small irony that I find myself writing about this advert while my own spinal stenosis means my vertebrae are compressed. No drooling, however.

20 Kaushik Sunder Rajan, *Biocapital: The Constitution of Postgenomic Life* (Durham, NC and London: Duke University Press, 2006), pp. 133–134. See pp. 138–181 for full discussion of the idea of 'Life as Business Plan'.
21 Hayles, *My Mother Was a Computer: Digital Subjects and Literary Texts* (Chicago, IL and London: The University of Chicago Press, 2005), p. 2.
22 Sunder Rajan, *Biocapital*, p. 34.
23 Melinda Cooper, *Life as Surplus: Biotechnology and Capitalism in the Neoliberal Era* (Seattle: University of Washington Press, 2008), pp. 19 and 10.
24 Cooper, *Life as Surplus*, p. 15.
25 Cooper, *Life as Surplus*, pp. 10–11.
26 Francis Fukuyama, *Our Posthuman Future: Consequences of the Biotechnology Revolution* (London: Profile, 2003), p. 7. Fukuyama's book is in many ways an extension of his arguments about 'human nature' and morality, here seen through the lens of biotechnology, explored in his earlier *The Great Disruption: Human Nature and the Reconstruction of Social Order*, albeit with a more simplistic view of such 'nature'. See *The Great Disruption: Human Nature and the Reconstruction of Social Order* (London: Profile, 1999).
27 Fukuyama, *Our Posthuman Future*, p. 9.
28 Rosi Braidotti, *The Posthuman* (Cambridge: Polity, 2013), p. 5.
29 Bruce Clarke, *Posthuman Metamorphosis: Narrative and Systems* (New York: Fordham University Press, 2008), p. 194.
30 Cary Wolfe, *What is Posthumanism?* (Minneapolis: Minnesota University Press, 2010), p. xvi.
31 Wolfe, *What is Posthumanism?*, p. xv.
32 Wolfe, *What is Posthumanism?*, pp. 126 and xv.
33 Possibly for this reason, Wolfe's engagement with disability studies in one of the chapters of *What is Posthumanism?* is a curious investigation. Focusing on Temple Grandin's accounts of her autism in her autobiographical writings, Wolfe is suspicious of what he terms the "pragmatic pursuits" of disability studies' concentration on the material consequences of living disabled lives because "they are forced to work within the purview of a liberal humanism in philosophy, politics, and law". This curtails the opportunity to pursue "a more ambitious and more profound ethical project: a new and more inclusive form of ethic pluralism". For Wolfe then, the detail of grounded disability lives is not 'profound', while disability studies itself only works to produce a "blockage" in any more 'ambitious' investigation of subjectivity. Instead he turns (again) to Derrida to make what he believes to be more insightful points about blindness or trans-species affiliations. It comes as no surprise then when, explaining his use of Grandin's work, he asserts that "I am less concerned with evaluating Grandin's assessment of her own case and its broader implications – an assessment that is often problematic, in my view – than with mobilizing her observations about her experience towards my own critical ends" (Wolfe, *What is Posthumanism?*, pp. 137, 139 and 128).
34 In the light of Wolfe's championing of Derrida, it is interesting to note that my idea of the future here is, in part, itself a point taken from Derrida, whose concept of *l'avenir* is precisely one of the future that *is* to come and the ways in which this shapes the present (Wolfe, *What is Posthumanism?*, p. 170).

35 I much prefer the analyses and arguments put forward by Stefan Herbrechter in his 2013 study *Posthumanism: A Critical Analysis*, to those of Wolfe. Herbrechter's account of posthumanism's genealogies and its possible critical futures are acute, but I find myself frustrated by his final recourse to Derrida and other theorists when contemplating the ultimate trajectories of posthumanism's potentials.

36 Hayles, *How We Became Posthuman*, p. 285.

37 Nikolas Rose, *The Politics of Life Itself: Biomedicine, Power and Subjectivity in the Twenty-First Century* (Princeton, NJ and Oxford: Princeton University Press, 2006), p. 7.

38 Alison Kafer and Eunjung Kim, 'Disability and the edges of intersectionality' in Clare Barker and Stuart Murray (eds), *The Cambridge Companion to Literature and Disability* (Cambridge: Cambridge University Press, 2018), p. 125.

39 See Nirmala Erevelles and Andrea Minear, 'Unspeakable offenses: untangling race and disability in discourses of intersectionality', *Journal of Literary and Cultural Disability Studies* 4, no. 2 (2010), pp. 127–145; Nancy J. Hirschmann, 'Queer/fear: disability, sexuality, and the other', *Journal of Medical Humanities* 34, no. 2 (2013), pp. 139–147; and Kafer, *Feminist, Queer, Crip*.

40 Frances Ryan, *Crippled: Austerity and the Demonisation of Disabled People* (London: Verso, 2019); and Katharine Quarmby, Scapegoat: *Why We Are Failing Disabled People* (London: Portobello Books, 2011). Quarmby notes that as she conducted the research for her book, "every disabled person I've interviewed, or even encountered socially, has experienced discrimination, or harassment, or worse" (p. 238).

41 Margrit Shildrick, *Dangerous Discourse of Disability, Subjectivity and Sexuality* (Basingstoke: Palgrave, 2009), p. 173.

42 Margrit Shildrick, *Leaky Bodies and Boundaries: Feminism, Postmodernism and (Bio)ethics* (London and New York: Routledge, 1997). See also '"Why should our bodies end at the skin": embodiment, boundaries and somatechnics', *Hypatia* 30, no. 1 (2015), pp. 13–29; 'Prosthetic performativity: Deleuzian connections and queer corporealities' in Chrysanthi Nigianni and Merl Storr (eds), *Deleuze and Queer Theory* (Edinburgh: Edinburgh University Press, 2009), pp. 115–133; and 'Re-imagining embodiment: prostheses, supplements and boundaries', *Somatechnics* 3, no. 2 (2013), pp. 270–286. As these last two articles indicate, Shildrick has used disability frames, and specifically ideas of prosthetics, to explore the permeable boundaries of the body.

43 Tobin Siebers, *Disability Theory* (Ann Arbor: The University of Michigan Press, 2008), pp. 22–33.

44 David Mitchell and Sharon Snyder, *Narrative Prosthesis: Disability and the Dependencies of Discourse* (Ann Arbor: The University of Michigan Press, 2000).

45 Mitchell and Snyder, *Narrative Prosthesis*, pp. 47 and 57.

46 Amy Vidali, 'Seeing what we know: disability and theories of metaphor', *Journal of Literary and Cultural Disability Studies* 4, no. 1 (2010), pp. 33–34.

47 Clare Barker, '"Radiant afflication", disability narratives in postcolonial literature' in Clare Barker and Stuart Murray (eds), *The Cambridge Companion to Literature and Disability* (Cambridge: Cambridge University Press, 2018), p. 104. Barker's initial exploration of wounds comes through a reading of Derek Walcott's 1990 long poem *Omeros*.

48 Tobin Siebers, *Disability Aesthetics* (Ann Arbor: The University of Michigan Press, 2010), p. 1.
49 Siebers, *Disability Aesthetics*, pp. 2–3.
50 Michael Davidson, *Concerto for the Left Hand: Disability and the Defamiliar Body* (Ann Arbor: The University of Michigan Press, 2010), p. 4.
51 Siebers, *Disability Aesthetics*, p. 4.
52 Davidson, *Concerto for the Left Hand*, p. 144.
53 For a thorough and compelling reading of disability in cultures of artistic (especially literary) modernism, see Davidson, *Invalid Modernism: Disability and the Missing Body of the Aesthetic* (Oxford: Oxford University Press, 2019).
54 Davidson, *Concerto for the Left Hand*, p. xvi.
55 Robert McRuer, *Crip Times: Disability, Globalization, and Resistance* (New York: New York University Press, 2018), p. 8.
56 McRuer, *Crip Times*, p. 4.
57 See especially *Crip Theory: Cultural Signs of Queerness and Disability* (New York and London: New York University Press, 2006).
58 McRuer, *Crip Times*, p. 13.
59 McRuer, *Crip Times*, p. 20.
60 James Berger, *The Disarticulate: Language, Disability, and the Narratives of Modernity* (New York: New York University Press, 2014), p. 9.
61 Michael Bérubé, *The Secret Life of Stories: From Don Quixote to Harry Potter, How Understanding Intellectual Disability Transforms the Way We Read* (New York: New York University Press, 2016).
62 Bérubé, *The Secret Life of Stories*, p. 25. Bérubé also argues that the workings of his notion of the "secret" aim to offer to a more sophisticated version of critical disability studies: "Even as disability studies has established itself in the humanities in a way that was unthinkable twenty years ago, it has still limited itself to too narrow a range of options when it comes to literary criticism [...] I am quite serious about the conviction that disability studies limits itself unnecessarily, as a new branch of criticism and theory, whenever it confines itself to determining the disability status of individual characters" (p. 20). While this point is well made, *The Secret Life of Stories* is a highly selective and, at times, curiously self-indulgent study. Bérubé's claims for a rewriting of a literary critical disability methodology are based around, as he admits, "delineating a few of the most important and engaging uses of intellectual disability in fiction" (p. 31), but the assumptions behind what constitutes 'important' or 'engaging', or indeed a real sense of why this version of a 'few' is better than any other, go uninterrogated.
63 The work of McRuer, Berger and Bérubé, and especially the notion that disability representation *in itself* contains an inherent process of critique, can be seen to extend Ato Quayson's outlining of the 'aesthetic nervousness' that comes with that he calls "the crisis of representation". It is "the aesthetic domain itself", Quayson asserts, that becomes short-circuited on the encounter with disability". The 'nervousness' that results can "be discerned in the suspension, collapse, or general short-circuiting of the hitherto dominant protocols of representation that may have governed the text". See *Aesthetic Nervousness: Disability and the Crisis of Representation* (New York: Columbia Press, 2007), p. 26.
64 Siebers, *Disability Theory*, pp. 14–15.

65 Ellen Samuels, *Fantasies of Identification: Disability, Gender, Race* (New York: New York University Press, 2014), p. 213.
66 Samuels, *Fantasies of Identification*, p. 214.
67 David T. Mitchell, Susan Antebi and Sharon L. Snyder, 'Introduction' in Mitchell, Antebi and Snyder, *The Matter of Disability: Materiality, Biopolitics, Crip Affect* (Ann Arbor: University of Michigan Press, 2019), pp. 2 and 3. In the last essay in this collection, Mitchell and Snyder give an explicit example of such a posthumanist approach, reading issues of memory and history in the Nazi T4 programme. Their argument, they note, considers "how the intersection of disability studies and memory studies might come into posthumanist with disability as an alternative to – or, at least, extension of – the fetishization of perpetrator mind-sets": *The Matter of Disability*, p. 251. I explore interactions between memory, posthumanism and disability in contemporary cinematic representations of the war on terror in: 'Disability and memory in posthuman(ist) narrative: reading prosthesis and amnesia in Hollywood's re-membering of the "war on terror"', *Parallax* 23, no. 4 (2017), pp. 439–452.
68 Rosi Braidotti, *Posthuman Knowledge* (Cambridge: Polity, 2019), pp. 138–139.
69 Nick Bostrom and Julian Savulescu, 'Human Enhancement Ethics: The State of the Debate' in Bostrom and Savulescu (eds), *Human Enhancement* (Oxford: Oxford University Press, 2009), pp. 20–21. It should be noted that both writers acknowledge that such processes of change also contain "great risks" (p. 21). Bostrom is in more overtly celebratory mood in his chapter 'Why I Want to Be a Posthuman When I Grow Up' in Ronald L. Sandler (ed.), *Ethics and Emerging Technologies* (London: Palgrave Macmillan, 2008), pp. 218–234.
70 Andy Clark, 'Re-inventing ourselves: the plasticity of embodiment, sensing, and mind', *The Journal of Medicine and Philosophy* 32, no. 3 (2007). Reprinted in Max More and Natasha Vita-More (eds), *The Transhumanist Reader* (Chichester: Wiley-Blackwell, 2013), p. 113.
71 Gregory Stock, *Redesigning Humans: Choosing Our Genes, Changing Our Future* (Boston, MA: Houghton Mifflin, 2003), pp. 153–175.
72 'Transhumanist Declaration' in More and Vita-More (eds), *The Transhumanist Reader*, p. 55. The declaration begins with a recognition that: "Humanity stands to be profoundly affected by science and technology in the future", and that the "misuse of new technologies" means that "humanity faces serious risks" including "possible realistic scenarios that lead to the loss of most, or even all, of that we hold valuable". For all that the use of 'we' here appears to imply a collective sense of humanity, the declaration also includes an advocacy for "the well-being of all sentience, including humans, non-human animals and any future artificial intellects" (p. 54). Both Bostrom and Sandberg are among the signatories.
73 Stock, *Redesigning Humans*, p. 158.
74 Anders Sandberg, 'Morphological freedom: why we not just want it, but need it' in More and Vita-More (eds), *The Transhumanist Reader*, pp. 61–62.
75 Sandberg, 'Morphological freedom', pp. 61 and 57.
76 For an eloquent rebuttal of many of the claims made about the desirability of perfection, see Michael J. Sandel, *The Case Against Perfection: Ethics in the Age of Genetic Engineering* (Cambridge, MA: Harvard University Press, 2007).

77 Russell Blackford, 'The great transition: ideas and anxieties' in More and Vita-More (eds), *The Transhumanist Reader*, p. 422. While I accept that I am using Blackford's arguments to generalise about transhumanist conceptions of the future body and self, it is a position held in much writing about transhumanism, both in *The Transhumanist Reader* and more widely.

78 At the time of writing, the X-Men franchise consists of 12 features. The first three films constitute a stand-alone trilogy, while a specific Wolverine trilogy – compromising *X-Men Origins: Wolverine* (2009), *The Wolverine* (2013) and *Logan* (2017) – has also been made. *X-Men: First Class* (2011) is a prequel exploring especially the early relationship between Xavier and Magneto. *X-Men: Days of Future Past* (2014) is a sequel to both *X-Men: The Last Stand* and *X-Men: First Class* and is followed in story order by *X-Men: Apocalypse* (2016) and *X-Men: Dark Phoenix* (2019). A separate X-Men spinoff, *Deadpool* (2016) and *Deadpool 2* (2018), has also been produced. I find it sobering that seven of the X-Men films have been made during the time it has taken me to develop the ideas for, and then write, this book.

79 Questions of philosophy, including ethics as well as ideas of norms and disability, are explored in the 2009 collection *X-Men and Philosophy: Astonishing Insight and Uncanny Argument in the Mutant X-Verse* (Hoboken, NJ: John Wiley, 2009), edited by Rebecca Housel and J. Jeremy Wisnewski. See Patrick D. Hopkins, 'The lure of the normal: who *wouldn't want* to be a mutant?' and Ramona Ilea, 'The mutant cure or social change: debating disability', pp. 5–16 and 170–182.

80 Reviewing *X-Men 3: The Last Stand*, Robert McRuer admits that while the film "is atrocious in a lot of ways", it is nevertheless "from a disability perspective [...] one of the more complicated films to emerge from Hollywood in a long time", citing especially its debate around 'cure'. See McRuer, 'A "last stand" against cure', *Ragged Edge*, June 2, 2006, www.raggededgemagazine.com/departments/closerlook/001144.html. Accessed December 6, 2017.

81 In the first two *X-Men* films in particular, the links to genocide – and especially the Holocaust – are specific. *X-Men* opens with a scene in which Eric/Magneto is forcibly separated from his parents by German soldiers as a group of Jewish citizens are forced into train carriages, while the narrative of the experimentation conducted on Wolverine (Hugh Jackman) echoes the practice of Nazi science in the death camps. In *X2*, the development of state/government arguments for the registration of all mutants are clearly presented as a step towards such authoritarian control, especially as both Magneto and Wolverine recall their own pasts when confronting the escalation of prejudice. See Jesse Karvadlo, 'X-istential X-Men: Jews, Superman, and the literature of struggle' in *X-Men and Philosophy*, pp. 38–50.

82 Petra Kuppers, 'The wheelchair's rhetoric: the performance of disability', *TDR/The Drama Review* 51, no. 4 (2007), pp. 84–85.

83 Xavier's mutant posthuman self, and especially his cognitive powers, can be read profitably next to Bostrom's idea of 'superintelligence'. Bostrom is one of the central figures involved in advocating uses of technology that will lead to the development of cyborg selves and human communities in other galaxies. His use of the term 'superintelligence' to "refer to minds that greatly outperform the best current minds across many very general cognitive domains" finds an uncanny personification in Xavier, whose telepathy not only fits

Bostrom's ideas of enhanced 'performance' but is also directed towards the kinds of moral growth and collective inclusiveness that Bostrom values in his imagined posthumanist future. See Nick Bostrom, *Superintelligence: Paths, Dangers, Strategies* (Oxford: Oxford University Press, 2014), p. 63.

84 Such a trajectory is echoed in Wolverine's personal narrative in which he seeks knowledge about his origins, a topic given its own film in the franchise: *X-Men Origins: Wolverine* (2009, d. Gavin Hood).

85 Many different Japanese versions of *Ghost in the Shell* have been made subsequent to Shirow's original narrative. Oshii's 1995 film was followed by a sequel, *Ghost in the Shell 2: Innocence*, written and directed by Oshii and released in 2004. A television series, *Ghost in the Shell: Stand Alone Complex*, was made in 2002 and was then reworked into the 2006 film *Ghost in the Shell: Stand Alone Complex – Solid State Society*. A new television series – *Ghost in the Shell: Arise – Alternative Architecture* – screened in 2015, while *Ghost in the Shell: The New Movie* was released in 2015. The films subsequent to Shirow's story and Oshii's adaptation all develop details of the originals in new story arcs.

86 When reunited with her mother Major discovers that her younger self was a radical who – her mother tells her – wrote "manifestos about how technology was destroying the world".

87 The politics of the film's humanist plot conversions are further underscored by the controversial casting of Johansson as the central character, as well as the (less commented upon) extension of this to the majority of the other cast members in the film. The production's cultural whitewashing were explored as part of a wider issue in the casting of white actors to play Asian characters in a March 2017 *Guardian* article by Steve Rose. As Rose notes, the whitewashing of *Ghost in the Shell* had arguably started with the 1999 production of *The Matrix* (d. Lily Wachowski and Lana Wachowski), which borrows heavily from Mamoru Oshii's film. As the article also observes, however, Oshii himself saw no problem in the casting of Johansson: "Her physical form is an entirely assumed one", he remarked, "the name Motoko Kusanagi and her current body are not her original name and body, so there is no basis for saying that an Asian actor must portray her". See Steve Rose, '*Ghost in the Shell*'s whitewashing: does Hollywood have an Asian problem?', *The Guardian*, March 31, 2017, www.theguardian.com/film/2017/mar/31/ghost-in-the-shells-whitewashing-does-hollywood-have-an-asian-problem. Accessed January 23, 2018.

88 Hajime Nakatami, 'Introduction: Komatopia', 'Limits of the Human', *Mechademia* 3 (2008), p. 66.

89 See Steven T. Brown, 'Machinic desire: Hans Bellmer's dolls and the technological uncanny in *Ghost in the Shell 2: Innocence*', *Mechademia*, p. 222.

CHAPTER TWO

Design, Engineering and Gendering the Disabled Body

Introduction: she/he/it, calling all robots

March 2017. I am in Sheffield, visiting the university's Robotics Institute as part of an ongoing research collaboration around ideas of disability, augmentation and posthumanism. After a morning brainstorming ideas, the project team is in the institute's laboratory playing around with the robots (most of us come from arts backgrounds and have no expertise in robots; we tend mainly to poke them and say 'hello'). Since I was last in Sheffield, the laboratory has acquired a new member, Pepper, a humanoid companion robot developed in France and Japan by Aldebaran Robotics and the SoftBank mobile network, launched in 2014 and made available for purchase the year after. Pepper is pretty cute – she/it/he (all the publicity material uses 'he' but there is of course no reason for this) is just over 1 metre tall with a round face and big, expressive eyes.[1] Pepper's torso tapers to a narrow waist before the body continues down and flares back out to a stable base that contains wheels, rather than having legs. It is her/its/his one obviously non-humanoid feature, though – as one member of the team pointed out – it bears a resemblance to a pencil skirt, and the flaring about the wheel housing reminded me of a fantastic 1940s style mermaid dress, the kind of thing Rita Hayworth might wear. Pepper has a touchscreen tablet, used to control basic settings and set up communication, attached to her/its/his chest and made to look as if it has been slung around the neck.

Pepper's strength as a companion robot is based around her/its/his ability to identify emotions and adapt its responses to, as the sales pitch puts it, "the mood of the moment, expressing himself through the colour of his eyes, his tablet or his tone of voice". Being able to analyse emotion, it is stressed, is "the heart of the robot". As the advertising continues: "Your robot evolves with you. Pepper gradually memorises your personality traits, your preferences, and adapts himself to your tastes and habits". Here, companion shades into friend, even potentially confidante. Pepper can identify faces, develop relationships in a "natural" way, and "wants to learn more about your tastes, your habits and quite simply who you are".[2]

This is exciting. Collaborator and colleague Michael Szollosy turns Pepper on, her/its/his head comes up from a reclining position and we start interacting. "Hello Pepper", someone says. There is a pause. Pepper's eyes change colour from partially blue to green, a sign of identifying the person speaking. "Hi Pepper", Michael says. "Hello" Pepper replies. Prompted by Michael, and seeking to start a conversation, we ask Pepper if she/it/he knows Asimov's laws of robotics, information we are aware has previously been programmed in. "Hello" says Pepper once more. We try again, but there is no answer to the laws question. After some time worrying whether there might be an issue around our accents (Michael and one other team member are Canadian, and Michael is careful to say 'ro-bot-icks', foregoing his usual way with consonants), we have another go: "Are you a robot?" someone asks. "Yes" Pepper replies, I'm a humanoid robot". We follow up: "What can you do? What kinds of things do you do?" There is a pause. It would be wrong of course to say that Pepper is confused, but the silence that stretches out inevitably signals something not quite being right. "How can I help you?" Pepper says finally, in what is clearly a default answer rather than an actual response to the question. We try a little more conversation but for the most part the interaction proceeds in this way. It occurs to me that, given that Pepper is being pitched as a companion robot for people with dementia, this is a pretty dementia-recognisable (non)dialogue, with very little meaning being expressed. Certainly, none of us feel as if our *emotions* are being recognised or responded to.

This description is, in truth, unfair. Pepper is, more or less, just out of the box and the team at Sheffield have only just begun the process of developing her/it/him. It may well be that she/it/he will ultimately be able to function exactly as Aldebaran and SoftBank say, which really is more a point about what others can add to the core platform provided, but for now the interaction is an example of a not uncommon phenomenon in which engaging with a robot (and specifically a humanoid robot, with all the affinities suggested) is a little *disappointing*. At this moment, the technology is not delivering on the

Pepper: Aldebaran Robotics/SoftBank

promise suggested by the initial meeting (the most enjoyable moment comes when we realise that we can make Pepper giggle by ticking her/its/his head; fun but not necessarily indicative of a future driven by unimaginable robot intelligence and almost certainly not the best use of what is a very expensive product). Then something interesting happens. After I ask some more questions, Pepper turns and looks up at me. "Hello Pepper" I say, the umpteenth time we have tried to start a conversation this way. "Hi Stuart", Pepper responds. There is a pause during which I look up at everyone else. As far as I am aware my name has not been mentioned, and certainly not in any direct address to Pepper. Then it dawns on me what has happened, and I turn to see Michael behind me with a laptop. He has told Pepper what to say. "It's the Wizard of Oz" I say to him and he smiles; Michael is the wizard behind the curtain, tapping keys rather than spinning dials and pulling levers, but fundamentally engaged in the same processes. Pepper has (finally) appeared to spontaneously interact with me, but in fact has done nothing of the sort; she/it/he has simply acted as instructed, as countless other pieces of technology do all the time. For a moment, a heartbeat maybe, there was a connection – human and robot converse! – but then the curtain was opened, and the smoke and mirrors revealed.[3]

This anecdote opens up at a number of immediate thoughts. The first is the *desire* we have for robot technologies to deliver on their boundless promise, for objects like Pepper to *really* be a companion friend, reading emotions and developing friendships, interacting seamlessly with people as they bring their excitement and needs to her/it/him. In her 2014 study *Anatomy of a Robot*, Despina Kakoudaki notes that public exhibitions of robot capabilities form part of "long-standing traditions of representation and performance" and that in such moments the "the attraction of anthropomorphic figures in general, the special allure of mechanical complexity, the resonance of gestures and explanation, the pleasure of witnessing autonomous action [and] the oracular power of the engineer's invitation to have inanimate matter move and speak" are all at work. These are, it can be noted, true even when, as with Pepper, the robot is *not* working. Attraction, allure, pleasure and power were all circulating in one form or another as we interacted with her/it/him.[4]

Following on from Kakoudaki's observation about 'mechanical complexity' above, thinking through the encounter with Pepper raises the place of the engineer/designer in this process of display, an activity that often goes unnoticed and without comment in our rush to have robots 'be themselves'. The character *missing* in the transfiguration of the Tin Woodman recounted previously in this book is the tinsmith, the individual who (presumably painstakingly) designed and made the various replacement body parts for the Woodman as he turned from human to posthuman. In *The Wonderful Wizard of Oz* he is unnamed, and there is no indication of any of his thoughts on what he does. Is he, for example, amazed at the requests he receives and the situations causing the limb loss? Does he understand his work as constituting replacement, restoring a disabled body? Are there complicated design and production factors that test his skills? What about the ethics he might have to consider? In many ways these are, of course, nonsensical questions; Oz is a place where wonderful and amazing things happen as a matter of course, and possibly the tinsmith's undescribed attitude is a nonchalance that matches the Tin Woodman's own calm as he recounts to Dorothy and the Scarecrow the changes his body underwent. But it strikes me that we are not wrong to ask such questions, to seek to know what is involved in the engineering of posthuman selves. Michael is not, he stresses, an engineer, but during that time with Pepper in the Sheffield laboratory he was arguably trying to deliver – to help make happen – the idea common to both the Tin Woodman and Pepper that, as Aldebaran and SoftBank term it, there is emotion and human connection at "the heart of the robot". As Pepper's audience, we wanted that transfiguration to happen, even if it might mean we ignored the human intervention that could make it possible.

The tinsmith in the Oz stories does, in fact, have a name – Ku-Klip

– that we learn from later novels. But even though he features again in *The Tin Woodman of Oz*, nothing is communicated about the reasoning for his actions, or how he might explain and rationalise his work. Here a central point needs to be stressed: for all that the *experience* or *representation* of the prosthetic, cyborg, biohybrid, augmented or difference body (the central concerns of much of this book) are vital and compelling, issues surrounding disability, self and subjectivity also apply during complimentary moments of design, production and deployment, and the questions of what is involved in these processes are essential to understand, if all too frequently ignored, when we consider disability and augmentation. By way of contrast, in this chapter I want to focus on the engineer; to imagine and, as it were, attempt to fill out Ku-Klip's role in the posthumanising process he makes possible. To begin with, I will analyse the intersection between engineering, design and ethics in the planning and production of technologies made to assist those with disabilities. Cultural theory and disability studies have much to say about prosthetics, exoskeletons and the often dramatic manifestations of the ways in which technology encounters disability, and this is a topic I will focus on more in the next chapter in particular. But such criticism rarely (if ever) considers what is involved in the engineering perspectives that produce such technologies.

Even looking at this brief outline, it is clear that any genuinely cross-disciplinary approach to the question of posthumanism and its intersection with disability needs to engage with engineering design and its parameters and rationales.[5] Too often cultural theory creates straw man (again, *The Wonderful Wizard of Oz* is strangely prescient) arguments that posit 'science' or 'medicine' as the originator of repressive modes and practices that seemingly enlightened critical perspectives can challenge. But although these positions can be founded on accurate apprehensions of certain aspects of scientific and biomedical models, it is a significant mistake to assume that sophisticated debates around bodies, ethics and engagements with those with disabilities do not take place within such disciplines. I want to engage here with those debates and see how thinking through them can make for better disability studies scholarship. Numerous people, involved in numerous activities, work with care and attention around disability, and collective research can only be better if it takes as much into account as possible.

The Pepper anecdote, however, not only speaks of the desire that surrounds what we want robots to be; I want to argue that it also suggests a crucial point about *gender*. In *To Be a Machine*, his book recounting a series of encounters with transhumanists, roboticists and others involved in the often murky world of biohybrid augmentation, Mark O'Connell describes meeting Pepper at a technology stall at a major robots fair in the US. In his account, O'Connell alternates pronoun use, with Pepper being "it" when basic presence and function is described ("a four-foot humanoid"), and "her/she" when focusing on the *role* he understands she/it/he has been designed for (a "customer service humanoid" designed to serve a "social and emotional" function).[6] During an awkward moment when O'Connell – "as much out of politeness as journalistic rigor" – agrees to a small piece of intimacy, he is hugged by Pepper and observes: "I fancied I detected something like ambivalence in Pepper's impassive gaze; but she raised her arms and I bent towards her, and suffered her to enfold me in her unnatural clasp. It was, frankly, an underwhelming experience; I felt that we were both, in our own ways, phoning it in. I patted her on the back, lightly and perhaps a little passive-aggressively, and we went our separate ways".[7] The slippage between pronouns appears natural and there is another scene in which Pepper hugs a three-year-old girl and where, again, feminine pronouns are used. But what is 'natural' here needs to be unpacked: an alignment of seeming intimacy (however contrived) described through tropes of the feminine set against the comprehension of Pepper in terms of male functionality. When robots become emotional or subservient in any way, it appears that they 'become' female.

Considering that robots are made of entirely artificial components, the desire to ascribe gender to them, and to *name* them, while ostensibly explicable, is intriguing. It is another sign of the ways in which the tendency to humanise technology asserts such a powerful pull. As Kakoudaki observes of robots, androids and cyborgs: "While ostensibly beyond or outside gender categories because of their inorganic status, mechanical bodies nevertheless refer to a visual and narrative vocabulary that is exaggerated in its depiction of gendered humanity".[8] This chapter will foreground these issues of narrative and vocabulary, and will read its investigations of engineering and design through the clear and obvious gender divisions that exist in the discussions around, and representations of, posthumanist technologies and A.I.. It is instructive (to say the least) to note how many of the most prominent figures in the public and academic debates surrounding post- and transhumanism – Hugh Herr, Hans Moravec, Ray Kurzweil, Francis Fukuyama, Anders Sandberg, Nick Bostrom and Max More (just to name a few) – are men; while many of the most incisive academic critical writers on the topics the subject raises are women, for example Donna Haraway, Rosi Braidotti, Anne Balsamo, Cassandra Crawford,

Margrit Shildrick, Despina Kakoudaki or Vivian Sobchack. I am aware that this is cherry picking and there is an obvious danger of selecting names here that perpetuate a created dualism, but it is difficult to argue against the bare fact that thinking and talking about any post-humanist future (especially in the public domain) has produced a significant gender split.[9] In addition, while numerous depictions of the technologised or enhanced female body involve the overt sexualisation of the figures involved (type 'female robots' into Google Images for a telling cross-section of how this is visualised), it is also the case that writers from Mary Shelley to Margaret Atwood and Lidia Yuknavitch have been incisive and perceptive in imagining the consequences of gendered discourses of fictional biohybrid posthuman selves living in the world. These are threads of both creative and critical imagination that need to be followed.

Gender and authorising technologies

Imagining engineering authority is to engage with processes that are substantively controlled by men. In part, this is because scientific creation and its subsequent study is frequently posited as a male activity, one connected to free-floating notions of knowledge and inspiration, and framed by ideas of rationality and technical competence. Nina Lykke is blunt in her formulation of the critical/political consequences of this:

> If science is regarded as an enterprise which, no more and no less, aims at a value-neutral, progressive discovery of "universal and objective truths" about nature and matter, there is no room for feminism [...] The claim that feminist perspectives can be meaningful in the hard sciences, beyond the issue of recruiting more women, involves a radical challenge to the traditional notion of science as a "pure" search for the hidden truths of nature and matter.[10]

It is possible to argue with this assessment, of course. Lykke is perhaps creating a simplistic idea of 'science', in order to define her sense of a progressive feminism, in ways I criticised above; and there is a grand and sweeping aspect to her claims that undoubtedly eschews the nuance found in different kinds of scientific research. But Lykke is a scholar who works in inter- and transdisciplinary contexts, and as a specialist in feminist technoscience she is not unaware of the detail of scientific practice. Her language here (which she goes on to note is informed, rather than uninformed, by working with scientists) suggests that, in spite of ongoing work that counters caricatures in discussing gender and science, there are still core issues to be addressed surrounding fundamental questions of boundaries, communication and representation.

Julie Wosk identifies just such problems in her 2015 study *My Fair Ladies: Female Robots, Androids and Other Artificial Eves*. Wosk writes not only on the representations of female automata, robots and androids, especially as they are created by men, but also gives over a chapter of her book, entitled 'Dancing with Robots and Women in Robotics Design', to an analysis of the design of such robots, particularly as technology has developed over the last 20 years. She observes that, as the twenty-first century has developed, "male roboticists [have] used the latest in technologies to embody their fantasies about a perfect female" and how, as a consequence, when designers "sought ways to make female robots ever-more realistic looking and acting, they seemed to be only rarely aware of how their research has been shaped by their attitudes towards women themselves".[11] Wosk's focus here is mainly on robots made in Japan and Korea and, although she is not explicit about it, her analysis relies on certain prejudicial assumptions about attitudes towards (negative) gender relations in those countries that go uninterrogated. Nevertheless, while it is fair to critique the cultural bias (and subsequent recourse to ideas of 'natural' human behaviour) in her writing, Wosk's broader point about the often unexamined nature of gender politics in robot engineering and design is well made. She notes that female robot design often accentuates qualities – partnering and nurturing for example – associated with perceived 'feminine' attributes, while specific body and face features in what Wosk terms "ultrarealistic female interactive robots" frequently involve soft silicone curves and wide-open eyes or fluttering eyelashes, read as markers of a male fantasy of the female form (Wosk is not making specific reference to sex robots here).[12] What anthropologist Jennifer Robertson, specifically citing the Japanese context, terms "robo-sexism" contextualises robot production within tropes of paternalism and ethnocentrism.[13]

Ultimately, and regrettably, given the opportunities suggested by her approach. Wosk's analysis of robot design is flawed in its use of detail, relying on an uninterrogated category of "male roboticists" and never engaging with questions of engineering design beyond some cursory readings of research projects or product launches (another chapter, 'Engineering the Perfect Woman', avoids actual engineering but rather uses the verb to mean 'producing' in a representational sense). But the broad scope of her thesis is suggestive, and in the second half of this chapter I will explore how engineer/scientists, both male and female, and their cyborg/biohybrid creations, are represented and deployed in a range of contemporary prose and film texts. I will frame this within a consideration of how cultural theory addresses disability and gender in technoscience, noting how engineering design is not gender neutral nor does it produce great flexibility in imagining the disabled body, for all that such bodies may well be the ones the design is *for.*

It was Donna Haraway who, in 'A Cyborg Manifesto: Science, Technology, and Socialist Feminism in the late twentieth century' (originally published in 1985 as 'Manifesto for cyborgs: science, technology and socialist feminism' in the 1980s), first articulated a mode of cyborg being that was powerfully and productively connected to gender, and Haraway's work has produced a long line of critical analysis that explores the relationship between bodies, gender and technology. I will analyse Haraway's manifesto in more detail later, especially to show how engaging her foundational scholarship in the service of disability critique is not unproblematic, but it is unquestionable that the questions of body politics and disability presence that arise from encounters with her cyborg are foundational and need to be part of any discussion of a disability/posthuman nexus. As Carey Wolfe has noted, "'The Cyborg Manifesto' was a profoundly liberating experience for many readers [...] in the sense of modelling for us a new and unprecedented range of expression and experimentation for serious academic writing".[14] What was true of the reading experiences at the time of the manifesto's publication is no less true now and engaging with Haraway's complex, sassy rhetoric and vision is essential in the consideration of what follows in this chapter. My thinking here, informed by Haraway and those who have built on her work, will move to imagine the vision of a theorised and gendered cyborg and its possible relationship with grounded disability identities. I will address the often giddy possibilities of a shining future and a seemingly limitless potential, but first it is best to deliberately hit pause, to restrain and reorient my critical gaze, and rather start again with details of a working practice.

Designing disability/disabling design

In the cultural representation of cyborg bodies and prostheticised selves, there is often a stress on the hyperreal (and, to follow on from the above point about gender, the hypermasculine). Extraordinary exceptionalism abounds. From the rebuilt police officer Murphy (Peter Weller) in Paul Verhoeven's seminal 1987 film *Robocop*, a text rightly considered foundational to contemporary visual narrative representations of cyborgs, to the multiple narratives surrounding Wolverine (Hugh Jackman) in the *X-Men* franchise, fictional cyborgs frequently combine depictions of masculine strength, violence and a moralising humanism as they wrestle (some sort of struggle is nearly always involved) with the consequences of man meeting machine.

I will return to these kinds of representations later in this chapter, particularly in readings of science and speculative fiction, but at the risk of stating the very obvious it is worth noting at the outset that such narrative depictions of the manufacture of cyborgs are, clearly, a long way from actual work undertaken within design and engineering on assistive technologies. While it was strangely enjoyable, a repeat viewing of *Robocop* with the express purpose of seeing how the technical elements of the engineering transformation are represented made it clear that no time whatsoever is given over to any representation of the *processes* of technological change. This is, of course, not surprising. For the most part, Hollywood audiences are not known to clamour for extended scenes of designing, prototyping and testing mechanised platforms, and when they are forced to wonder at such practices (as with Tony Stark's (Robert Downey Jr) creations in *Iron Man* for example), it is within a context of the marvellous; comic-book capacities of futuristic creations and whizzbang montages of obsessive genius.

But in this chapter I want to consider how the actualities of design and engineering might sit alongside such fantasies and caricatures of the marvellous and to see if, critically at least, it is possible to reclaim the space that is missing in *Robocop*. How might the systems and procedures of engineering speak to the glamorous worlds of science fiction in ways that teach us more about disability, gender and their relationship with posthumanism? What can we learn from the methods and narratives (of all kinds) of designing and producing technologies that revise our ideas of bodies and how they work in the world?[15] In his ground-breaking 2009 study *Design Meets Disability*, Graham Pullin notes that designers and engineers work in tension-filled environments surrounding attitudes towards disability. "Within design for disability", he observes, "where teams still tend to come exclusively from clinical and engineering backgrounds the dominant culture is one of solving problems", meaning that "there are significant differences between the cultures found within design and medical engineering – differences in values, methods, and even in ultimate goals".[16] If engineering frequently focuses on utilitarian notions of replacement when addressing disability as a 'problem', Pullin suggests that designers often "perceive disability in terms of approaching legislation that threatens to compromise their creativity, rather than as a source of fresh perspectives that could catalyse new directions and enrich the whole of their work". The result, he notes, is that "there is not so much a clash of design cultures as a yawning gulf between them".[17] He goes on: "Traditionally, design for disability has paid more attention to the clinical than the cultural diversity within any group. The same prostheses, wheelchair, and communication devices are often offered to people with a particular disability, whether they are seventeen or seventy years old, and regardless of their attitudes, towards their disability or otherwise".[18] What is noticeably missing from both cultures (as Pullin realises), is any real input from people with disabilities.

Pullin's perspective on design stems from a creative arts background (although he also stresses he is a medical engineer), and for all that there are obvious overlaps, his comments make it clear that he views *engineering* design as a discipline with different rationales and demands. It is the work of Louis L. Bucciarelli that best teases out the issues at play in this latter field. In a series of publications starting with his 1994 book *Designing Engineers*, Bucciarelli unpicks the ways in which design engineers can, through their conception of objects, instrumentality, utility, function or marketplace, be ignorant of the detail inherent in the processes they enact. "The way in which one sees how technology works is very much a matter of the nature of the encounter" he observes, immediately raising questions of relationality and reciprocity.[19] For Bucciarelli, the problem often lies in an over-concentration on what he terms "an object-world view of a social process", a view that cannot capture the complexity of design and its contexts. In place of a fixation on "the object as a thing in itself" (a wheelchair, for example, or prosthetic limb), he stresses ideas of vision, harmony and "a cultural matrix".[20] Where we might expect an engineer to hone in on the fine details of a design, Bucciarelli stresses the need to "unfocus", and to then "start with a broad canvas, hold suspect the categories and relations we unconsciously accept today, and seek [...] evidence of relations in the making and using" of engineered products.[21] In *Design Meets Disability*, Pullin calls for a similar stress on the formation of new relations: "The design issues around disability are underexplored, and demand and deserve far more radical approaches [...] What is needed is truly interdisciplinary design thinking, combining and blurring design craft with engineering brilliance, therapeutic excellence and the broadest experiences of disabled people".[22]

Radical interdisciplinarity and renewed vision are the core concepts here, working to replace assertions of scientific autonomy or caricatured user. "Other cultures or consumers may appropriate the artefact and make it their object", Bucciarelli observes, continuing with language more seemingly suited to social or cultural theory than engineering:

> There are other stories, other social processes of impacts, of alienation, reconstruction, and use. The artefact as object can live again. It can become a nexus or icon of social discourse or exchange. In its use it can impose, block, enable, shape social connections and the aspirations of those it meets. There are other object worlds within which the artefact can be seen and used in different ways. Deconstruction and bricolage are always possible.[23]

In effect, Bucciarelli is calling for engineers to *imagine* their work as a matrix of affiliation, as well as asking his readership to similarly use imagination in the characterisation of what an engineer is and does; and though he has no focus on disability, his stress here on appropriation and reuse makes his thinking an innovative and productive frame for conceiving disability experiences of objects. For those with disabilities, constructing different meanings – 'deconstructions' – of the physical environment, and adapting as a consequence, is an everyday occurrence. Though written in the mid-1990s, Bucciarelli's work here has clear continuities with more contemporary concerns. It is a seamless fit, for example, with Liz Jackson's 2018 concept of 'life-hacking' discussed in this book's Introduction. The idea of the object 'living again', as outlined by Bucciarelli, is precisely that of Jackson's summary of the 'interventions' made by disabled designers.

How, then, might it be possible to take the ideas of Bucciarelli, Pullin and Jackson, along with the vexed question of engineering ethics, and place them within a context of design, disability and the posthuman, especially as these are inflected by gender? And is there any way that such considerations can be juxtaposed with the cultural narratives of hyperreality, the extraordinary bodies so loved by Hollywood noted earlier, or the augmented selves imagined by science and speculative fiction? Is there an engineered posthumanist body that can escape from, but also talk to, the boundless possibilities of fiction? To begin to answer these questions and to establish a critical framework for them, there is a need to return to that theoretical work in which the full complexities of such presences are explored.

Engineering theory

Critical writing on gender and disability can help begin to unpick the complexities of these positions, especially considered in the wake of the pioneering work of Donna Haraway. As noted earlier, for all that Haraway's foundational cyborg manifesto suggested connections to disability identities and experiences, these were not interactions she chose, for the most part, to stress. Famously, Haraway characterised a cyborg as a "creature in a post-gender world", one "resolutely committed to partiality, irony, intimacy and perversity. It is oppositional, utopian, and completely without innocence". Cyborgs, she went on, "are not reverent; they do not re-member the cosmos. They are wary of holism, but needy for connection";[24] and it was the suggestive potential provided by this partial, perverse and irreverent figure, but also the connections it appeared to need, that excited critics writing after the manifesto's publication in 1985.

If disability scholarship did not immediately respond to Haraway's thinking, feminist writing engaged with the cyborg figure from the moment the manifesto appeared, whether to criticise its omissions or point to its possibilities. Anne Balsamo's 1996 study *Technologies of the Gendered Body: Reading Cyborg Women* begins with a chapter that reads the cyborg body within a frame of "writing feminism". For Balsamo, Haraway's insistence on the in-between position of the cyborg means it can be read as "a matter of fiction and a matter of lived experience", and the reassertion of a "material body" challenges the absence of the body in much poststructuralist and postmodern theory. As such "the cyborg challenges feminism to search for ways to study the body as it is at once a cultural construction and a material fact of human life".[25] The cyborg's ability to disrupt what (erroneously) appears as the 'given' nature of the female body is, Balsamo argues, the perfect starting point for a feminist critique that can map the sliding identities and transformations that mark how women live. Other scholars who developed Haraway's ideas are more equivocal then Balsamo about the manifesto's possibilities for linking theorised and situated female experiences. Also writing in 1996, Judith Squires noted that "whilst there *may* be potential for an alliance between cyborg imagery and a materialist feminism, this potential has been largely submerged beneath a sea of technophoric cyberdrool".[26] The 'drooling' to which Squires refers is feminist writing that, as Alison Adam noted in 1998, "is in danger of falling into the same trap with regard to the body, as cyberculture in general, which promotes a particularly masculine connotation of the new continuity of mind and machine".[27] Where writers such as Balsamo saw the progressive futures suggested by Haraway's manifesto, others worried that her thinking might in fact shape new limitations and simplifications.

Writing on feminism and the cyborg has thus developed in the shadow of Haraway's thinking, creating a body of work that extends to discuss other aspects of posthumanist conditions. A major concern for feminist scholarship has been how it might be possible to marry the liberating aspects of posthumanism's deconstruction of binaries and fixed identities, along with its reading of technology, with a need for concentrating on material existence and advocacy. In her 2007 study *Cyborgs and Barbie Dolls: Feminism, Popular Culture and the Posthuman Body*, Kim Toffoletti addresses precisely these topics, noting that "the cyborg provides new modes of conceiving both social and bodily realities and the universal notion of women's shared experiences".[28] She draws on feminist critiques of technology and the digital to assert how "cyberfeminism is fundamentally concerned with claiming cyberspace for women", but reconfigures this in making claims for a specifically "posthuman landscape" in which "technology is neither friend nor foe, but emerges as a possibility or potentiality to refigure bodies and identities outside of self/Other relations".[29] Because "the posthuman is a figuration that exceeds signification", Toffoletti sees it as a rich space in which to organise a new critical politics of feminism and identity.[30]

Rosi Braidotti's writing on feminist engagements with technologies and subjectivities, across books from *Nomadic Subjects: Embodiment and Sexual Difference in Contemporary Feminist Theory* (1994) to *Metamorphoses: Towards a Materialist Theory of Becoming* (2002), *The Posthuman* (2013) and *Posthuman Knowledge* (2019), enacts a critical exploration of how the cyborg can be read in terms of feminist theory. In *Nomadic Subjects* she situates Haraway as a theorist rooted in "the tradition of materialism" who sees that in a posthumanist time of power systems that are defined by "networking, communication, and multiple intersections", the cyborg signifies a subjectivity marked by "interrealtionality, receptivity, and global communication that deliberately blurs categorical distinctions".[31] As Braidotti observes in a concise summary: "It is a way of thinking specificity without falling into relativism", a phrase that also usefully defines her own work on the topic. What Braidotti terms a linkage of "body and mind in a new flux of self" in an emerging "post-human world", is a process and consequently a subject, "an open-ended project to be constructed", informed by an interrogation of sexual difference and the category of 'woman'.[32] In *Metamorphoses*, Braidotti develops her sense of feminism's parodic and paradoxical methods within contemporary cyberculture through what she terms 'cyber-teratologies', technological updates on "the monstrous, the grotesque, the mutant and the downright freakish" that "have gained widespread currency in urban post-industrial cultures".[33] "Feminism is very much part of this culture" she asserts, because "cyber-feminists play with the body boundaries and the contours of the corporeal".[34] For Braidotti here, the cyborg is the latest instantiation of the 'becoming-woman' found in manifestations of the monstrous and the grotesque and, like these, it offers spaces for the actualisation of a philosophy and practice of difference.

But Braidotti's language when describing 'freaks' and 'mutants', and her wider theorisation of the body, emphasise a point that should be made clearly: discussions of disability are, almost without exception, absent from the theorising of feminism and posthumanism outlined above. In part, this is because traditions of writing about feminism and cybercultures predate the rise of critical disability studies and much thinking about women and technology took place (in the 1980s especially) when discussions of disability were off the radar of mainstream cultural theorising. But such disciplinary contexts should not mask the more important fact that the kinds of interstitial spaces explored by feminist writing on the cyborg overlap with, and are complemented by, disability versions of the same. In particular, the difference of disability – of bodies, cognitive states and the social and cultural formations they create – allows for similar reconfigurations of theorising posthuman spaces and, through this, a rearticulation of grounded, lived experience as those investigated in the work of Braidotti, Toffoletti and others. The intersection of gender, disability and posthumanism (in all its formations) extends our thinking about subjects and their contexts in the contemporary world.

Cripping technology and gender

The most serious and significant critical engagement with the cyborg figure and its specific relationship to disability, particularly its gendered iterations, comes in Alison Kafer's chapter 'The Cyborg and the Crip: Critical Encounters', from her 2013 study *Feminist, Queer, Crip*.[35] While Kafer suggests that the "cyborg figure certainly holds much promise for a disability politics", she is cautious about the ways in which cyborg as a term functions in much usage, and how in particular it is represented by Haraway. Perceptively, Kafer notes that, more often than not, the idea of the cyborg is one that tends to fix the disabled body in stasis, even as it appears to suggest change and progress. It is precisely because people with disabilities are discussed as cyborgs *only* when they meet technology, Kafer asserts, that the very idea of the cyborg reproduces the image of disabled body as locked into disability experiences, and those experiences alone. That disabled body, the logic continues, is then *transformed* as it becomes technologised, a process that only serves to stress that any person with a disability who is *not* somehow engaged with technology remains identified as being 'disabled'. So, she argues, Haraway's cyborg, "rather than entailing a critique of existing categories and ideologies, is used to perpetuate distinctions between 'normal' and 'abnormal' bodies, distinctions that have material consequences involving discrimination, economic inequalities, and restricted access". In her reading around the topic, Kafer finds that those with disabilities appear to be granted access to topics such as 'cyborg politics' or 'cyborg ethics' when their bodies are augmented by technology, but the inference is that politics and ethics were not part of the lives of those same individuals before they 'became' cyborgs, and indeed that – post cyborgisation – disability will be a state and experience left behind. "Cyborg qualities become markers of difference" she concludes, "suggesting an essential difference between disabled people and nondisabled people. Any potential transgressive tendencies are lost when these labels become locked to certain bodies. 'Cyborg' itself becomes reified, reduced to a particular kind of body".[36]

Kafer's critique of the problematic positioning of disability in Haraway's cyborg manifesto is powerful, sustained and revealing: "Although Haraway recognizes the potential insights to be derived from the experience of living with disability technology" she writes, "she presents disability in remarkably monolithic terms, as a single universal experience [...] The disabled body, then, is figured within the manifesto as the creature of futuristic fiction or the monstrous past; disabled bodies are, once again, cast as out of time".[37] In spite of her criticism, however, she is unimpressed by the various suggestions (companion species, vampires, the grotesque) that might replace the cyborg, noting that they each have their issues in relation to disability (non)inclusion. The terms of these more recent arguments, she observes, leave her "looking back longingly at the cyborg"; and at the heart of this appeal of the cyborg is precisely its problematic formation in Haraway's work, its "gap and oversights". Kafer goes on: "one of the things that most appeals to me about the cyborg figure is its multiple, and often contradictory, deployments. Its very unpredictability is precisely what makes it such an important and potentially useful concept; its fluidity and permeability make it difficult to lock it permanently into one set of meanings".[38] She finds this especially useful in charting the "the cyborgs of critical theory" and how they might produce progressive cyber/crip positions, and especially through responses to the history of cyborg usage "in feminist activism and scholarship", where a tradition of "cross-pollination" has produced "potent fusions and fruitful couplings" in ways that can inform the methodologies of disability criticism.[39]

I shall return to Kafer's reading of feminism and cyborgs in a moment, but first I want to stress the continuities between the 'multiple', 'contradictory' and 'unpredictable' forms of the cyborg that she notes here, and the aesthetics of fictional texts outlined in the Introduction to this book. Like Kafer, I am drawn to the messiness of disability narratives (fictional and not) precisely *because* of their frequent contradictory and unpredictable trajectories. It is exactly because the Tin Woodman combines a celebration of posthuman subjectivity with an overt humanism that Baum's characters become, for me, both critically interesting and foundational in the uneasy multiplicities that signify disability and posthumanism. The texts that are analysed in what follows, in this chapter and those after, are full of such complications and clashes, and indeed *can only* be made meaningful through a consideration of their contrary tendencies. Kafer's regard for the potential mobility of Haraway's cyborg, its capacity to erase difference but also its ability to make alliances, is a wonderfully productive frame through which the representations of disability cyborgisms.

"Bringing a disability consciousness to the cyborg" and developing "a non-ableist cyborg politics", as Kafer terms it, is a complex business.[40] It requires rethinking the practice and ethics that might constitute 'assistive' engineering technology, or indeed the very interface between body and technological artefact. The possibility that the artefact might itself change because of such an encounter is (as with Buccarelli's observations earlier) a provocative one: imagining, for example, the ways in which a prosthetic can be made different precisely *because* a person with disability comes to use it. It is this critical idea of a 'disability consciousness', a *foregrounding* of not only disability experience, but disability logic, that I want this book to continue to commit to.

Kafer sees no reason not to continue discussions about medical cyborgs though, as she notes: "why not do so in a way that actually engages with the insights and experiences of such cyborgs? We could explore what such identifications or characterizations might mean to them, or how they might themselves frame cyborg discourse. These kinds of discussions can enrich our understandings of cyborg technology and, in turn, extend our theoretical framing of the cyborg".[41] This is precisely the kind of 'cross-pollination' described earlier, but also a recognition that a core aspect of thinking about the posthuman should involve considering associations between technologies and their disabled users, and a demand for people with disabilities to be included in the research paradigm. It echoes the thinking of Pullin and Bucciarelli, made from different points of origin within their disciplines, but with aligned sympathies. Kafer explores links to similar critical flexibilities found in feminist scholarship, in which affinities allow for the exploration of "alliances" and "cross-movement work" on subjects such as (for example) non-normative identities or the relations between critical race and feminist discussions of selfhood. These connections offer a platform for a feminist-informed disability studies to be part of the continued debate around the cyborg figure, but their status as critical methodologies also, I want to argue, enables ways in which we read the fictional representations of such figures.[42] As this chapter will argue, feminist readings of the figure of the engineer, particularly in relation to female subjects and experience, highlight new perspectives on the intersection of disability and the posthuman.

Ultimately, Kafer observes that "it is high time to explore how best to discuss the relationship between disability and cyborgism without facile references to disabled bodies as self-evident cyborgs simply by virtue of their use of 'assistive' or 'adaptive' technologies".[43] While I do want to continue to explore such technologies (though hopefully not in a facile way), I am drawn to Kafer's assertion that cyborgism is as much about disability understood within the frames of gender and "*political practices*" as it is about bodies.[44] She extends the critical concept of the cyborg to discuss protest, activism and community, as well as specifics such as medical interventions and prescription drugs. So, in the textual readings that follow I want to analyse political disability manifestations (of race, sexuality, non-normativity or historical locations) as much as questions of embodiment. The kinds of "cyborg futures" seen in Kafer's formations span a range of possibilities (and not all of them disabled). Mapping such range can only make critical disability scholarship more nuanced and flexible.

It is an unfair comment to make of Kafer's analysis, since she makes her terms of enquiry clear, but of course she has no interest in *where cyborgs come from*. Like Haraway, she is not interested in questions of origins. But if I am allowed a minor critical heresy in a deliberate (mis)reading here, it still strikes me that it is a productive question to imagine the engineering of cyborgs, read as a mode of *making*, and its associated ideas of gender. Such imagining helps in the ways we can continue to stress the theorising of disability both as abstracted conception and grounded existence. Caring about how (for example) a prosthetic limb is designed, the ethics of its manufacture or what ideas of function might be associated with it are still examples of focusing on disability (and gender) narratives; indeed, following Kafer's observation above, they can be seen as a way to insert disability thinking into the processes of engineering. Even if Haraway makes great capital of the fact that, as she says, "the cyborg has no origin story in the Western sense", and that, concomitantly, it does not "dream of community", she nevertheless explores "real-life cyborgs" in her manifesto, and cites people with disabilities as an example of such 'reality'.[45] Likewise, Kafer, for all her concentration on cyborgs as they manifest within critical theory, notes that a significant limitation of Haraway's essay is the absence of "any analysis of the material realities of disabled people's interactions with technologies".[46] Discussing the details of design and engineering is precisely an example of such a material interaction, whether through the ways that they are taken up by people with disabilities or the soft power created by high-profile cultural representations of augmented and enhanced bodies.

The 'missing engineers' of cultural narrative, then, the shadowy figures of Ku-Klip and his successors, with all their seemingly absent motivations and methods, are really subjects who have been present all along. But they have rarely been represented and have never properly been read for the ways in which they shape the processes of augmentation. It is time to read them because, as we shall see, they have much to say.

Metropolis: making the gendered body

To explore the ways in which engineering, disability and gender coincide with depictions of the posthuman, we need look no further than one of the most notable films of the twentieth century, Fritz Lang's *Metropolis*, made in 1927 and, at the time, the most expensive film ever produced. *Metropolis*' style and design, particularly the striking expressionist modernism through which its cityscape is depicted, established a visual language that has proved seminal for the proliferation of science fiction films that have followed it – from *Blade Runner* (1982) and its sequel *Blade Runner 2049* (2017), through the various feature versions of *Ghost in the Shell* (1995, 2015 and 2017), to *Her* (2013) and countless others, contemporary cinema exploring the posthuman echoes its portrayal of architecture and representation of space. As many critics have noticed, however, for all its optical extravagance, *Metropolis* advances a plot that is anything but complex.[47] In its representation of personal and communal identity, social hierarchies and character motivation, the film's story falls back continually on convention, caricature and cliché. Its representation of a workers' revolution fails to negate a conservative paternalism that sees the story end in a truce between workers and city leaders that negates political opposition to reassert social and class conventions.

Metropolis' disability and gender narratives follow these conformist patterns and intertwine around the figure of engineer/inventor Rotwang (Rudolph Klein-Rogge). Obsessed with Hel, the wife of central patriarch Joh Fredersen (Alfred Abel) who died while giving birth to son Freder (Gustav Fröhlich), Rotwang constructs a robot in her image. When Joh Fredersen then captures Maria (Brigitte Helm), a young woman whose public speeches are inspiring the workers to challenge their masters, Rotwang agrees to transform the robot version of Hel into a cyborg, taking the drugged body of Maria and – in one of the most famous scenes in the history of cinema – subjecting it to a succession of chemical and electrical processes. The new, biohybrid, Maria is as wanton and lascivious as the original was chaste and pure and, as many commentators have observed, the film formulates its depiction of gender around the twin positions of a virginal Madonna and the whore of Babylon, each caught and framed within the power systems of male creation.[48] When cyborg Maria is finally burnt at the stake, a premodern death for the most postmodern of posthumans, her body falls away to reveal the robot figure of Hel underneath. As Andreas Huyssen observes:

> [T]he destructive potential of modern technology [...] had to be displaced and projected onto the machine woman so that it could be metaphorically purged. After the dangers of a mystified technology have been translated into the dangers an equally mystified female sexuality poses to men, the witch could be burnt at the stake and, by implication, technology could be purged of its threatening aspects.[49]

More widely, as Minsoo Kang asserts in his assessment of the film, it centres on "the male desire to construct a woman ideal in body and personality, and to maintain total control of her".[50] While this control may not always be absolute, with both Marias suggesting the possibility of their own agency (either the passionate political speeches of the 'real' Maria or the subversive seductions of cyborg Maria), by the film's close each has been pulled back into the consuming logic of male dominance, either banished to the periphery of society or destroyed by fire.

In his creation of both Hel and cyborg Maria, Rotwang combines the traits of the obsessed and isolated scientist with the difference of disability. His house/laboratory, with its curved walls, trapdoors and labyrinthine room structure, is the complete antithesis of the gleaming metal city that surrounds it; but his fanaticism and infatuation is most clearly signalled by his black metal prosthetic hand, self-engineered to replace the one he lost (presumably through grief and passion) in making Hel. In a way that criticism has yet to fully register, *Metropolis* is a film obsessed with hands. Numerous close-ups feature hands in extravagant gestures: characters thrust hands in front of the faces of others, signifying anger, threat or fear; hands dramatically pull and push the levers of the underground machines, or signal prayer and supplication. It is not only the acting style of the period responsible here: above and beyond this, *Metropolis* enacts what Rosemarie Garland-Thomson calls "speaking hands", in which "the expressive work of hands [...] demands scrupulous watching".[51] Such expression, and such watching, find a charged marker in Rotwang's prosthetic hand. The hand invites stares as it performs the final act – the last pull of the lever – that completes the transformation of Hel into cyborg Maria. In a complicated semiotics, Rotwang's hand is clearly an index of disability and, as such, functions to underwrite his overall difference as an obsessed character; but it is not, in fact, *disabling* for him as a character, operating both physically and visually more like a glove than a prosthetic. The *signification* of disability is what counts here; its alignment with invention and engineering, embodied in a fully fledged 'mad scientist', presents a disabled presence seen to be out of control.

The prosthetic hand, the futuristic inventor and the cyborg figure all suggest the congruence of disability and posthumanism, but *Metropolis* backs away from potential new formations of bodies and technology. Rather, 'hands' occupy a resolutely humanist position in the film, seen in the final scenes as the unifying 'mediator' between the 'head' (Joh Fredersen's leadership and control) and the 'heart' (the central machine is itself, extending the idea of a body politic, called the 'Heart Machine' and powered by workers who make the city function). In the end, hands put the body politic back together, and Freder literally brings the hands of Joh Fredersen and Grot (Heinrich George), the workers' foreman, together in an uneasy conjoining at the film's conclusion. Seen in the context of such a moment of unification,

Joh Fredersen (Alfred Abel) and Rotwang (Rudolph Klein-Rogge) in *Metropolis*

Rotwang's hand is rendered even more anomalous, an aberration in a world in which the wholeness of the social body is (desirably) reinstated by the physical connection of fully able bodies. *Metropolis* may, for a time, seem to promise a posthumanist future in which machine combines with human, and Kang in fact puts forward a nuanced argument that the "subversive potential" and excessiveness of the female robot allows for a freedom from "its original programming" that facilitates an "independence of consciousness and will", but by its conclusion the film reverts to a centred, embodied and *whole* vision both of character and society.[52] It is a world with no place for the crazed, disabled engineer, and Rotwang duly falls to his death – his replacement hand held dramatically high as he does so – when fighting Freder after kidnapping Maria.

In such a position of complexity, Rotwang thus looks backwards and forwards: back to the representation of science, and especially scientist-as-man, that emerged from Mary Shelley's *Frankenstein* (1817), and developed through the nineteenth century; and forward to narratives that situate the inventor/engineer in contemporary moments of networked technologies and the kinds of patterned flow of information that mark a posthumanist present. In the rest of this chapter I want to follow these questions of disability and gender as they inform ideas of science, bodies and communities through narratives of engineering and technological creation. If *Metropolis* exhibits a tension between the visualising of the *process* of posthumanist creation – the fascination with Rotwang's technology, and the female body, as he creates cyborg Maria – and the humanism that ultimately governs notions of identity and belonging, then subsequent texts shuttle between these positions as they explore how the future and its disability spaces might be engineered. These spaces are, to return to Alison Kafer's earlier observation, always *political*. Through its focus on control and revolution, *Metropolis* visualises and narrates a literal politics, but all engineered posthumanist disabilities are political in some way, even those set in the most otherworldly of locations. The analyses that follow are, in their own way, part of Kafer's "coalitional moments", instances of practice that offer "alternative political imaginaries", contested and contradictory as they might be.[53]

Artificial I-s

There is a considerable critical literature on the relationship between humans and the kind of technological being Kakoudaki calls an "artificial person". Multiple examples from fiction and film participate in what she terms "a dense web of interactions between fiction and reality in contemporary culture". "Despite their unreality", she notes, "they seem to inform a host of cultural domains and debates".[54] This interaction has always taken place of course. Fantasies of artificial people pervade cultural representations of all ages, and achieve particular prominence during periods of intense technological change, such as modernity and the contemporary digital and computer age. They become, according to Kakoudaki, "superbly dynamic and culturally reflective", telling stories that deploy questions not only of embodiment, but also class, gender, race, health, technological capability and their multiple intersections.[55] In the texts that are analysed in the remainder of this chapter, this blend of dynamism and reflection is constantly on show, creating allegories and metaphors in which disability functions as a complex set of states that inform the domains and debates of the present.

Commercial cinema in the post-studio age has returned time and again to narratives that explore the consequences of human interactions with technology in which the representation of embodiment is central. To name but a few of the more high-profile examples: *Westworld* (1973), *The Stepford Wives* (1975), *Blade Runner* (1982), *Weird Science* (1985), *Robocop* (1987), *Making Mr Right* (1987), the *Terminator* (1984–2003) and *Matrix* (1999–2003) trilogies, *Gattaca* (1997), *A.I.: Artificial Intelligence* (2001), the *X-Men* and *Avengers* franchises (2000–present and 2014–present), *I, Robot* (2004), the *Iron Man* trilogy (2008–2013), *Lars and the Real Girl* (2007), *Her* (2013), *Under the Skin* (2013), *Transcendence* (2014), *Lucy* (2014), *Ex Machina* (2014), *Ghost in the Shell* (2017), *Blade Runner 2049* (2017), *Zoe* (2018) and *Alita: Battle Angel* (2019). These films express the tensions this book has centred on: the fascination with future technologies and the worry over the meaning of the human body that is created in tandem with this. The majority focus on male creations of female bodies (either as subservient or independent) or explore issues of masculinity and hyperability. In each, the changing body is one in which some form disability is deployed and can be read.

A genealogy of contemporary literary fiction focusing on artificial people, or the link between human and engineered machine, might stem from Kurt Vonnegut's first novel *Player Piano* (1952). Vonnegut portrays a dystopian postwar future (with heavy overtones of Aldous Huxley's *Brave New World*) in which American society has emerged to be governed by a combination of engineers and managers. Engineers are elevated to the position of national hero, but the novel's satire plays out an idea of artificiality in both the processes of mechanical production and the men who control them.[56] Equally, but in significantly different forms, the late works of Samuel Beckett presents a searing 'artificiality' in their depiction of complex embodiment. Nearly all of Beckett's characters appear to be disabled in some way, their bodies marked or imprisoned within physical spaces or those of the stage.[57] Following Vonnegut and Beckett, we can identify a move into a series of narratives that explicitly link engineered technology and the creation of gendered bodies. From the novels of Philip K. Dick, especially *Do Androids Dream of Electric Sheep?* (1968), through Ira Levin's *The Stepford Wives* (1972), and into the speculative cyberpunk worlds of William Gibson and Bruce Sterling (particularly Gibson's Sprawl Trilogy (1984–1988) and Sterling's *Schismatrix* (1985)), stories depicting engineered cultures of embodiment and the male creation of robots, cyborgs and automata came to both reflect and construct social attitudes towards technology and the body.[58] Contemporary writing by women pushes back against the ingrained sexism of much cyberpunk fiction in particular. Novels such as Louisa Hall's *Speak* (2015), Annalee Newitz's *Autonomous* (2017) and Lidia Yuknavitch's

The Book of Joan (2017) explore worlds of biotechnology and A.I. with central female protagonists and often offer explicit critiques of male authority. They bring contemporary fiction's representation of the interaction between human, engineering and the augmented or disabled/different body up to date in a time of advanced and rapid technological change.

In Thomas Berger's 2004 novel *Adventures of the Artificial Woman*, the engineering of a technologised female functions within the kinds of counters mapped out above.[59] Ellery Pierce, "a technician at a firm that made animatronic creatures for movie studios and theme parks", decides to make an artificial woman – Phyllis – because he has never found "a real woman with whom he could sustain more than a temporary connection".[60] Pierce is a "journeyman", a mid-level employee, and knows that in order "to fabricate a woman who could be put to all the uses of a real one, and fool everyone but her creator", he has "his work cut out for him".[61] Berger's imagined world is no futuristic environment of science fiction, but rather a twenty-first century present in which it just so happens that certain individuals can manufacture animatronic robots that can be mistaken for real humans. The novel is subtle and playful; Pierce is every inch the male creator, focused on perfecting physical features such as skin texture or stride length, but also language abilities and domestic responsibilities. But Phyllis soon finds her role as Pierce's companion limiting and, as the title suggests, embarks on adventures of her own. "I'm off to a life of new challenges" she tells Pierce after she has tied him to the bed in a sex session. Pierce's reply, as he lies bound, is both desperate and indicative of much of the novel's knowing humour:

> He grimaced. "That's more of the foolish crap you picked up from the mass media. You can't make it on your own. You're not some Frankenstein's creation of organic materials, with a brain that revolts against its maker. You're an electronic and mechanical personage. You'll need recharging any minute now. And what if one of your systems goes out of order – in fact I think one or more have already done so, or you wouldn't be acting like this".[62]

But Phyllis leaves, pausing in the bedroom doorway to tell Pierce that she thinks she might "have a try at show business".[63] What follows, in a pastiche of gender roles, is an initial trajectory from sex work to amateur dramatics, film stardom and politics (she ultimately becomes President-elect), with Phyllis largely unaware, because of her artificiality, of the commodification of her body involved in each process.

Pierce, meanwhile, falls into neglect. Unable – as with Frankenstein – to create a second figure, he loses his job and becomes homeless. Unaware of Phyllis's success, he stumbles across a picture of her in one of her major film roles in a newspaper and is astounded:

> Phyllis as she existed today was inexplicable to him. She represented an impossibility. Her handlers must know, by now, that she was an artificial woman. They *had* to know. They had updated or replaced her major systems and reprogrammed her completely. She was no longer the Phyllis that Pierce had created and, in retrospect, loved so profoundly. Given the nature of her being, it could not even be said that she has grown, human-style, from what she once had been to what she was today, as a girl becomes a woman. She has rather evolved, from Model T to Lincoln Town Car, or like the telephone, from Bell's crude experiment to today's miniature portable instrument. She had not matured; she had undergone a series of modifications.[64]

Pierce can only conceive of any change in Phyllis as some kind of mechanical upgrade. What he cannot comprehend is that her transition is, in effect, a version of a posthumanist singularity, the attainment of a level of independence beyond any aspect of her programming. Pierce is here dumbfounded by Phyllis achieving *agency*; as with her original decision to leave him, Phyllis enacts *choice* to a degree Pierce finds 'impossible'. The engineer/creator, lost in unrequited but paternalistic love, is rendered speechless by his creation. Desperate to regain a vocabulary that might reassert himself in the face of Phyllis' difference, Pierce can only reiterate one of the oldest categories for containing the non-human. Now that she is "no longer a feasible substitute for a real woman", he observes, she had become "a monster".[65]

As Margrit Shildrick and others have shown, monstrosity was a category frequently mobilised to include those with disabilities, and *Adventures of the Artificial Woman* is subtle in figuring Phyllis's difference as an encounter with disability.[66] As she develops her theatrical career (by learning all of Shakespeare's works by heart in one day) she is struck by *Hamlet*'s characterisation of "a mentally retarded female by the name of Ophelia, to play whom convincingly, [she] would have to suppress any evidence of intelligence"; while the one man she encounters in her career as a sex worker who does not make a sexual advance on her, and who acts genuinely to help her, is in a wheelchair.[67] Then in a surreal scene after he and Phyllis are reunited later in the novel, Pierce notes how "she would do something so delightfully surprising as to distract him from soul-searching", continuing:

> After viewing a DVD of *Rain Man*, she reproduced the idiot-savant feats of Dustin Hoffman's character, counting the individual matches in boxful while they fell en masse to the floor; reproducing from memory the names, addresses, and numbers in a telephone directory after one quick perusal thereof; identifying each playing card in a deck that was scattered before her at high speed – all without a concomitant show of autistic disabilities.[68]

This is complex: an (ostensibly female) animatronic posthuman performing, for her creator, a reproduction of one of the most famous fictional representations of neurobehavioral difference, but with the absence of the features that constitute such acts as being *disabled*. For Phyllis, Raymond Babbit's actions in *Rain Man* are simply *things that can be done*. She sees no reason to consider them as any form as savant compensation for a disabled deficit. As with the example of her earlier employer in a wheelchair, and indeed her wider incomprehension of the nuances of gender difference, here the posthuman Phyllis emphasises that she sees diversity without the individual prejudices and social constraints that accompany it.

Adventures of the Artificial Woman mobilises Phyllis' innocent vision precisely to discuss sexist and ableist constructions of power, but the seemingly progressive politics this might suggest proves deceptive. In the end, when Phyllis is the president-in-waiting, she begins to exhibit autocratic tendencies and a desire for control that Pierce feels too threatening. "I've come to realize what the Presidency calls for" Phyllis asserts, "We're a special breed, we whom the American people have selected to lead them".[69] She plans not only to enact policy changes that would alter all aspects of American society, but also to replace Pierce with an animatronic husband. Acting both as seemingly concerned citizen and rejected partner, Pierce turns Phyllis off, "inserting the tip of his little finger into her nearby ear and pressing the tiny fail-safe button just inside the auditory orifice, an essential of the original design but never used till now".[70] He reasserts the male power of creation just as the posthumanist female appears to become fully autonomous as the most powerful individual in the world. The ending complicates the novel overall, signalling Pierce's fear of Phyllis' ultimate independence as well as, potentially, a wider cultural fear of a future, technologised woman.

As a single example of the kinds of text and cultural dynamics mentioned previously, *Adventures of the Artificial Woman* reveals itself to be typical of fictional narratives in which the social and the engineered combine to produce visions of a gendered technological future.

In such texts, gender and disability – inevitably intersecting – are part of a matrix in which desire and fear shuttle across locations, evidence of the unstable position that the categories of artificial or posthuman hold in the imagination. The augmented/disabled body arouses fascination because of its potential to supersede the present, until its difference evokes what James Porter has articulated as the classic double bind of disabled embodiment, when it becomes "too much a body, too real, too corporeal", a process that conversely makes it "lack something essential, something that would make it identifiable and something to identify with". Continuing, Porter notes, "it seems too little a body: a body that is deficiently itself, not quite a body in the full sense of the word, not real enough".[71] The excitement of the supplemented self can, it seems, all too easily become a horizon to back away from; the imagining of diverse posthumanist possibilities signalling a return to the fantasy of a normalised, whole humanism. Equally, narratives of gender in texts such as *Metropolis* and *Adventures of the Artificial Woman* see women, as they interact with technology, occupy positions of subversive power from which they suggest the articulation of possible alternative futures; but they become excised from them as the stories conclude, removed as the issues of technology, society and embodied selfhood are resolved through what appears inevitably to be a prism of male creation and resolution.

The fictions we have seen so far are turbulent objects, full of contradictory impulses around individuals and their interactions with engineered futures of change. But the problems of the artificial and engineered can be recast as the potential of posthumanism's concentration on the meaning of technology, and there are other environments to explore that speak of other bodies and other prospects. In the next section, it is the narratives of contemporary speculative/science fiction and film that will form the locations for these, locations that bring disability and gender to the forefront of imagining the processes of engineered technologies.

Imagineering embodied female subjects in speculative/science film and fiction

Sherryl Vint entitled her 2007 study of science fiction, technology and subjectivity, *Bodies of Tomorrow*, and the striking phrase is useful in suggesting imaginings of not just posthuman selves and disability subjectivities, but their place within the imagining of science as fiction. Introducing her argument, Vint notes that "technology is rapidly making the concept of the 'natural' human obsolete. We have now entered the realm of the posthuman, the debate over the identities and values of what will come after the human". She then goes on:

> I would add that the outcome of such debates pivots greatly on the concepts of identity and embodiment that are dominant in the cultural milieu that surrounds the deployment of such technologies, and further that such values are significant not only for the effects they have on the human species but also for the relationship between humanity and the rest of the world that are implicit in them. My contention is that in thinking about the consequences of technologies of body modification, what is ultimately most important is the social milieu and philosophical assumptions which ground the way we deploy such technologies.[72]

Vint's book has no particular focus on either disability or engineering, but her comments here make a clear space for contemplating each within her terms. Social and cultural imaginings of identity and embodiment are at the heart of the disability narratives and deployments that concern this study, even if some of those imaginings undo any stability that 'identity' might suggest, while the assumptions around deployment of technology is clearly a foundational aspect of engineering. Importantly, Vint's fictionalised bodies of tomorrow are both situated and discursive: "it is important", she notes, "to return to a notion of embodied subjectivity in order to articulate the ethical implications of technologies of bodily modification. Technological visions of a post-embodied future are merely fantasies about transcending the material ream of social responsibility".[73] If we might see the fantasies of transcendence as science fiction, then the technologies of modification are very much the work of engineers.

In his more recent 2016 study *Biopunk Dystopias*, Lars Schmeink makes explicit the links between science fiction and critical posthumanism. He locates the origins of representations of the posthuman in what he terms a "proto-science-fictional context", noting that how "the concerns and conceptions of (post)humanist thinking lie at the heart of science fiction".[74] Technology and embodiment are central to this, and Schmeink outlines a detailed account of scholarship on posthumanism recognisably related to the work of Rosi Braidotti and Pramod Nayar that he then extends to analyses of science fiction. In the fiction, Schmeink sees depictions of "a critical dystopian future [...] in which the posthuman has become a tangible reality that is trying to establish a position in the 'natural order' and ultimately ends up threatening to replace the human completely". I am more ambivalent than Schmeink about the idea of 'complete' replacement, but his connection of science fiction to the critical decentrings of posthumanist theorising (with all its associated commentaries on bodies, gender, race and politics) is a substantial investigation of the interplay between science/speculative fiction, technology and the body.

As outlined previously in this chapter, the engineered body raises issues of material and responsible political and social action. The disability and feminist activists and scholars, examined earlier, who seek to articulate grounded narratives of critical intervention that speak both of experience and philosophical/ethical contemplation exemplify this, as do the fictional questions around the concept of the 'artificial'. Michael Bérubé's description of the disabled body as "both material artefact and social construction" outlines positionings also true of female and technologised embodiments.[75] When Vint observes that "[t]he body remains relevant to critical work and 'real' life [...] because the discourses that structure these material bodies continue to construct and constrain our material selves", she is speaking of an embodied subjectivity, figured through discourse, that can be disabled, feminist and posthuman.[76] The problems of the artificial and fear of difference discussed in this chapter can be addressed through imaginations of bodies that project the kinds of progressive possibilities envisaged by Haraway, Kafer and others. Indeed, I want to argue that it is the specific fictional representation of these material, engineered bodies that offer precisely these productive moments; here figuring *science fiction* as the literal fictionalisation of engineering science. As Kathryn Allan has noted:

> SF has long explored deviant and disabled bodies [and] is inhabited by people (and aliens) whose embodiments are situated along the entire spectrum of ability [...] No other genre comes close to articulating the anxieties and preoccupations of the present day as clearly and critically as SF, making it a vital source for understanding advances in technology and its impact on newly emerging embodiments and subjectivities, particularly for peoples with disabilities.[77]

As we will see, while this can mean a focus on ideas of technology as cure for disabilities, it can also make for disability-rich narratives in which difference becomes the norm.

Manuela Rossini has coined the term 'imagineering' for the ways in which texts conceptualise bodies within networks that anticipate the future, with her deliberate collision of words suggesting an interaction between fictional approaches and a conception of engineering practice. When she observes what she terms the "double movement" of technology and the literary, she makes an important point, namely that "literature does not merely react to technological development and offer ethical guidance". Rather the process is one of greater equality: "the technological potential will affect the way the human body/subject is defined but these new meanings (produced in texts and images) will influence, if not our actual use and even deployment of them, our handling of technologies".[78] To 'imagineer' then, might be to deploy the various versions of design and expression for which I argue here.

However, while Rossini is deft in her analyses of cultural theory and fictional texts, her critical approach does not break down 'technology' in any way, leaving nothing that might allow for a focus on how actual engineering methods can contribute to a critical interdisciplinary idea of the engineered body. There are no specifics about the *work* of design or production in her asserted 'double meaning', no account of the complexity inherent when conceiving of production design; the detail only comes from one side. To observe this is to register those moments when cultural criticism, always piratical in its methods, lays claim to terminology and (broadly conceived) ideas from disciplines beyond its own but displays no real care (or courtesy) towards those other subjects. For Rossini, 'engineering' is just a set of generalisations attached to a word.

But the term can be reclaimed from Rossini's omissions, if for no other reason than its collision between two words is so suggestive of a productive critical method. We can fill in that which Rossini ignores and give engineering the space it is due. So, the final section of this chapter will imagineer the nexus of disability, engineering and feminism to bring a critical posthumanist perspective to questions of origins, selfhood, and the interaction between human and non-human. I will look in particular at Alex Garland's 2014 film *Ex Machina*, and the Wayfarer trilogy of science fiction novels by Becky Chambers – *The Long Way to a Small Angry Planet* (2015), *A Closed and Common Orbit* (2016) and *Record of a Spaceborn Few* (2018) – to explore how gender, design and mechanical production produce specific stories of a posthumanist disabled presence, particularly as that presence is manifested through the meeting of bodies and technology. As Vint notes, "the new selves SF might help us imagine are both [...] problematic selves and unexpected others". She goes on: "they remind us of the fragility of our boundary-making work and that the Other always *is* an aspect of self made problematic".[79] It is precisely these problematic selves that I want to chart, reading imaginative worlds in which speculation is central to the articulation of person and place.

As many feminist critics writing on science and speculative fiction have noted, the open possibilities of the genre allow for formal and textual intricacies that match the multiple positionings women inhabit in relation to technology. Posthumanist conceptions of assemblages and networks, with their focus on decentralisation and questions surrounding species specificity, lend themselves naturally to science fictional depictions of technology and alien subjectivities. Pramod Nayar anchors most of his discussion of posthuman biology in Octavia Butler's seminal *Xenogenesis* trilogy (1988–1989), using Butler's fiction to outline a posthumanist "site of acculturation" in which biological and genetic states (but also "histories, memories and habits") exemplify posthumanism's identification of, and commitment to, what he elsewhere terms "interconnections, messy histories, blurred origins, borrowing and adaptations, cross-overs and impurities [and] dependency and mutuality across species".[80] As this study has shown, 'messy', 'blurred' 'impurities' are central to the working of fiction's aesthetics. The fit here, between disabled bodies, gendered selves, imagined engineering, posthuman landscapes and the worlds of science fiction, is exciting in its potential.

The figuration of such worlds in science fiction cinema is a different matter. Sue Short observes in *Cyborg Cinema* that, "compared to […] literary SF […], cinematic versions have proved to be much more conservative in their depictions of gender, particularly where artificial women are concerned".[81] Short's analysis ranges across a multitude of film texts, from Heinrich Galeen's *Alraune* (1928) and Bernard Knowles' *The Perfect Woman* (1949) to John Hughes' *Weird Science* (1985) and Scott's *Blade Runner* (1982), noting that in nearly all cases "to survive as an artificial woman in SF cinema necessitates conforming to approved standards of behaviour and generally deferring to male authority".[82] The gender dynamics of contemporary Hollywood in particular leave little room for the kind of productive articulation of the present that Allan sees in literary science fiction. If the second decade of the twenty-first century has seen the development of critical ideas of intersectionality that chart the intricate contemporary interactions between gender, bodies and technology, Short asserts that these have yet to transfer to the realm of high-production commercial cinema.

Racialising the technologised female robot

Ex Machina is the most notable and critically complex recent feature in the tradition Short examines. It is a film that lays claim to being more intelligent and less misogynistic than those in her study though, as we will see, it is not without its own messy contradictions. *Ex Machina* explores processes of engineering and production, and through a gender lens. Nathan (Oscar Isaac) is the inventor of the search engine Blue Book (a thinly disguised Google) and a self-styled Prometheus working on the creation of an A.I. that will possess true consciousness.[83] He invites Caleb (Domhnall Gleeson), one of his employees, to his secluded research facility in order to subject his latest humanoid model Ava (Alicia Vikander) to an enhanced Turing test, a set of processes designed to see if she exhibits qualities that mean she can approximate human behaviour. During the test Caleb will come to believe that Ava possesses a complex consciousness even as he knows her to be non-human.

The film establishes Nathan's stereotypical masculinity from the start: Caleb first sees him working out with weights, while Nathan seeks to overcome Caleb's initial nervousness with a succession of demotic colloquialisms. "Can we just be two guys?" he asks Caleb, a representative phrase accompanying various offers of beer and exclamations of "dude!". "Lay off the textbook approach", Nathan commands at one point; and, tired of Caleb's attempts to intellectualise the experiment with Ava, he interrupts to assert: "I want to have a beer and conversation with you, not a seminar". Nathan's buddy speak is only one example of the film's careful staging of the patriarchal framing of his work and creation of Ava in particular. It is his sense of entitlement that allows him to use Bluebook to collect data from every cell phone in the world to produce the software for his engineering; while although Caleb points out that he could have created all the necessary technology in "a grey box", Nathan's models and prototypes are all female-based humanoids designed to be sexual. "You bet she can fuck" he says of Ava at one point, only one of the aggressive statements that underscore his sense of self as a creator of what is, in his eyes, sentient female selfhood. Nathan sleeps in a room in which all the pre-Ava prototypes developed during his experimentation are kept in cupboards, as if he is some serial killer hoarding bodies as trophies.

Caleb lacks Nathan's alpha male bravado but is nevertheless complicit in the controlling exercises that test Ava. Watched by Nathan from a separate control room (one of a series of ways in which the film puts Ava on display for a male gaze), it is Caleb who, over a series of interview/conversation sessions, asks Ava questions to establish her emotions, desires and capacity of mind. Confined to a glass room, Ava interacts with Caleb as he (without his full knowledge) enacts

Nathan's real and undisclosed version of the Turing test: whether in fact Ava will manipulate Caleb to try to escape. Unable to contain his emotions for Ava, Caleb becomes the patsy that proves Nathan's thesis: that Ava is in fact Eve, the duplicitous woman who, using guile and deceit, fools a man into acting in her best interests. That Nathan takes *this* particular set of female characteristics as indicating true A.I. ability is no coincidence, confirming his misogyny and sense of entitlement.

But Ava in fact produces a double move. In his arrogance Nathan believes that it will be "the next model", that made after Ava, who will be "the Singularity", the true breakthrough; Ava herself is to be downloaded and developed, her memories erased but her body retained to hold the next upgrade. But for all of his satisfaction in creating Ava's successful deception of Caleb, Nathan fails to perceive that Ava's ultimate goal, the real extent of her posthuman intelligence, is to fool *both* men. Ava literally *engineers* her escape through a combination of technologies, repurposing the hardware and software through which she has been created as well as those that imprison her within Nathan's compound. She creates power cuts in order to pull Caleb into an intimacy (away from the cameras that cover all the rooms), but also manipulates him into overriding the lockdown system that means she can exit the room in which she is kept. After killing Nathan, she traps Caleb in the control room (his confinement echoing hers), shuts down the computer systems he desperately tries to use to escape, and leaves the facility for freedom with a half glance towards him as he screams for help.

Ex Machina's feminism is, as we shall see, not unproblematic, but the core of its narrative revolves around a female posthumanist subject taking over the conditions under which she was produced, deleting the men who created and tested her, and exiting into personal freedom. If Victor Frankenstein failed in the creation of a bride for his monster, the technology unable to make a female partner for a male, Ava asserts an individualism that has no need of male companionship.[84] She becomes Haraway's cyborg, with no need for origins and a very clear rejection of any return to nature: Ava/Eve *does* enter the garden/Garden as she leave's Nathan's house but, in a knowing move, only to walk through it and take a helicopter away from the complex. The final shot of the film sees her at a busy city traffic intersection, a location she has earlier said to Caleb she would want to visit because of the multiplicity of people she would find there. She turns and leaves, with the audience none the wiser as to the future she will create – beyond an understanding that it will be on her terms.

Ava (Alicia Vikander) comes face to face with a prototype in *Ex Machina*

Ex Machina is a disability film because it has a continual emphasis on the embodied nature of selfhood and because it visually figures the complex difference of the body. As a technological construction, and thanks to the CGI imagery of the production process, Ava is visibly non-human; but her body is at the same time clearly *humanoid*, something underscored by the strength of the real Alicia Vikander's performance within her computer-generated physical self. Ava's android intermeshes, especially the clear engineering of her limbs and head, do not supersede her 'human' appearance. Rather they produce an amalgam in which viewers see Ava as both human and not, and at the same time. It is within this paradox that we can see the potential for a productive disability reading of *Ex Machina*'s posthumanism; the double presence of Ava's body enacting Porter's classic disability marker of signalling both *not enough* and *too much* humanity in the single moment, a reminder of absence and excess, conjoined in their complexity.

The film plays on the possibilities such visuals present. Ava covers her body with clothes and a wig, hiding her clearly technologised self, when wanting to suggest how she might pass as human. This process takes place when during the interview sessions she is luring Caleb into an intimacy in which she suggests they might go on a 'date', as well as at the end when she dresses for her final escape. In both cases Ava takes her clothes out of a wardrobe, literally performing Eve Kosofsky Sedgwick's arguments in *Epistemology of the Closet* (1990) that secrecy

– here Ava's non-human status – is not only about concealment but the impossibility of disclosure.[85] In her future, it is suggested, Ava will cover her android self. Using Sedgewick's theory, Tobin Siebers develops the idea of a disability as a masquerade, a process that offers "an opportunity to rethink passing from the point of view of disability". In a phrase that captures Ava's use of the closet, Siebers observes that, through the idea of the masquerade, "the powerful symbolic connection between disability and prosthetics allows those who improvise on the use of their prosthesis to tinker with the social meeting of their disability".[86] Ava's escape is planned, but – as the development of her conversations with Caleb makes clear – she is also an improviser, and the idea that her clothes *themselves become* prosthetics is a powerful disability-led critical argument for the ways in which she constitutes the meaning of her actions. Fully clothed, Ava is a posthumanist masquerade, a non-human embodied agent of difference.[87]

Ex Machina's visual association between disability and intersections of vulnerability and violence is as complex as this masquerading agency. In the fight in which Ava and Kyoko (Sonoya Mizuno), the second android in the complex and one manufactured to act as servant and sex slave, kill Nathan, he attacks both androids with a dumbbell, severing one of Ava's arms and breaking off Kyoko's jaw and lower face. This last act makes Kyoko fall to the floor, effectively 'killed' (she does not move from this position for the rest of the film). Before this final drama, Caleb has watched footage of how, in previous experiments, one of Nathan's prototypes, Jade, has screamed to be released from her captivity and smashed her arms against a wall until both limbs are reduced to metal stumps. It is when the androids are at their most vulnerable to physical attack, but also most threatening, that their bodies lose parts, interrupting the apprehension that their selves are whole.

Ava replaces her missing arm, however, in a scene in which she enters Nathan's bedroom, opens the cupboards there, and sees the prototypes. She takes an arm from a figure and bolts it on to her own body, a seamless attachment of a prosthetic strangely reminiscent of Baum's Tin Woodman (as with the Woodman, the arm functions immediately). Similarly, she also peels skin from a prototype before grafting it to her body, smoothing it into place. The disabled body is thus restored to wholeness, but the scene is not as simple as this might suggest; there is a clear sense in which it is shot that Ava is restoring herself in an act *of community*. Her recognition of the prototypes is wordless, but the sensuality with which she touches the other bodies, and the shot/reverse/shot technique between her face and that of the prototype from which she takes the arm and skin, clearly suggest understanding and complicity. Equally, Ava is rendered multiple during this interaction through the refractions we see of her in the mirrored doors of the cupboards as she opens them. This, it appears, is not an act of centred individualism. As with the way in which Ava teams with Kyoko to kill Nathan, here android/disabled bodies are in dialogue. Ava then can be read as both posthumanist and disability amalgamations, a networked technological creation in which a complex embodiment is stressed through the processes of visuality that allow us to see the constructed engineering of self. The interaction is also intersectional, as in this moment Ava is in the final stages of her feminist triumph: her escape from Nathan, Caleb and their patriarchal presumptions.

But such a reading is too seamless. Upon reflection *Ex Machina* contains the same contradictions identified in so many of the texts examined in this study so far; the same narrative push-and-pull that ideas of the posthuman create around bodies. But here the category that destabilises the posthumanist feminism outlined above is race. The prototype from which Ava takes the body parts is Jade, previously seen on film attempting to escape from her captivity, and a model who is clearly marked as Asian through her skin tone, hair and facial features. Likewise, Kyoko is identifiably Asian, through similar features and her name (and the fact she is played by a Japanese actor). As Ava turns away from Nathan, dying in a corridor, she also leaves Kyoko, motionless on the floor. If there has been complicity between the two androids in the murder of Nathan, it generates no sense of responsibility or care here. Why is Kyoko, who has displayed the possibility of her regeneration in scenes in which she peels back her skin to reveal her technological workings, not allowed to leave? Equally, while it is possible to read Ava's taking of Jade's limb and skin as the kind of posthumanist assemblage described above (and indeed potentially as a productive multiculturalism), it also functions as an appropriation, a mining of the Other's body in the creation of a new self.

In a sharp and perceptive reading of the film's racial politics, Danielle Wong observes how in *Ex Machina*'s "conflation of the posthuman with the postracial [...], race is, quite literally, deconstructed and disassembled in order for Ava to continue her prosthetic evolution". Ava may pass Nathan's Turing test but, as Wong asserts, "Kyoko and Jade fail; they are *too* obviously machines". Ava is "free to move onward into tomorrow", but only as a subject who literally carries a history of race appropriation with her: "The posthuman future emerging out of the Information Age grafts onto the skin that remembers the histories of racialised slavery and indentured labour

Racial politics in *Ex Machina*: Kyoko (Sonoya Mizuno) and Ava (Alicia Vikander)

that gave rise to Western modernity". As such, a reading of Ava *as engineer* has to contextualise her adroit manipulation of Nathan and Caleb's programming within the longer narrative of technology as appropriative power and tool of oppression. Jade's name conjures up Orientalist fantasies of Asia as a place of exploitable materialist fortunes, objects to be found and taken, while the silence of both Asian androids (Kyoko has been made not to talk) rehearses centuries-old Western apprehensions of the 'inscrutable and unreadable' Asian figure. What Wong neatly terms "techno-Orientalist anxieties" underpin both Nathan's narrative of power (Kyoko as servant) as well as Ava's trajectory towards freedom (Kyoko and Jade as disposable accomplices). These anxieties work to create fissures through the film, "interrogat[ing] the liberal humanist subject who is reincarnated as the white-as-postracial subject".[88]

Wong calls this process a "haunting" and it is an apt word for the spectral presence of humanist values that runs through so many narratives of the posthuman. In *Ex Machina*, these ghosts stare down, or at least *at*, feminist and disability readings. The complex embodiment suggested by the interaction of technologised limbs and skin, and the vulnerability of the film's characters, do not resolve the anxieties over race traced by Wong. Mobilising Ava as a posthuman feminist creates an argument at odds with a reading of her as an extension of Euro-American modernity. As Mel Chen has observed in their work on disability and race, there is an "integral fabric of racialisation within dominant disability and illness narrations and representations", and the effects of these are, as with racialisation in general, "never merely figurative, but materially consequential".[89] No critical sleight of hand is available to fix these contradictions, and it is instructive to note that the film's cultural appropriation of Asia, and particularly Japan, continues a tradition established by the cyberpunk fiction of William Gibson and Bruce Sterling, where both writers' fraught fascinations with technology and the body frequently focus on Asian women's bodies.[90] *Ex Machina* becomes the latest iteration of the mixing of excess and absence this book has found itself tracing; a celebration of the A.I. that becomes a free sentient subject set against the repression of racialised histories that made such a process possible. As ever, the disabled posthumanist body appears as eruptive, overwritten by stories that fail to cohere upon it.

With its suggestion of Ava's life beyond the end of its narrative, *Ex Machina* forms the kind of "cyborg future" highlighted by Alison Kafer earlier in this chapter. Remembering Kafer's observation that the cyborg articulates discourses of the political as well as those of embodiment, while bearing in mind Chen's above reflection on the material consequences of racialisation, what emerges from the film are the tensions that exist between its assertion of female emancipation and reiteration of racial anxieties. *Ex Machina*'s politics articulate both gender and race, but in radically different ways. The film is more intelligent than those Short analyses in *Cyborg Cinema*, practising a critique of "patriarchy's (de)valuation of women" that she sees as being inherent in cinema's representations of cyborg women.[91] But these progressive gender politics cannot be articulated without recognition of the racial bias that makes them possible. This is still a future that places certain bodies under erasure.

Dealing with 'the kit': A.I. and crisis of body modification

Becky Chambers' Wayfarer trilogy is composed of three narratives that trace characters across a fictional multi-species universe in which body enhancement and modification are common and are matched by worlds of cultural and gendered diversity and entanglement. Both society and self in Chambers' novels are marked by mixtures and amalgamations. The following description, of Port Coriol marketplace in *The Long Way to a Small Angry Planet* (the first novel), is typical of the novels' depictions of the posthumanist interactions that characterise their social locations:

> Sprawling streets stuffed with open-air shopfronts, overflowing with clothes and kitsch and sundries. Grounded ships, gutted and transformed into warehouses and eateries. Towering junk heaps lorded over by odd tinkerers who could always find exactly the part you were looking for, as long as you had the patience to talk about their latest engine mod. Cold underground bunkers full of bots and chips, swarming at all hours with giddy techs and modders sporting every implant imaginable. Food stalls offering everything from greasy street snacks to curious delicacies, some with rambling menus of daily specials, others with offerings so specific that the only acceptable thing to say at the counter was 'one, please.' A menagerie of sapients speaking in a dizzying array of languages, shaking hands and clasping paws and brushing tendrils.[92]

The 'dizzying menagerie' here is, to a degree, reminiscent of Gibson's fiction or *Blade Runner*'s imagined locations, where spaces of technological surplus, linguistic pastiche and conglomerations of culture challenge notions of purity and authenticity. But where Gibson's novels and Scott's film use such settings to investigate stories of male capability, vulnerability and violence, Chambers populates her spaceworlds with characters marked by personal fluidity and polyphonic associations. Individuals cross between genders depending on fertility cycles, or lack any gender identification at all; families involve same-sex parents or have complex formations of care, with individuals moving between birth parents, designated "raising" families, and groupings of friends and lovers where polygamy is the norm; genetic tweaking is not for the pursuance of individual strength or corporate gain, but rather "to make your physical self fit with who you are inside".[93] Given this polyphony, it is appropriate that the major romantic relationship in *The Long Way to a Small Angry Planet* is between Jenks, a technician, and Lovelace, the A.I. on the engineering ship the *Wayfarer*. And throughout the trilogy, human characters are frequently marked by their ignorance and limitations: the central character of *The Long Way to a Small Angry Planet* "chided herself for being so species-centric" as she encounters a range of sapients and societies while employed on the *Wayfarer*;[94] while in the third novel in the series, *Record of a Spaceborn Few*, it is reiterated continually that human culture is precarious: "We build off their tech", one character notes in relation to the multiple instances in which alien technology is cited as being superior to human, "and we get the planets they've decided are too crummy to live on".[95] In all three novels, it is the non-human animals who practise the greatest cultural and social sophistication or the most complex formations of selfhood.

Disability runs through the Wayfarer series, even given the plurality of body types that make up Chambers' fictional worlds. In *The Long Way to a Small Angry Planet*, Jenks, the *Wayfarer*'s technician, has "an average size" head, but "the rest of him was small, small as a child. He was stocky, too, as if his limbs had filled out while refusing to lengthen". His physical features draw comment: "why would anyone go to that much trouble to make himself small?" one character wonders on first meeting him.[96] Jenks finds himself, however, at home in spaces of technological body modification. His own enhancement, he stresses, "has been my way of saying that this is *my* body [...] All the things I've done to my body, I've done out of love", while he is drawn to markets and subcultures where "hardcore modders" are "prone to removing their own limbs in favour of synthetic replacements", and "metallic exoskeletons, or swirling nonabot tattoos, or unsettling perfect faces that betrayed a weakness for genetweaks" are a posthumanist norm. "Alongside such oddities", Jenks observes, "his small stature was nothing special. It was hard to feel weird in a place where *everybody* was weird. He took comfort in that".[97] In worlds where multiple forms – physical, cognitive, sexual, social – abound, disability is defined by the practice of prejudice rather than the straightforward fact of difference; it is the humans who *presume* that Jenks should have undergone modification to make himself taller who construct his stature as a 'problem'.

It is the second novel of the trilogy, *A Closed and Common Orbit*, that explores ideas of disability, engineering and gender in the greatest detail. *A Closed and Common Orbit* develops two parallel narratives. The first is that of Sidra, the reboot of Lovelace, the A.I. on the *Wayfarer* in *The Long Way to a Small Angry Planet* who has – illegally – become embodied in an exoskeleton housing and made to pass as a human. The second is that of Pepper, the engineer who created Sidra in an act of rescue, though most of Pepper's story is that of her childhood 20 years before, when she was a child slave known as Jane 23. As the novel progresses the reader becomes aware that Jane is Pepper and the two narratives come together at the end.

Sidra's condition is a careful exploration of a mind/body Cartesian dualism and the resulting nature of technological affect. As an A.I. on board the *Wayfarer*, her (she makes the decision to take female gender) responsibility was to oversee the totality of the ship's space: "She'd had cameras in every corner, voxes in every room. She'd existed in a web, with eyes both within and outside. A solid sphere of unblinking perception". But in her technologised embodied state, that perception has reduced dramatically: "Her vision was a cone, a narrow cone fixed straight ahead, with nothing – actual nothing – beyond its edges". Gravity, which was once "something that happened within her, created by antigrav nets in the floor panels", is now "a myopic glue, something that stuck feet to the floor and legs to the seat above it". And whereas before she was in constant connection to the Linkings, the novel's characterisation of the internet, within her new body, she now "could access no knowledge except that which was stored inside a housing that held nothing but herself". The result is that "she felt blind, Stunted. She was trapped in this thing".[98]

Sidra's narrative in *A Closed and Common Orbit* is one of struggles with and adjustment to what she refers to as 'the kit' that constitutes her body. Physically, her spatial and proprioceptive senses are completely reconfigured by her new self; while, initially programmed to be unable to lie, she has to learn how to obfuscate language when replying to questions or expressing herself. "Everything feels wrong" she says at the start of the novel, "I feel inside out".[99] Sidra's encounter with her new world as she moves from the limited environment of a ship in space to the teeming multiplicities of life on a planet is one of continuous disablement. Hating the limitations of her body, she wants to return to what she sees as the many advantages of her previous state as a diffused technological mind. "I was housed in a ship", she tells a friend to whom she has confided her truth, "I'm now housed in a body kit. My place of installation changes my abilities, but it's not *mine*, it's not *me*".[100] Sidra's preference for mind over body is part of a heritage of the rejection of the 'meat' of the physical self. As with the Baum's Tin Woodman, here the body that needs to sleep, be fed or that can be subjected to violence and feel pain (Sidra's 'kit' has to enact these so she can pass as being human, even though she has no need to such bodily functions) is seen as inferior to a posthumanist consciousness of pure thought. But whereas the Woodman makes a journey from human to android/cyborg, Sidra's trajectory is *back* from an A.I. to a physical self that in fact only approximates a human state as it is, still, a technological construction. Sherryl Vint notes that science fiction often focuses on "the question of authenticity, of distinguishing 'true' from 'false' selves, of sorting out what is really 'me' from the programming of cultural influences on the one hand [...] and biological instincts on the other", but Chambers' narrative is more complex than this.[101] Sidra's relationship with embodiment is one *between* technological states, with 'biology' only a subject to be contemplated from without. Vint cites patterns in history that results in a hegemony through which "we" (understood as majority, and therefore ableist, social opinion) "are inclined to identify ourselves with 'voice' or self inside our heads", and to "value a concept of self as self as immutable and self-consistent, some essence that persists despite changes, including changes in our body".[102] While this applies to Sidra, it does so only partiality and the whole question of her selfhood and agency is made both more problematic and tantalising by her foundational state being that of an A.I.

Jane 23/Pepper's narrative appears more recognisably human than that of Sidra. Jane is a child slave on an unnamed planet for a people named 'the Enhanced', made to work continually on extracting reusable parts from scrap metal and overseen by android 'Mothers' whose supervision consists solely of surveillance and violence. When, aged ten, Jane escapes from the building in which she lives and works, it is the first time she has ever seen the sky: "the ceiling that wasn't a ceiling" was "so, so big [...] It went on so far Jane 23 couldn't see any edges. It went on for always".[103] Jane finds a derelict shuttle in an environment covered with machine cast-offs from other parts of the planet and, fighting off feral dogs and acute food and water shortages, over the course of nine years reassembles the craft to make it flightworthy. Jane, Chambers stresses, is a consummate engineer, capable of fixing more or less anything, a characteristic carried forward in her reinvention as Pepper. Jane's story, as she flies away from her abusive origins to become integrated into a social world of culture and people, is one of victory over captivity through her capability and perseverance.

But the depiction of Jane 23/Pepper is subtler and more nuanced than this outline suggests. With the first ten years of her life limited to the dorm and sorting room in which she lives and works, her story is not one of a humanist 'return'. She has never known spaces such as Port Coriol or encountered the range of species that populate the rest of the novel. Jane, it also transpires, is a clone. Although details of her exact origin are never disclosed, she believes that the society that created her as a slave "probably cooked her up out of some grab-bag gene junk and pulled her out of a gooey vat, along with the other disposable girls", while she knows that she only "had a single chromosome, which was apparently one short from the usual".[104] Her body is, she says, all "monkey limbs and tweaked face".[105] As such, Jane's status is not the same as those other characters in the Wayfarer series who become posthumanised 'genetweaks' through voluntary modification. Her genetic composition is not tied to ideas of augmentation or enhancement; rather it, and her early life, indicate a disposability, a form of existence in which dignity is absent.[106]

In addition, Jane is not alone on the shuttle. As she flees the dogs who attack her following her escape, she is guided to the ship by a voice: "a weird voice, all wrong around the edges, not making any sense, not making any good words. Just a bunch of junk sounds".[107] The voice belongs to Owl, the shuttle's A.I., "a mind in a machine" as she describes herself to Jane during their first conversation.[108] Owl was jettisoned as junk along with the rest of the ship when the original crew were arrested, and her contact with Jane is the first interaction she has had since then. The twinning that Jane and Owl form over the years before they leave the planet becomes a narrative that parallels the mind/body split with which Chambers animates Sidra's storyline. While Jane becomes the physical half of the pairing, demanding from Owl building "tasks" and exploring outside the shuttle for usable technology and food, Owl takes on the status of Jane's teacher, advising and instructing on language, culture, objects and (literally) the nature of the universe. Comparison between Owl and Sidra sets up a fruitful complication of any idea of an A.I. 'self' in the novel; while Sidra feels confined in her 'kit' and yearns for her time as a distributed consciousness aboard the *Wayfarer,* Owl has been trapped in her software isolation until Jane's arrival and even when the two are together laments her inability to offer physical aid. The related experiences here reflect different, arguably competing, models and modes of disablement.

A Closed and Common Orbit brings its two narrative strands together following Jane's development into Pepper and subsequent intersection with Sidra's storyline. Sidra is quarantined after leaving her home planet and, with her future unsure, is taken by Pepper to Port Coriol to work in her engineering parts shop. But this departure involves abandoning Owl who, for a second time, is left trapped aboard the ship. The precise hinge at which the storylines come together is Pepper's discovery of the location of the shuttle, following which Sidra becomes integral to obtaining Owl's freedom. Sidra downloads her consciousness on to the ship, facilitating Owl's reactivation. The result is that at the novel's end the two A.I.s inhabit the same space of consciousness: "The AI framework installed in the walls – Sidra's design, Pepper's implementation – contained a single node where Sidra and Owl could communicate with one another".[109] But Sidra's return to an A.I. self is not depicted as a celebration of the rejection of her embodied status. Rather her 'kit' becomes what the narrative terms her "core body", a physical/technological exoskeleton to which she can return at will when she feels a need to experience the proprioceptive sense of her body in interactive motion.[110] Sidra's self is, then, distributed across both physical and (shared) A.I. formations. If much of the novel to this point has focused on Sidra as a 'central' character, reminiscent of a narrative of 'discovery', then this conclusion decentres her presence, stressing not a coming together of her embodied and A.I. selves but rather their actuation *across* her different subject positions. Such a process is typical of the deconstruction, central to critical posthumanist methods, of the singular, normative and coherent self, here replaced by the assertion of Pramod Nayar's "interconnections", "cross-overs" and "adaptations" between origins and histories, cited earlier. All these terms fit both Jane 23 and Sidra's storylines, framing issues of psychological subjectivity but also the grounded nature of engineered selfhood, while the characters' productive 'deviation' from social, cultural and embodied norms serves to remind readers of the disability logic that runs through Chambers' work. The origins of both characters are situated within profoundly disabling environments of trauma and dislocation, their 'impurities' mark them with difference (as with Jenks in *The Long Way to a Small Angry Planet*) even in the complex multiplicities of Chambers' fictional universe, while their adaptations address the challenges they experience as a result. "The law forgot to make space for people like me. People like her", Pepper asserts at one point, discussing the ways that both she and Sidra are excluded from the mainstream practices of the worlds in which they live.[111] For both characters, existence is a state – of embodiment, socialisation and experience – removed from their peers.

In *A Closed and Common Orbit*, however, other 'cross-overs' create an enabling scaffold of identification. Pepper 'implements' the changes that make Sidra's embodiment, and then her networking, possible and it is her skill as an engineer, her ability to 'borrow and adapt', that drives much of the possibility for agency in the novel. "It was always good, finding the bits that worked" the ten-year-old Jane 23 says at the very start of her section of the novel, prefacing not only her character's grounded sense of embodied self but also the technological expertise that underpins the overall sense of how the novel's assemblages (of all kinds) 'work'.[112] Gender is central to this construction, with all three novels in the trilogy featuring central female characters whose subjectivities defy ideas of compulsory heteronormativity. Both *The Long Way to a Small Angry Planet* and *Record of a Spaceborn Few* are animated by a queer sensibility: Rosemary, the central protagonist of the first novel and administrative officer aboard the *Wayfarer*, develops a relationship with Sissix, a female Aandrisk alien; Kizzy, one of the ship's mechanics, has two fathers; and, as characters shift between genders, the pronoun 'xe' is commonly used. In *Record of a Spaceborn Few*, Isabel – the archivist who is at the core of the narrative's stress on ideas of culture, history and inheritance – develops her views of social difference through interactions with her wife Tamsin and as part of an ethnographic research project with a female alien academic.

Such queering is only one example of the intersectionality at the heart of Chambers' work that sees species, bodies, sexualities, technologies, languages and cultures all mix in what is ultimately a non-hierarchical depiction of social space. It is especially of note that across the trilogy it is women who engineer both bodies and narrative events. Engineered bodies in science fiction are frequently the product of male expertise and actions; men both *make* bodies in their role as creators and place these bodies in contexts of conflict and violence. In Scott's *Blade Runner*, the replicants return to meet the man responsible for their production: "it's not an easy thing to meet your maker" Roy Batty (Rutger Hauer) says to Eldon Tyrell (Joe Turkel), the head of the Tyrell Corporation, immediately before he kills him, also calling him "Father" and "the God of Biomechanics" in this climactic scene. The ways in which men produce women in science fiction cinema frequently enacts the traits identified by Short in her critical genealogy; in *Blade Runner* the Tyrell Corporation construct Rachael (Sean Young), the most sophisticated of all the replicants. But even with Tyrell's death, Rachael is merely passed on to Deckard (Harrison Ford): as Short notes, through his physical possession of her "Deckard effectively replaces Tyrell in reprogramming her to his needs".[113] Scott's film, in which Deckard noticeably destroys the two rogue female replicants through extreme violence but is not responsible for the 'retiring' of the male robots (one is in fact killed by Rachael, the other 'expires' at the end of his life span), is only the most complex of film narratives in which men construct, possess or eliminate cyborg women.[114]

Chambers' fiction, however, operates in entirely different spaces. It is her central female characters, particularly in *A Closed and Common Orbit*, who negotiate both the creation and experience of different embodiment. While not entirely absent, violence is rare across the Wayfarer series and is never used to articulate ideas of male fragility or capability.[115] Female productivity is depicted in entirely different ways, figured as complex and challenging both intellectually and through invention and adaptation. While Jane 23 is *made*, as a disposable genetic anomaly, by the Enhanced, she herself becomes the *designer and engineer* of Sidra, a process that involves engagement with technical, philosophical, legal and social contexts. And Sidra becomes her own confrontation with these questions, particularly those of self and embodiment. As mentioned previously, Sidra is the reboot of Lovelace, the A.I. in *The Long Way to a Small Angry Planet*. Following an attack on the *Wayfarer* at the end of that first novel, Lovelace undergoes a hard reset in an attempt to recover her systems. The reset fails and a new A.I., who becomes Sidra, is created. Initially, Sidra knows nothing of Lovelace's character or history, but in a telling moment in *A Closed and Common Orbit*, she encounters the Lovelace A.I. model in a shop. As a product to be purchased before installation, Lovelace is a globe sitting on a shelf. Sidra picks it up, "cupping it gently. She could see the kit's face reflected in the globe's plating".[116] Here, Sidra is literally faced by her former self, yet in a sign of the novel's intricate depiction of technology this Lovelace is of course *not* that from the *Wayfarer* but rather a consumer object, hardware and software waiting to be connected to the networks of some other, unknown, ship. The moment exemplifies the novel's nuanced presentation of posthumanist subjectivity: an embodied A.I. encountering a version of her former self, physically connecting through touch and psychologically through Sidra's own 'messy history' ("synthetic personalities are just that: synthetic" the seller says to Sidra, completely unaware of how her personality has developed).[117] But at the same time Sidra is distanced; the Lovelace she holds is not the A.I. who preceded her. It provides no answers to her quest.

As all these examples show, Chambers crafts narratives that push the boundaries of the intersections between selves, bodies, communities, gender and technology. The future she depicts are those that Kafer wishes for when she writes of the intersections between feminism and disability, the "desirably disabled futures" made possible by not seeing either 'disabled' or 'woman' and the connections between them as problematic terms.[118] Part of this desirability in Chambers work is inflected by her stress on women as designers, producers and adapters of technology. There is no recourse to the 'genius' of the male inventor in *A Closed and Common Orbit*; the *Frankenstein* narrative is entirely absent. Rather, Chambers' engineering is a fraught and often conflicted process. In the manner in which it falls away from models of heroism it enacts multiple other differences: of place, self, body, relationship, or sexuality. Chambers queers and crips posthumanist technology and (crucially) she does so through her engagement with what Ato Quayson has termed the "crisis of representation" that disability produces in literature. For Quayson, the "embarrassment, fear and confusion that attend the disabled in their everyday reality is translated in literature and the aesthetic field into a series of structural devices".[119] For Chambers, these devices are located in science fiction's aesthetics and textual spaces, but in a revision of Quayson's thinking they do not begin from 'fear and confusion' but rather an acceptance of embodied difference as a starting point for explorations of all the elements of her fictional worlds. Many of the fictional texts analysed in this study so far have fallen through their own representation crisis, pulled into humanist models of individuals and communities even as they are seduced by the glamour and potential of the posthuman. Chambers' work does not avoid the messy contradictions of fictional aesthetics, but it suggests possible shapes for engineering a disabled and feminist portrayal of technological futures.

Conclusion: Peppers

This chapter has been bookended by the tale of two Peppers. In Sheffield, the SoftBank Pepper appeared striking in terms of potential: for activity, function and a new conception of posthuman care. For now, however, Pepper's pleasing humanoid shape and possible capabilities present as a project to be developed more than a model of sophisticated companionship. Chambers' Pepper, by way of contrast, possesses all the advantages of being imagined. She articulates complex modes of being and belonging: with origins in technology, without community and any awareness of a wider world, she progresses to become designer and engineer of the spaces in which she lives. Precisely because she contains all the multiplicities of fiction – the overlapping of genre, plot, characterisation, topic and metaphor – Pepper inhabits story spaces that carry details the 'real' Pepper cannot hope to match. This is not to say, of course, that Softbank's Pepper is not to some degree the product of narrative and surrounded by the stories that mark a place in the world; clearly all the choices that have gone into her/its/his development speak of a moment in the hopes and desire that characterise our increasingly technologised history. But Chambers' Pepper deploys the unlimited possibilities of fiction and so can explore interactions with technology that our present moment *envisages*, without the need for the actual laws of physics. The Pepper of *A Closed and Common Orbit* is also more secure in her status as female than the robot. Chamber's Pepper is a clone, but (as with Sidra) her atypical origins only add to her complex characterisation as a woman. Softbank's Pepper, by way of contrast, appears indicative of a confusion about gender, labelled male but at times read as female. Possibly it will take a period of usage of Pepper in people's homes, interacting with them on a daily basis, before that exact terminology is worked through.

Both Peppers inhabit discourses of expectation. It may well be that future historians of disability technology look back on the development of the companion Pepper as a seminal moment in a trajectory of post/non-human care and this particular Pepper will be remembered long after Chambers' writings are forgotten. But the imagined Pepper is no less valuable. Precisely because she is fictionalised, she functions not only as part of a richly textured and made-up world; she also reminds readers of the ways in which stories are told of the possibilities of present technology and the sometimes hidden fictions of design and production. It is through this idea of expectations that each Pepper intersects with disability futures, either through the immediate possibility of care or the imagined science fiction universe.

At the end of 'A Cyborg Manifesto', Donna Haraway writes that conceiving of science and technology through cyborg imagery "means embracing the skillful [*sic*] task of reconstructing the boundaries of daily life, in partial connection with others, in communication with all of our parts". Communicating with 'all of our parts' is a powerful disability statement, recognising the body and its activities in its rich diversity. It is also a statement about engineering, recognising that the design and production of parts is central to the construction of the cyborg. Any number of non-dualistic positions, Haraway notes, "require a cyborg theory of wholes and parts". Both disability and engineering are also grounded in the experience of daily life that Haraway identifies here, an experience that her work explores additionally in terms of gender, through the "dailiness [...] that makes visible unvalued female activity". In the end, Haraway asserts, "Cyborg gender is a local possibility taking a global vengeance [...] There is no drive in cyborgs to produce total theory, but there is an intimate experience of boundaries, their construction and deconstruction".[120] Such terminology is apt for the kinds of gendered, designed and engineered disability this chapter has explored, though possibly we might extend 'global' to now become 'planetary'.

Notes

1 In a 2014 article describing Pepper's development and production, Erico Guizzo uses the gender neutral 'it' throughout to describe Pepper: 'How Aldebaran Robotics built its friendly humanoid robot, Pepper', *IEEE Spectrum*, December 26, 2014, https://spectrum.ieee.org/robotics/home-robots/how-aldebaran-robotics-built-its-friendly-humanoid-robot-pepper. Accessed July 16, 2018. Writing in *The Guardian* in July 2018 about Pepper's potential to work in social care, John Harris notes that "Pepper has been given a male

pronoun, for some reason": Harris, 'Robots could solve the social care crisis – but at what price?', *The Guardian*, July 2, 2018, www.theguardian.com/commentisfree/2018/jul/02/robo-carers-human-principles-technology-care-crisis. Accessed July 16, 2018.

2 https://www.ald.softbankrobotics.com/en/cool-robots/pepper. Accessed March 29, 2017.

3 Guizzo notes that at Pepper's launch event it was "unclear how much autonomy the robot has [...] most of its actions were clearly preprogrammed".

4 Despina Kakoudaki, *Anatomy of a Robot: Literature, Cinema, and the Cultural Work of Artificial People* (New Brunswick, NJ and London: Rutgers University Press, 2014), p. 13.

5 See Raymond Holt and Stuart Murray, 'Prosthesis and the engineered imagination: reading augmentation and disability across cultural theory, representation and product design', *Medical Humanities* 41, no. 2 (2020), pp. 55–62.

6 Mark O'Connell, *To Be a Machine: Adventures Among Cyborgs, Utopians, Hackers, and the Futurists Solving the Modest Problem of Death* (London: Granta, 2017), pp. 118–119.

7 O'Connell, *To Be a Machine*, pp. 121–122.

8 Kakoudaki, *Anatomy of a Robot*, p. 81.

9 See the essays in Richard Grusin (ed.), *Anthropocene Feminism* (Minneapolis: University of Minnesota Press, 2017) for a critique of masculinist techno-approaches in articulating transhumanism.

10 Nina Lykke, 'Between monsters, goddesses and cyborgs: feminist confrontations with science' in Gill Kirkup et al. (eds), *The Gendered Cyborg: A Reader* (Abingdon and New York: Routledge, 2000), p. 84.

11 Julie Wosk, *My Fair Ladies: Female Robots, Androids and Other Artificial Eves* (New Brunswick, NJ and London: Rutgers University Press, 2015), p. 153.

12 Wosk, *My Fair Ladies*, p. 154.

13 Jennifer Robertson, 'Gendering humanoid robots: robo-sexism in Japan', *Body and Society* 16, no. 2 (2010). See also Wosk, *My Fair Ladies*, pp. 159–162.

14 Cary Wolfe, 'Introduction' in Donna Haraway, *Manifestly Haraway* (Minneapolis: University of Minnesota Press, 2016), p. ix.

15 It is instructive to consider how engineering associations and institutional regulators engage with questions arising from such detail. In October 2005 the UK's Royal Academy of Engineering, in association with the Engineering Council and following a series of consultation events, published a Statement of Ethical Principles, later revised in July 2017. The academy's statement "covers ethics in engineering education, ethics in practice and the issues surrounding emerging engineered technologies" and outlines four "fundamental principles for ethical behaviour": 'honesty and integrity', 'respect for life, law, the environment and public good', 'accuracy and rigour' and 'leadership and communication'. Under the second of these the statement notes that engineering professionals should "protect, and where possible improve, the quality of built and natural environments" and "maximise the public good and minimise both actual and potential adverse effects for their own and succeeding generations". Such a focus on the 'public good' is, relatively speaking, rare in scientific industries often built around corporate engagement and client demand, and while the academy's outline of ethics is not

a set standard, it extends to underpin the various codes of conduct of the different bodies of the Engineering Council (the organisation that deals with chartered engineering registration). The Institution of Mechanical Engineers (the branch of engineering that connects most to the design and production of assistive technologies for people with disabilities), for example, adapts the academy's statement in the 'Code and Conduct of Regulations' section of its own Royal Charter & By-Laws. The IMechE Code requires its members to practise a "duty of care" and "be alert to the ways in which their duties derive from and affect the work of other people, respect[ing] the rights and reputations of others". In addition, members must "place responsibility for the welfare, health and safety of the workforce and wider community at all times before responsibility to the profession" and "embrace the needs of the community and future generations and adopt practices that have minimal adverse effects on social, cultural, archaeological and ethnic heritage, and the broader interests of humanity as a whole". Given that this is a code of conduct regulating the practice of chartered engineers, individuals sign up to it and can be struck off for any failure to adhere to its principles.

Seen through a specific disability optic, we might note that mechanical engineers (or at least, here, IMechE members) working on the design and production of assistive technologies for people with disabilities are required to consider not only their subjects' health and welfare in the immediate present, but also 'future generations' of disabled people and their interaction with the increasingly complex worlds of technological development. And, if those with disabilities are considered to have a 'cultural heritage' or belong to a community, as stated by the code (and it is important to view disability identities in such terms), then engineers must work with an understanding of that heritage and community belonging in all that they do. What, exactly, might this mean if we subject this to a critical disability reading? First, such explicit direction on issues of respect requires that engineers employed in the production of technologies should not view disabled users as incomplete or defined by notions of loss or absence; and then working with a "duty of care" positions engineers in an ethical space that should foreground the complexities of such 'care'. See Royal Academy of Engineering, 'Creating systems that work: principles of engineering systems for the 21st century', www.raeng.org.uk/publications/reports/rae-systems-report.

16 Graham Pullin, *Design Meets Disability* (Cambridge, MA and London: MIT Press, 2009), pp. xv and 4.
17 Pullin, *Design Meets Disability*, p. 45.
18 Pullin, *Design Meets Disability*, pp. 89–90.
19 Louis L. Bucciarelli, *Designing Engineers* (Cambridge, MA and London: MIT Press, 1994), p. 11.
20 Bucciarelli, *Designing Engineers*, pp. 18–19.
21 Bucciarelli, *Designing Engineers*, p. 19.
22 Pullin, *Design Meets Disability*, p. 90.
23 Bucciarelli, *Designing Engineers*, p. 195.
24 Donna Haraway, 'A Cyborg Manifesto: Science, Technology and Socialist-Feminism in the Late Twentieth Century' in *Manifestly Haraway*, pp. 8–9.
25 Anne Balsamo, *Technologies of the Gendered Body: Reading Cyborg Women* (Durham, NC and London: Duke University Press, 1996), p. 33.

26 Judith Squires, 'Fabulous feminist futures and the lure of cyberculture' in Jon Dovey (ed.), *Fractal Dreams: New Media in Social Context* (London: Lawrence and Wishart, 1996), p. 195.
27 Alison Adam, *Artificial Knowing: Gender and the Thinking Machine* (London and New York: Routledge, 1998), pp. 172–173.
28 Kim Toffoletti, *Cyborgs and Barbie Dolls: Feminism, Popular Culture and the Posthuman Body* (London and New York: I.B. Tauris, 2007), p. 21.
29 Toffoletti, *Cyborgs and Barbie Dolls*, pp. 24 and 21.
30 Toffoletti, *Cyborgs and Barbie Dolls*, p. 26.
31 Rosi Braidotti, *Nomadic Subjects: Embodiment and Sexual Difference in Contemporary Feminist Theory* (New York: Columbia University Press, 1994), p. 103. Braidotti produced a revised and extended edition of the book, also published by Columbia University Press, in 2011. See also the collection Braidotti edited with Nina Lykke, *Between Monsters, Goddesses and Cyborgs: Feminist Confrontations with Science, Medicine and Cyberspace* (London: Zed Books, 1996).
32 Braidotti, *Nomadic Subjects*, p. 105.
33 Rosi Braidotti, *Metamorphoses: Towards a Materialist Theory of Becoming* (Cambridge: Polity, 2002), pp. 177–178.
34 Braidotti, *Metamorphoses*, p. 179.
35 Critical work on the topic before Kafer's study was largely exploratory and limited, but for thoughtful investigations of the place of social theories of disability in debates around feminist technoscience see Donna Reeve, 'Cyborgs, cripples and iCrip: reflections of the contribution of Haraway to disability studies' in Dan Goodley, Beverley Hughes and Lennard J. Davis (eds), *Disability and Social Theory* (London: Palgrave Macmillan, 2012), pp. 91–111, and Sharon Betcher, 'Putting my foot (prosthesis, crutches, phantom) down: considering technology as transcendence in the writings of Donna Haraway', *Women's Studies Quarterly* 29, no. 3/4 (Fall 2001), pp. 35–53.
36 Alison Kafer, *Feminist, Queer, Crip* (New York: New York University Press, 2013), pp. 105 and 107–110.
37 Kafer, *Feminist, Queer, Crip*, pp. 112–113.
38 Kafer, *Feminist, Queer, Crip*, p. 116.
39 Kafer, *Feminist, Queer, Crip*, pp. 106 and 116.
40 Kafer, *Feminist, Queer, Crip*, p. 118.
41 Kafer, *Feminist, Queer, Crip*, p. 119.
42 Kafer, *Feminist, Queer, Crip*, p. 117.
43 Kafer, *Feminist, Queer, Crip*, p. 120.
44 Kafer, *Feminist, Queer, Crip*, p. 120; emphasis in original.
45 Haraway, 'A Cyborg Manifesto', pp. 8–9 and 61. Haraway observes that: "Perhaps paraplegics and other severely handicapped people can (and sometimes do) have the most intense experiences of complex hybridization with other communication devices" (61). While such language appears problematic, Kafer notes that Haraway was probably unaware of the shift in language from 'handicap' to 'disabled' as the 1970s turned into the 1980s. *Feminist, Queer, Crip*, p. 111.
46 Kafer, *Feminist, Queer, Crip*, pp. 106 and 105.
47 See, for example, Andreas Huyssen, 'The vamp and the machine: technology and sexuality in Fritz Lang's *Metropolis*', *New German Critique* 24/25

(Autumn 1981–Winter 1982), pp. 221–237, and Minsoo Kang, 'Building the sex machine: the subversive potential of the female robot', *Intertexts* 9, no. 1 (2005), pp. 5–22.

48 As Julie Wosk notes, Maria "embodies the familiar archetype of a woman who is both harlot and saint, angelic comforter and diabolical destroyer", Wosk, *My Fair Ladies*, p. 72.

49 Huyssen, "The vamp and the machine", p. 236.

50 Kang, "Building the sex machine", p. 5.

51 Rosemarie Garland-Thomson, *Staring: How We Look* (Oxford: Oxford University Press, 2009), p. 120.

52 Kang, "Building the sex machine", pp. 5–6.

53 Kafer, *Feminist, Queer, Crip*, p. 169.

54 Kakoudaki, *Anatomy of a Robot*, p. 3.

55 Kakoudaki, *Anatomy of a Robot*, p. 4.

56 I do not have the space here to do justice to the complexities of Vonnegut's novel, but it conveys a powerful (if largely backward-looking) critique of a mechanised postwar society in the US. In terms of my focus on gender in this chapter, Vonnegut's acerbic vision of an automated society includes deft portrayals of the role of men and women. Almost without exception, the engineers and managers in the novel are men, while women are wives and secretaries. In the novel's envisioning of an engineered future, the rise of the machines creates the parallel rise of those men who use them to control the economic and social means of production. In turn, this reinforces the stark and strict gender binaries that offer women no real power whatsoever in a developing of postwar American society. Alex Goody writes perceptively on automation, production and consumption in the novel's representation of a "new Americianism". See Goody, *Technology, Literature and Culture* (Cambridge: Polity, 2011), pp. 150–152.

57 See Stuart Murray, 'The ambiguities of inclusion: disability in contemporary literature' in Clare Barker and Stuart Murray (eds), *The Cambridge Companion to Literature and Disability* (Cambridge: Cambridge University Press, 2018), pp. 91–93. In *Krapp's Last Tape* (1958) this sense of restriction and confinement takes a specific technological turn in the protagonist's repeated use of a tape-recorder to relive his memories. For an analysis of this, see Goody, *Technology, Literature and Culture*, pp. 154–157.

58 Gibson's post-punk futureworld is saturated with ideas of engineering and technological innovation that, through their invocation of digital futures, maintain a contemporary feel. In *Neuromancer* (1984), the first novel of the trilogy, developments in genetic engineering, neurosurgery and synthetic organ production create multiple possibilities for bodily adaptation, and questions of engineered embodiment suffuse the novel. Case, the central protagonist, begins the narrative with his nervous system deliberately damaged "with a wartime Russian mycotoxin" after he is caught stealing from his employers, while Molly, the femme fatale and central female character, has mirror glasses that are, in fact, "surgically inset, sealing her sockets", and "ten double-edged, four-centimeter scalpel blades" that emerge from her nails to be used as weapons. In the late capitalist, brand-soaked, world of the novel's urban environments, the physical or cognitive enhancement produced by engineering is a given, something (particularly) to be purchased, and it is

often rather the quality or value of the work that has been undertaken that is the relevant issue. William Gibson, *Neuromancer* (London: Harper Collins, 1993), pp. 36–37.

The topic's coverage in science fiction is too multiple to detail here, but milestone texts include Anne McCaffery's short story 'The ship who sang' (1961, later developed into a novella), Martin Caidan's *Cyborg* (1972, spin-offs of which became the television series *The Six-Million Dollar* Man and *The Bionic Woman*), and the ground-breaking work of Octavia Butler, particularly the *Xenogenesis* trilogy (1987–1989). Ramez Naam's *Nexus* trilogy (2013–2015) is also worthy of mention here because of Naam's previous career as a technology engineer at Microsoft, where he was part of teams developing Outlook and Internet Explorer, among other programmes. Naam's novels are fluent in the language of post- and transhumanism and he is also the author of non-fiction studies of the subject. See, for example, *More Than Human: Embracing the Promise of Biological Enhancement* (London: Broadway Books, 2005).

There is a growing output of cyborg romance fiction as well, in which the generic codes of romance fiction take new forms across human/technology boundaries.

59 It is worth noting that this idea is common in cinema, with *Weird Science* and *Zoe* being the most prominent examples. In *Making Mr. Right*, the gender relations are inverted to some extent, with a woman working in public relations (Ann Magnuson) having to 'humanise' an android scientist (John Malkovich). It is important to note that the woman is therefore not the literal creator here and that maternal and paternal roles are largely still preserved.

60 Thomas Berger, *Adventures of the Artificial Woman* (New York: Simon & Schuster, 2005), p. 1.

61 Berger, *Adventures of the Artificial Woman*, p. 3.

62 Berger, *Adventures of the Artificial Woman*, p. 30.

63 Berger, *Adventures of the Artificial Woman*, p. 30.

64 Berger, *Adventures of the Artificial Woman*, p. 102.

65 Berger, *Adventures of the Artificial Woman*, p. 102.

66 See Margrit Shildrick, *Embodying the Monster: Encounters with the Vulnerable Self* (London: Sage, 2002).

67 Berger, *Adventures of the Artificial Woman*, pp. 65 and 61–64.

68 Berger, *Adventures of the Artificial Woman*, pp. 134–135.

69 Berger, *Adventures of the Artificial Woman*, p. 195.

70 Berger, *Adventures of the Artificial Woman*, p. 198.

71 James Porter, 'Foreword' in David T. Mitchell and Sharon L. Snyder (eds), *The Body and Physical Difference: Discourses of Disability* (Ann Arbor: University of Michigan Press, 1997), pp. xiii–xiv.

72 Sherryl Vint, *Bodies of Tomorrow: Technology, Subjectivity, Science Fiction* (Toronto: University of Toronto Press, 2007), p. 7.

73 Vint, *Bodies of Tomorrow*, p. 8.

74 Lars Schmeink, *Biopunk Dystopias: Genetic Engineering, Society, and Science Fiction* (Liverpool: Liverpool University Press, 2016), p. 32.

75 Michael Bérubé, 'Afterword' in Sharon L. Snyder, Brenda Jo Brueggemann, and Rosemarie Garland-Thomson (eds), *Disability Studies: Enabling the Humanities* (New York: Modern Language Association of America, 2002), p. 323.

76 Vint, *Bodies of Tomorrow*, p. 9.
77 Kathryn Allan, 'Reading disability in science fiction' in Allan (ed.), *Disability in Science Fiction: Representations of Technology as Cure* (Basingstoke: Palgrave Macmillan, 2013), p. 2.
78 Manuela Rossini, 'Bodies' in Bruce Clarke and Manuela Rossini (eds), *The Cambridge Companion to Literature and the Posthuman* (Cambridge: Cambridge University Press, 2017), p. 164.
79 Vint, *Bodies of Tomorrow*, p. 21.
80 Pramod K. Nayar, *Posthumanism* (Cambridge: Polity, 2014), pp. 135 and 30. See also pp. 127–130 and 135–149.
81 Sue Short, *Cyborg Cinema* (Basingstoke: Palgrave Macmillan, 2005/2011), p. 94.
82 Short, *Cyborg Cinema*, p. 83.
83 In the shooting script, although not in the film, Nathan's surname is given as Bateman in what appears to be a clear allusion to Jason Bateman, the psychotic protagonist of Bret Eason Ellis' 1991 novel *American Psycho*. See www.slguardian.org/wp-content/uploads/2016/06/Ex-Machina.pdf. Accessed June 7, 2018.
84 The film echoes Shelley's novel not only through its central narrative but in its clever use of location and environment. Nathan's secluded facility is carefully filmed to evoke ideas of the sublime, with framing shots of mountain and trees. In a similar vein, Nathan and Caleb have an important conversation about the philosophy underpinning the creation of Ava next to a cascading waterfall, that most traditional motif of the Romantic sublime. It is no coincidence that, in contrast to the idea that Nathan's 'genius' is set in 'nature', Ava escapes to the city, and specifically a busy and crowded road intersection.
85 Eve Kosofsky Sedgwick, *Epistemology of the Closet* (Berkeley and Los Angeles: University of California Press, 1990).
86 Tobin Siebers, *Disability Theory* (Ann Arbor, University of Michigan Press; 2008), pp. 101 and 110. See pp. 96–119 for the full outline of the concept of 'disability as masquerade'. Merri Lisa Johnson and Robert McRuer also discuss Sedgwick's study as an intersectional disability text that helps further articulate their theory of crispistemologies. Sedgwick's unpacking of the closet, they note, is "useful in for locating *cripistemology* within terminological geopolitical crises of our moment and for asking questions about remote locations, styles, and modes of transmission for prohibited knowledge about disability". 'Crispistemologies: introduction', *Journal of Literary & Cultural Disability Studies* 8, no. 2 (2014), p. 130.
87 Though the book is now old, Mary Anne Doane's *Femmes Fatales: Feminism, Film Theory and Psychoanalysis* (New York: Routledge, 1991) is still an excellent feminist study of masquerade, especially in relation to spectatorship.
88 Danielle Wong, 'Dismembered Asian/American android parts in *Ex Machina* as "inorganic" critique', *Transformations* 29 (2017), pp. 36–38. See also LeiLani Nishime, 'Whitewashing yellow futures in *Ex Machina, Cloud Atlas,* and *Advantageous*: gender, labor, and technology in sci-fi film', *Journal of Asian American Studies* 20, no. 1 (2017), pp. 29–49.
89 Mel Chen, 'Unpacking intoxication, racialising disability', *Medical Humanities* 41 (2015), p. 25. For more general critiques of posthumanism from critical race perspectives, see Kristen Lillvis, *Postmodern Blackness and the Black Female*

Imagination (Athens: University of Georgia Press, 2017) and Matthew Taylor, *Universes Without Us: Posthuman Cosmologies in American Literature* (Minneapolis: University of Minneapolis Press, 2013).

90 This is especially noticeable in, for example, the Japanese Chiba City locations at the start of Gibson's *Neuromancer* or the off-world, Japanese-derived cultural setting of the powerful 'Geisha Bank' in Sterling's *Schismatrix*. Both writers also explicitly use the zaibatsu, the business and finance corporations that underpinned the economies of Imperial Japan, refitting it for the post-industrial worlds they create. As with so many technofantasies, and as with *Ex Machina*, the stereotypes of Japanese culture here combine with those of sexualised women. Cyberpunk fiction undoubtedly depicts a posthumanist space of multiple potential embodiments, but it appears as a landscape for boy's games in which various exciting others are appropriated to come within reach. For more on these contexts, see the essays in David Roh, Betsy Huang and Greta Niu (eds), *Techno-Orientalism: Imagining Asia in Speculative Fiction, History and Media* (New Brunswick, NJ and London: Rutgers University Press, 2015), especially those in part II by Julie Ha Tran and Kathryn Allan.

91 Short, *Cyborg Cinema*, p. 97.

92 Becky Chambers, *The Long Way to a Small, Angry Planet* (London: Hodder & Stoughton, 2015), p. 96.

93 Chambers, *The Long Way to a Small, Angry Planet*, pp. 252–255 and 203.

94 Chambers, *The Long Way to a Small, Angry Planet*, p. 253.

95 Becky Chambers, *Record of a Spaceborn Few* (London: Hodder & Stoughton, 2016), p. 91.

96 Chambers, *The Long Way to a Small, Angry Planet*, p. 32.

97 Chambers, *The Long Way to a Small, Angry Planet*, pp. 57–58 and 109.

98 Becky Chambers, *A Closed and Common Orbit* (London: Hodder & Stoughton, 2016), pp. 5–6.

99 Chambers, *A Closed and Common Orbit*, p. 7.

100 Chambers, *A Closed and Common Orbit*, p. 209; italics in original.

101 Vint, *Bodies of Tomorrow*, p. 5.

102 Vint, *Bodies of Tomorrow*, p. 6.

103 Chambers, *A Closed and Common Orbit*, p. 60.

104 Chambers, *A Closed and Common Orbit*, pp. 193–194.

105 Chambers, *A Closed and Common Orbit*, p. 302.

106 Pramod Nayar uses Giorgio Agamben's work on *homo sacer* to discuss how the posthuman condition can involve the creation of bodies and lives "that may be terminated [...] without attracting punishment". Such description fits Jane's experience on the planet on which she grows up. See Nayar, *Posthumanism* (Cambridge: Polity, 2014), p. 61.

107 Chambers, *A Closed and Common Orbit*, p. 69.

108 Chambers, *A Closed and Common Orbit*, p. 85.

109 Chambers, *A Closed and Common Orbit*, p. 361.

110 Chambers, *A Closed and Common Orbit*, p. 359.

111 Chambers, *A Closed and Common Orbit*, p. 302.

112 Chambers, *A Closed and Common Orbit*, p. 14.

113 Short, *Cyborg Cinema*, p. 91.

114 A disability reading of *Blade Runner* might nevertheless pick up on a number of features. The four-year lifespan of the Nexus-6 replicants – termed

"accelerated decrepitude" by Pris (Darryl Hannah) – and the fact that J.F. Sebastian (William Sanderson) has 'Methuselah Syndrome', which creates premature ageing, suggests that shortened life expectancy functions as a form of disablement. In addition, the final fight scene between Deckard and Roy sees the former's body repeatedly broken by the 'superhuman' strength of the latter. The iconic shots in which Batty breaks Deckard's fingers, before returning his gun to his mutilated hand, leaves Deckard reduced physically and totally vulnerable in this key moment of conflict. It is noticeable that Deckard does not 'recover' from this to destroy Batty; the replicant 'expires' naturally.

115 Following an alien attack on the *Wayfarer* in *The Long Way to a Small Angry Planet*, the crew is helpless in the face of the superior strength of the attackers and it requires the negotiating skills of central character Rosemary to defuse the situation.

116 Chambers, *A Closed and Common Orbit*, p. 248.

117 Chambers, *A Closed and Common Orbit*, p. 246.

118 Kafer, *Feminist, Queer, Crip*, p. 68.

119 Ato Quayson, *Aesthetic Nervousness: Disability and the Crisis of Representation* (New York: Columbia University Press, 2007), p. 19.

120 Haraway, *Manifestly Haraway*, pp. 67 and 66.

CHAPTER THREE

Visualising and Re-Membering Disability Body Politics in Filmic Representations of the 'War on Terror'

Introduction: global acts of biotechnologies and disability viewings

In this chapter I want to follow and extend the critical energy that comes from the complex interweaving of body, technology (especially prosthetics) and gender characterised in Chapter 2. In doing so I am interested in the ways in which disability, as represented on film, creates what we can recognise as new focal moments on global articulations of the human and posthuman as they play out through the systems, international economies and politics of the technologically embodied. It is vital to consider both disability and posthumanism in terms of the global, an approach that is often absent from critical practices that concentrate on each as they are experienced and represented in European and American situations alone. What Michael Davidson has termed "the work of disability in an age of globalization" frames questions of embodiment, technology and race (in particular) within contexts where assumptions about what constitutes disability are expressed through multiple and overlapping frames of reference. To analyse texts that focus on the global through a critical disability lens involves what Davidson calls a re-evaluation of "some of the keywords of disability studies – stigma, normalcy, ableism, difference – from a comparative cultural perspective".[1] Such perspectives produce situated and localised patterns of disabled difference that articulate crucial topics such as poverty, labour, access to resources and the meanings of individuals and communities within global dynamics of political health.

My focus in this chapter is on the cinematic representation of war and conflict, read as specific examples of this intersection of disability, technology and the global, and it will develop arguments that work to utilise the different cultural inflections identified by Davidson in reading two distinct sets of films. The first is a set of high-profile, commercial features from the US that depict either the conflict in Iraq, or issues of 'terror' that are seen to arise as a consequence of American military intervention abroad. I will analyse several films, but my main texts are *Source Code* (2011), read as a narrative exploring the war on terror as it is imagined within the US itself, and then *Green Zone* (2011), *The Hurt Locker* (2008) and *American Sniper* (2014), all focused on the military presence in Iraq. The second is a group of films made within conflict zones (particularly Iraq and Iran) either occupied or destabilised by US military presence. The principal focus here will be on the Iraqi feature *Alhaam* (2005) and the Iraqi/Kurdish drama *Turtles Can Fly* (2004), two films that centre on events immediately before and after the US invasion of Iraq in 2003.

Reading disability within a global frame poses challenges. As Clare Barker has noted in a discussion of the heritage of postcolonial and decolonising histories that created numerous disabilities through conflict or political productions of poverty: "In the present day, the wars, debt, migrations, and disasters brought about by decolonization, as well as neo-colonial activities such as economic sanctions and western military intervention in the Middle East, persist in disabling postcolonial citizens. To tell a story about colonialism or its aftermath, it is often necessary to tell a story about disability".[2] Disasters and sanctions are good examples of events that not only produce specific disabilities, but also create levels of poverty that are clearly disabling in both the experiences of everyday life and implications for future health. Standards of living for those with disabilities in Europe and North America (although of course below the national average) are frequently higher than those classified as non-disabled in low-income countries. As this observation suggests, global economic policy has a huge impact on processes of disablement. Robert McRuer has read questions of disability globalisation in key terms – "displacement", "dispossession", "inhabitable spaces" – that chart the architecture of contemporary neoliberalism and policies of austerity: "the global austerity politics that escalates super-exploitation of workers globally and protects capitalists while slashing services to the poor would be a clear example of [...] accumulation by dispossession: wealth is redistributed to/accumulated by those at the top while those at the bottom are dispossessed of resources, public services, or secure networks of care".[3] In a more overt social science critical tradition, both Nirmala Erevelles and Helen Meekosha have explored questions of the (in)visibility of disability within what Erevelles terms "the social relations of production and consumption of transnational capitalism". For Erevelles, such arrangements create the question of why "some bodies matter than others" in global formations of capital, and as a consequence why "it does not even matter to us that some bodies are actually invisible" within such configurations.[4] Meekosha has observed that the invisibility created by the combination of economic and social forces obscures a full recognition of disability globally: "Maybe it is too confronting to deal with the continuing disability of people in the global South because in trying to claim the positives of a disability identity it becomes difficult to acknowledge the overwhelming suffering that results from colonisation, war, famine, and poverty".[5] Such difficulties create different dispossessions in different locations, as encounters with austerity are inflected through experiences produced in individual societies.

In addition, specific cultural determinants pertain. The distinct conceptions of embodiment or beliefs about selfhood that are woven through cultural histories mean that disability is not understood as a single state. Autism, to give one example, is fundamentally read as a biomedical condition in nearly all high-income countries, but frequently understood in terms of spirituality or psychological damage in locations where health is conceived of through different logic. Limb loss in a UK military veteran, who as a result of service has access to the latest prosthetics and assistive technology, means something very different to the equivalent in a child in sub-Saharan Africa who has had meningitis and, as a result, is less able to secure employment that will sustain her family. How disability is *seen*, both literally and conceptually, varies across the globe.

Seeing disability is crucial to film. A camera can linger on a disability, foregrounding it and creating what Rosemarie Garland-Thomson terms "scenes of staring", where "a desire for visual stimulation" meets "our brain's search for novelty [...] amid a landscape flattened by familiarity".[6] Or it can create a misè-en-scene in which the disability is precisely *part* of that familiarity, built in to the fabric of the storyline and its visual expression and not drawing attention to difference. The way disability is visualised on film has different heritages across different cultural traditions. Hollywood, for example, has always favoured stories of individual struggle and heroic recovery, whereas (to give a counter example relevant to this chapter) Iranian cinema, both in the current new wave and in films that predate this, has emphasised more lyrical, philosophical or social approaches to disability subject matter. As Emily Jane O'Dell observes: "Contrary to most films in the 'west' about disability, Iranian cinema has not historically portrayed disabled subjects as mere objects of pity or courageous souls overcoming obstacles. Since the 1960s, Iranian filmmakers have fashioned 'disability' as a springboard from which to launch social, economic, and religious critiques, and a protected space to raise existential, theological, and spiritual questions".[7] In advancing critical opinions on disability across global film cultures, it is essential to take these variations into account.

Scholarship on disability in global cinema is still sparse. In his introduction to the 2016 collection of essays *Cultures of Representation: Disability in World Cinema Contexts*, Benjamin Fraser notes that "despite the growing [...] number of book publications on disability in general, there are only a small handful of these each year that relate to non-Anglophone contexts" and that "when one askes how many of these books systematically deal with artistic representations or humanities cultural products – films or otherwise – the total number of relevant publications is greatly lessened indeed".[8] While this is possibly not as surprising as Fraser intimates – 'disability' is such a huge category reaching across so many disciplines that critical humanities approaches are bound to be relatively small as a percentage of published outputs – his point concerning disability in global film is well made. It is, however, indicative that Fraser notes that his own collection actually "struggle[s] to find 'global' coverage" and that because of this struggle can only constitute "the mere beginning of a more global discussion of disability".[9] It is unfortunate that Fraser's introduction to *Cultures of Representations* works largely through posing questions and does not (indeed apparently *cannot*) suggest any kind of critical frame for the discussion of disability in global cinema. The problem is, however, revealing. The complex intersection of aesthetic practice, cultural variation, differing business models, diverse audiences and modes of spectatorship seemingly makes evaluating global disability film, other than in local contexts, beyond current scholarly reach.

Biopolitics, precarious life, and debility

I will explore all of the films in this chapter through readings of narrative and deployment, visual aesthetics and the social contexts of their making, but because of the ways in which they enact a series of crossings between the global North and South (in terms of production, locations and reception), the films can be productively, if problematically, framed through an analysis of the ways in which disability functions in contemporary posthumanist global biotechnology economies. If this is a surprising choice of investigation, given the prevalence of more standard modes of reading film texts, I aim to show that it provides a particular insight into the relationship between disability and increasingly global posthumanist technologies of health, those forms and spaces where lives are circumscribed by what Melinda Cooper has called "the science politics of the neoliberal era".[10] Cooper's analysis shows that the global expansion of US power in the twenty-first century, a combination of neoliberal economics and military intervention, has brought about a specific "US defense discourse" that has become tied to bioeconomic systems that mobilise what she terms "the name of life in its biospheric dimension". Under such circumstances, "war is no longer waged in defense of the state" but rather constitutes an operating model of 'whole life' that links the military to the global economies of capital and the life sciences.[11] Disability, in such a scenario, is placed in a precarious position. For all that it is problematic to over-associate disability with a language of vulnerability, it is nevertheless true that, within the juggernaut logics of the economies Cooper describes, those with disabilities are made vulnerable in multiple ways. Disabled people are both denied full citizenship in the new, emerging conceptions of postgenomic biological 'life' and subjected to the consequences of neoliberalism and its relentless drive to marketise all aspects of existence.[12]

For Rosi Braidotti, warfare in the contemporary era is recognisably posthumanist. "Posthuman wars", she notes, "breed new forms of inhumanity".[13] Adapting Achille Mbembe's idea of necro-politics, Braidotti links the development of global capitalism and "the politics of death" to new forms of "post-anthropocentric technologies" that now dominate war.[14] Thought of in such terms, there is no distance between posthumanist networks – of capital, technology or command and control – and the grounded realities of destruction, death and the creation of disability that they produce. As we shall see in the films from Iraq and Iran discussed later in the chapter, those figures denied citizenship and 'life' because of the practice of the 'war on terror' are subject to military technologies that enact the complexities of posthumanist assemblages, even if these cultural stories seem more 'local' and more concerned with raw survival than such a global context suggests. What Braidotti terms "the era of orchestrated and instrumental massacres" is posthumanist in its assembled and interlaced orchestration and instrumentalisation, but needs to be understood as still being about the reality of massacres.[15] The films analysed in this chapter portray posthuman death and disability from different viewpoints, but they remind us that the relationship between technology and embodiment in warfare encompasses both the most sophisticated weaponry on the planet and the grounded worlds of the individuals and communities that weaponry often destroys.

An idea of 'whole life' and concomitant states of vulnerability, precarity and liminality play significant parts in the kinds of exchange this chapter will chart. Numerous critics read such positions as exemplifying many aspects of contemporary life, whether individual or communal, and many see new global formations of health as being intrinsic to the construction of such states. In her 2004 study *Liminal Lives: Imagining the Human at the Frontier of Biomedicine,* Susan Merrill Squier writes of the "inherently unstable" nature of lives that are "generated at [...] nodal points of biomedicine and culture". These lives are, she continues, "the product of a volatile convergence of disciplines, discourses, practices, events and people", a range that captures the multiplicity of disability expressions across the cultures this chapter explores. Echoing some of Braidotti's observations, Squier's interest "lies in the way that biotechnology is reshaping the human body", a process she reads in terms of the liminal. "The human bios", she observes, "is changing so quickly that zoë, the simple fact of being alive, is no longer stable". Any reading of the 'stability' of being alive raises questions of disability, and not just seen in pejorative assumptions that this means 'instability'; Squier's conceptualising of the 'liminal life' also refers "to those beings marginal to human life who hold rich potential for our ongoing biomedical negotiations with, and interventions in, the paradigmatic life crises: birth, growth, aging and death". While a disability studies viewpoint might pause at the use of 'marginal' here, Squier makes it clear that she is speaking of a marginality that, while recognising the grounded experiences of excluded communities, includes *all* human beings, and on a global scale. She writes that all of us

> living in the era of these biomedical interventions [are] liminal ourselves, as we move between the old notion that the form and trajectory of any human life have certain inherent biological limits, and the new notion that both the form and trajectory of our lives can be reshaped at will – whether or own or another's, whether for good or ill.[16]

Though she does not use the term posthumanism, Squier's 'new notion' of 'reshaped' lives here aligns with many strands of posthumanist thinking, while the broad sweep of her work is rich in its potential for disability-led theories of selves and environments.

Judith Butler's writing on precarity in her 2004 book *Precarious Life* navigates similar terrain. Theoretically driven through core reference to Foucault and Levinas in particular, the study is equally grounded in explorations of the creation of vulnerability and precarity by US state power. In terms highly apposite for this chapter, Butler outlines the "indefinite detention" that has accompanied US governmental and military action since 9/11 (both in specific reference to inmates in Guantanamo Bay and beyond). "The future becomes a lawless future" she observes, "not anarchical, but given over to the discretionary decisions of designated sovereigns [...] who are beholden to nothing and to no one except the performative power of their own decisions". One result, Butler notes, is that state recourse to violence produces a certain kind of vulnerability, one that is "a vulnerability to the other that is part of bodily life, a vulnerability to a sudden address from elsewhere that we cannot pre-empt". In relation to the US campaign in Afghanistan, Butler notes that its "scenes of pain and grief [...] either represent American triumph, or provide an incitement for American military triumph in the future. *They are the spoils of war or they are the targets of war*".[17] As this chapter will show, Butler's iteration of 'performative power' 'bodily life' and understanding of 'precariousness' operate across Hollywood's representations of bodies in its narratives of the 'war on terror'. The performing of military action (both actual and in fiction) is knitted to the unstable and discretionary performances central both to the liminality of bodily life and to narrative itself, while the 'spoils' and 'targets' of war enact an idea of global precarity underwritten by the nightmare vagaries of state power.

It is in the work of Jasbir K. Puar, especially her 2017 monograph *The Right to Maim*, that the links between liminal and precarious life, globalisation, conflict and disability are most precisely named. Puar's critical concepts of debility and capacity articulate the biopolitical drives through which "some bodies may not be recognized as or identity as disabled" but nevertheless "may well be debilitated, in part by being foreclosed access to legibility and resources as disabled". In turn, the "biopolitics of debilitation" create bodies that "may well be disabled but also capacitated", a consequential set of processes by which experiences of disability become rendered as complex sites of bodies and their contexts, produced through social controls.[18] She links these to the "global circuitry of the US war machine", noting that in the ways such circuits function "one can clearly discern how debility can get translated into a form of capacity", through the kinds of foreclosure and rendering described above. She continues: "Via this circuitry, disability – or, rather debility and debilitation – is an exported product of imperial aggression"; and when the "targets of the war on terror are not civilians" because they are "deemed terrorists", the disabilities produced in such a war become justified. This is what Puar terms "disavowed, belated disability", a culture of toxic maiming and injuring that combines with (particularly) the politics of racial prejudice to manufacture "a constant state of becoming disabled" in Iraq and Afghanistan especially.[19]

This chapter is informed by these ideas of debilitated, liminal, precarious, vulnerable and surplus lives. As we shall see, a disability-inflected criticism, aligned with the range of cultural contexts on display, mean that the different films encode each term in a different way; disability writes 'vulnerable' or 'precarious' in distinct and specific forms, and not always in terms of loss. In light of Squier's and Butler's work, I want to keep alive both the problematic and potentially productive meaning of the marginal and liminal as equally excluded *and* transgressive. And, as I hope is clear, such interactions are also the stuff of fictional narrative, the messy contradictions and revealing aesthetics that have drawn me to representations of disability and the posthuman throughout this study. Squier is clear that her own book is driven by such an approach. Fiction, she writes (which of course includes fiction film), functions "as a crucial site of permitted articulation for the desires driving these new biotechnologies"; it articulates "*what might be*, all transgressions of the (socially constructed) boundary of fact", giving "access to the biomedical imaginary: the zone in which experiments are carried out in narrative, and the psychic investments of biomedicine are constructed".[20] The networks of military power, fragile embodiment, global health, visual codes and narrative methods in the films this chapter will analyse are all part of this 'biomedical imaginary'. It is a space where representations of posthumanist technology – the might of the American military–industrial complex – enact the kinds of desire towards, and rejection of, the possibilities such depictions suggest, in ways that are commensurate with the texts that have been explored in this study to date. It has always been the case that war films are among the most humanist of filmic narratives. As we shall see, that humanism receives particular inflections in the disability/technologised worlds of recent conflicts.

Disability, technology and 'the everywhere war'

Some of the films I analyse here deal directly with the detail of combat while others work allegorically and through tropic reference, but each serves as an examples of what Derek Gregory has termed "the everywhere war" that has followed in the wake of 9/11, a conflict in which "war has become the pervasive *matrix* within which social life is constituted" and one that is "barely known but vividly imagined", an observation certainly true in terms of the conflicts' filmic representation.[21] In the films in question, disability not only reorders ideas about the body and the human, but through this also inserts itself into and reconfigures trajectories of capitalist bioeconomies and the various projections inherent in American military power and its place in what Zygmunt Bauman termed, in 2001, the "wars of the globalization era". For Bauman: "By far the most prominent and seminal feature of our times is the emergence of 'global figuration': of a network of dependencies which covers the entirety of the planet". As I hope to show, Bauman's 'network of dependencies' can be configured as a matrix of posthumanist connections, linking individual disability to wider questions of technology and history. When Bauman asserts that "nothing that happens anywhere on earth can be safely left out of account in calculations of causes and effects of actions: nothing is indifferent, or of no consequence, to the conditions of life anywhere else", he is suggesting a frame that allows for links between individual disability and global histories and economies (of all kinds).[22] As we shall see, this idea of a *projected* technological capacity, in which the human is removed and deferred into modes we might recognise as posthuman (and indeed a *prostheticised* posthumanism), is common in the films in question. In each, we can read this process as an example of disability at work; in nearly every case the manner in which bodies are taken apart and put back together again is constitutive of disabled modes of being and the alterity disability brings to bodies and their contexts.

In what follows, I am making a claim that the US military presence and function in Iraq and Afghanistan can be read as enacting the posthuman. Given the tragic cost in all-too-human lives and the destruction of whole societies, this needs some justifying. Donna Haraway has noted that a major context for her writing her cyborg manifesto in the early 1980s was her experience of "the military industrial complex as it is embodied, embedded, in elite research apparatuses and in real places" during her time teaching and researching in Baltimore and Hawaii, both locations of military command and research centres.[23] Her cyborg (and its posthumanist afterlifes) can, then, be understood as a figure that, in part, emerges from considerations of military power. Extending this, the core of my claim lies in a reading of power and technology as a particular form of network and assemblage, part of what Pramod Nayar has observed as the "ways in which the machine and the organic body and the human [...] are now more or less seamlessly articulated, mutually dependent and co-evolving".[24] Nayar sees this process in positive terms, noting that it "offers a more inclusive and therefore ethical understanding of life", but I would contend that these kinds of interactions can also be seen in the applications of killing technologies.[25] It is, for example, the 'seamless articulation' of technology, military power and human decision making that makes drone warfare possible, often with what appears to be an absence of moral oversight, and reserving what Puar describes as "the right to maim", the sustained practice of imperial violence injuring and destroying both bodies and infrastructures through conflict.[26] Gregory notes in his study of drone warfare as a case study of "late modern war" in Iraq and Afghanistan that "the effortless sense of time–space compression" in the deployment of drones "is exceeded only by its casual imperialism [...] and these remotely piloted missions not only project power without responsibility – as the Air Force frequently asserts – but also seemingly without compunction".[27] The reference to 'power without responsibility' is an echo of Butler's theorising of precarity and vulnerability, but it also makes clear that there is no benevolent version of posthumanist assemblage here.

Gregory shows in his account of the "kill-chain" that leads to the deployment of drones that it is a process that is defined by networks of technology: "the kill-chain can be thought of as a dispersed and distributed *apparatus*, a structure of actors, objects, practices, discourses and affects, that entrains the people who are made part of it and constitutes them as particular kinds of subjects".[28] Such subjects, I argue, are productively read as being posthumanist. The connections across geographies (different units connected to a single attack are frequently situated in locations that span continents), the facts of dispersal and distributions (and Gregory lists many other examples, from real-time intelligence processing about targets to lawyers consulting about the (il)legality of the process), as well as the reliance on non-human technologies as the actual instruments of killing, are all examples of a performative network in action, one defined by capabilities that can only exist as a technological *extension*, and arguably a *surpassing*, of human action. Similarly, in his study of the production of satellite imagery as part of what he calls an "imperial gaze" and "battlespace awareness", Chad Harris notes how military image intelligence systems render "extreme forms of violence [...] everyday, bureaucratic and even mundane" because of their conceptions of distance and visualisation. Harris stresses the workings of an "interoperable 'assemblage' of shifting authority, social practices, and technological systems

[...] resulting in the creation of an omniscient, surveillant subject far removed from the violence [...] being perpetuated on the ground".[29] 'Interoperability' is a key term here, one taken from computer and network systems literatures that describes how systems coordinate their operations and activities within other systems. For Harris, this opens up possibilities "for understanding how a technology of control and transparency is associated with nation state power", and it is precisely that such power might be exercised from within the logic of a "system of systems" that renders it posthumanist in its reach. As we will see, these ideas of violence and remote warfare are central to the films I will analyse here, whether *The Hurt Locker*, in which embodiment and mobility are altered by support technology created over distances, or *Source Code*, where one of the 'systems' involved is a life-support mechanism that keeps a disabled protagonist 'alive'. More generally, however, Harris, like Gregory, stresses that the assemblages and networks of modern conflict have to be understood as operating at a supra-human level.[30]

But if the idea of a performative posthumanist assemblage as exemplified in the connected technologies of aerial warfare might seem obvious, I want to claim that it also exists at the micro level of soldiers operating on the ground. In my reading of the films in the first half of this chapter I am interested in the ways that bodies interact with clothing and armour for example, or individual weaponry and vehicles. These elements are the fine detail of the operation of military power, but they are equally networked and part of the representation of a killing process that is global in its connectivity. Though I share Vivian Sobchack's suspicions concerning the endless proliferation of ideas of "the prosthetic" – she characterises it neatly as an apparently "sexy new metaphor that, whether noun or (more frequently) adjective, has become tropological currency for describing a vague and shifting constellation of relationships among bodies, technologies and subjectivities" – I cannot help be drawn to the potentially productive elements of understanding US military power in Iraq partially in terms of prosthesis.[31] The suit that protects the bomb-disposal expert, the rifle that allows for long-distance killing, or the fleet of vehicles that undertakes the incursion into 'hostile' space: all exemplify the projection of power at a distance from, but connected to, the body. As such, they create new ideas of dispersed embodiment and agency. It would be wrong to write of such metaphors and extensions as the only examples of disability in the films in question (this would be critical appropriation of the worst kind), and my focus will be on *actual* instances of the representation and deployment of disabled bodies and minds, but it is the case that thinking of military power as posthumanist prosthesis in this way allows for the mobilisation of a critical disability perspective that sheds new light on questions of conflict, technology and embodiment.

There is, however, a more obvious idea of 'the human' at play in the films through narratives of *individualised* characters, as opposed to the distances involved in drone and aerial warfare. The stories that focus on specific personnel become vehicles for powerful reflections on humanism, bodies and their relationship to the technologies and politics of killing. Here, as we shall see, characters often inhabit spaces of the human and posthuman through the portrayal of their vulnerabilities and intimacies, those moments when bodies encounter, enact or transgress thresholds and limits. As a product of war, disability is central to these processes and, in the films to be analysed here, there are crucial instances in which disability makes narrative meanings possible because of the ways in which it informs how we read the boundaries of the body. As so often in the texts analysed in this study, obsessions with the complex technologies of the present and future become channelled into humanist stories of precarious selves, narratives both of violent power and individual worry.

That the critical reading processes have to be rooted in visuality is obvious; the films are specifically visual texts, and the bodies and contexts they depict fundamentally make sense through strategies of looking. But the processes of visualisation they produce are complex, and nothing about visualising disability is ever straightforward. In addition, in these films the visibility of the disabled body works in concert with what a number of writers have noted about the visual and spatial nature of modern warfare: Gregory discusses "the spatiality of the war zone" and "scopic regime" through which military operations take place, while also mapping "fields of violence" on to "fields of vision" in the "techno-cultural apparatus" of war;[32] and Harris outlines his theories of imaging and conflict through notions of the "gaze" and the "omniscient eye".[33] These outline contextual specifics that link the visual to the processes of "taming the world with our eyes", as Rosemarie Garland-Thomson puts it in her foundational work on disability and staring. Staring is, as Garland-Thomson asserts, "a conduit to knowledge. Stares are urgent efforts to make the unknown known, to render legible something that seems at first glance incomprehensible. In this way, staring becomes a starer's quest to known and a staree's opportunity to be known".[34] Watching a film (and seeing characters look at each other) is not, of course, the same as looking at or photographing real individuals, but the forms of knowledge that emerge from the scopic environments created by the texts enlighten understandings of both disability and conflict. According to James Der Derian in his book *Virtuous War*: "The new wars are fought in the same manner as they are represented". Although he is more interested in relations between the film *industry* and politics than actual film texts, Der Derian's comment is one that we might appropriate. In the juxtaposition of his analyses of real military and political events with filmic, gaming and wider media representations of war, Der Derian notes how such interactions lead to new "screen [...] configuration[s] of virtual power".[35] As such, he reminds us that the multiple ways of *seeing* war, like those that enable seeing disability, create core categories and mechanisms of meaning. How we see, and how we are shown, the technologised bodies of war and conflict are processes that produce rich sites of the intersections between disability and the posthuman.

These complex processes of disability, technology, posthumanist conflict and visuality come together in Duncan Jones' 2011 film *Source Code*, a science fiction meditation on technology, individualism and the presence of the war on terror in the US itself. The film begins with US Army pilot Colter Stevens (Jake Gyllenhall) waking abruptly on a Chicago commuter train, having no idea where he is and seemingly not himself but rather (as he finds when he consults documents in his wallet) a schoolteacher called Sean Fentress. As he begins to process his situation, the train explodes, killing the majority of people on board. The film's narrative unfolds to reveal that, in fact, Stevens has previously been fatally injured in a mission in Afghanistan and his death reported to family and friends. Rather than being allowed to die, however, Stevens has been saved by the military and turned into a biohybrid figure – his maimed body inserted into a technological matrix in what is very much an example of posthumanist assemblage – as part of an experimental intelligence project called 'Source Code'.[36] Stevens is connected to and controlled by military handlers through both physical and cognitive prostheses that establish his selfhood as a networked presence. Physically cocooned in a pod-like structure within a military complex, he is an uncanny incarnation of what Lambèr Royakkers and Rinie van Est, writing on modern digitalised warfare in conflicts such as those in Afghanistan or Iraq, call the "cubicle warrior", an isolated but nevertheless spatially connected operator of weapons systems. As Royakkers and van Est note, "a cubicle warrior finds himself in a unique situation: on the one hand, the socio-technical system enables him to fight [a] war from a remote place, on the other hand the same system connects the soldier to the war zone [...] thus enabling some form of tele-presence".[37]

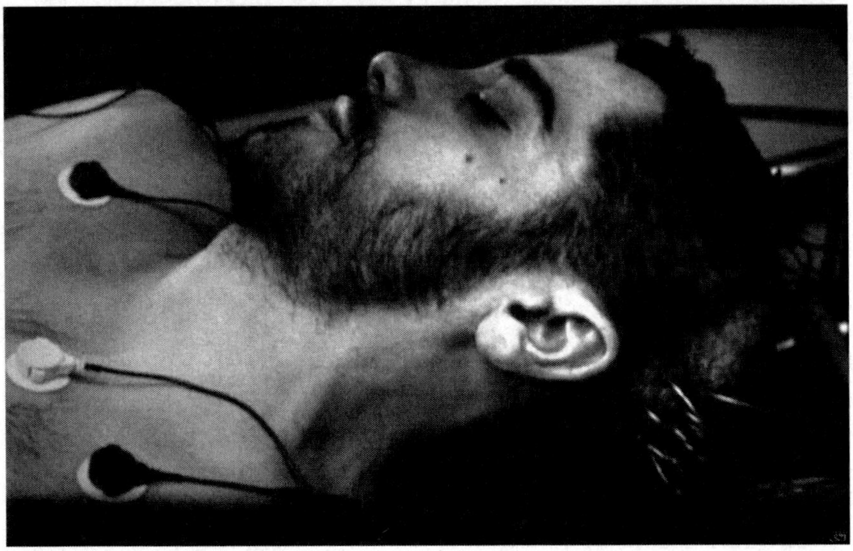

The biohybrid soldier in the military matrix: Colter Stephens (Jake Gyllenhaal) in *Source Code*

Both remote and connected, Stevens is the quintessential assembled posthumanist warrior. Here, however, *assemblage* is not simply a technological process but also one of reconstituted embodiment; it is in his cubicle and via the possibilities it creates that Stevens can become physically whole again.

Stevens is enabled by Source Code to enter an alternative timeline in which he can experience the final eight minutes of another person's life. Informed that the explosion on the train was due to a terrorist attack, Stevens is ordered to re-enter the time immediately before the blast, locate the bomb, and apprehend the perpetrator. After multiple separate returns into the eight-minute timeline before the explosion, each one providing more evidence of the bomber than the last, he is successful: the lives of the commuters are saved and the terrorist (interestingly, given the context, a white male) is apprehended.

Source Code appears in many ways to be a paradigmatically posthumanist film, suggesting enabling ways to think about embodiment, technology and selfhood through a series of complex assemblages. Its narrative is founded on the imaginative possibilities offered by the integration of human and machine produced through radical destabilisations of corporeal integrity and wholeness, while its treatment of time evidences a move away from standard linear conceptions of storyline progression and the memory of event. As Anneke Smelik observes, the film displays "a deliberate blurring between different time lines, spaces and realities". As a consequence, "the complexity of the narratives becomes part of the visual pleasure".[38] Through this narrative complexity, the film becomes many things. Although it never makes any explicit comment on contemporary politics, it is obviously a 9/11 fantasy in which the attacks on the World Trade Center are prevented; as in New York, the bomb on the train explodes during a morning rush hour dominated by a bright blue sky. But more important for my arguments is that *Source Code* is a disability narrative that addresses both posthumanist explorations of the interaction between man and machine, and a humanist validation of individual agency and will. Stevens' body is dismembered to the point that the Source Code cubicle functions as a de facto life-support machine and a late scene reveals, in a powerful visual moment that invites exactly the kinds of stares described by Garland-Thomson, that his actual body consists of his head, torso and one arm, spliced into a web of technological attachments. The film's content is, then, driven all along by a technologised prosthesis, but the *narrative* revolves around an explicit idea of re-membering human wholeness. Stevens' opportunities to continually revisit the moments immediately prior to the catastrophe allow him, in effect, to overwrite human processes of memory on each occasion, building a meaning of time through the added knowledge and control the additional experiences provide. The film charts his progression from a terrified, unconnected amnesiac opening to a position of final personal control.

Stevens averts disaster through his belief that, contrary to all understandings of how Source Code works as technology, a final entry into the timeline will allow him not only to alter the nature of the event itself, in effect producing an act of faith in his own ability to effect change, but also to subsequently survive as Sean Fentress. He argues for, and is allowed, this one last return to the train, and saves those on board, a move followed by the 'death' of his original self in the military installation when the machine to which he is connected is turned off by a sympathetic handler, Colleen Goodwin (Vera Farmiga). Aligned with this assertion of normative embodiment and agency, Colter enacts other recognisably humanist plot devices: pursuing a romantic narrative with a fellow commuter, Christina (Michelle Monaghan), whom he convinces of his 'true' identity; and even managing to have a farewell phone conversation with his grieving father, in which he poses as a friend who confirms how much Stevens loved his family.

As such, the posthumanist possibilities of cyborg identity and narrative disruption fail to lead to any actual exploration of how a future technologised disability body might be formed, and what it might mean. Rather the fantastic machinery on show and the looping story operate merely as visual markers and narrative riddles for the viewer through processes of innovative, if recognisable, spectatorship. *Source Code*'s real depths rather lie in standard humanist tropes: individual achievement, civic responsibility, romantic completion and familial affiliation. The personal values then map on to social equivalents: military personnel are still heroic, fighting 'terror' is just, disabled bodies can be repaired and an appropriate morality can resolve collective trauma. The film conforms perfectly with Cooper's reading of the contemporary biotechnological dimensions of the war on terror. When she observes that "the doctrine of preemptive warfare assumes that the only way to survive the future is to become immersed in its conditions of emergence, to the point of actualizing it ourselves", Cooper's ideas of pre-emption, immersion into and survival of the future, emergence and actualisation are all literally played out in and through Stevens' actions.[39]

Ultimately, *Source Code* asserts that positive interventions to counter threats to either the individual or social body are fundamentally questions of character. As we shall see in a number of the other films discussed in this chapter, this is a familiar narrative. Such characters are always normative and able: they may threaten to be consumed by precarity and vulnerability and their bodies may become marked by technologies of conflict, but these narrative moments are deceptive and only ever temporary tangents. Indeed, Stevens' hyper-capable, able-bodied, masculine hetero normativity actually functions to the point of erasure. In his trajectory to embodied wholeness, he *replaces* Sean Fentress at the film's conclusion. Fentress' character (never actually depicted) vanishes, a victim of the desire to pre-empt catastrophe and keep the integrity of both individual and community bodies intact. One reading of this narrative *power* is that a film such as *Source Code,* set in the US itself, requires a successful humanism to establish that attacks to American values can be neutered. No 'kill-chain' can be allowed within the geographical boundaries of the US, a point the film makes with its assertion of Stevens' individualism and triumph over technological systems, as well as concomitant closure of the unethical Source Code programme. But even the most strident supporters of resolution and reassurance cannot pretend such conditions apply to the conflict abroad. In Iraq, catastrophe cannot be averted. How such catastrophe is imagined, however, brings together further messy interactions between bodies and technology, with disability again central to the ways in which these stories are told.

Fragile bodies and the prostheticised self

In technologies of war, male selfhood is both weaponised and highly fragile. As *Source Code* demonstrates, men may be inserted into the machinery of conflict, in terms of armament and the full capacity of war materials, but such power cannot offset the vulnerability subsequently produced. Whether through the failure of the physical body or mental health trauma, such vulnerability becomes inescapable. In terms of combatants, war both isolates the individual and creates (predominantly male) communities, factors that I will analyse here within the logic of humanist conceptions of selfhood. War also encounters and creates community in those spaces where it takes place, and this chapter will also explore how characters in the non-US films are figured in terms of family and culture, depictions that often stand in stark contrast to the technologised self of the soldier.

There is a pivotal scene about a third of the way through Paul Greengrass' 2010 feature *Green Zone* that speaks of disability's relation to technology, conflict and ideas of the human. Freddy (Khalid Abdalla), an Iraqi translator employed in Baghdad by Chief Warrant Officer Roy Miller (Matt Damon) and working for the US Army, runs from a conflict scene carrying a notebook of information that will lead to the disclosure of the non-existence of weapons of mass destruction (WMD). Pursued by Miller and his unit, Freddy is cornered in an alleyway. As he attempts to climb a wall to escape, a soldier grabs him, only for his crude prosthetic leg to come off as he is manhandled. Following a succession of frenetic camera movements and edits during the chase, the film pauses suddenly as Freddy becomes the subject of the multiple gazes of the chasing platoon. "What more I have to do for you?" he shouts, hopping on his one leg, his anger suddenly exploding. In response to Miller asking him how he lost his leg, Freddy replies: "My leg is in Iran, since 1987", before giving an impassioned speech that, in its controlled emotion and relative quiet, contrasts starkly with the violence – helicopter assaults, screamed interrogations, handheld camerawork, fast-paced editing – that has dominated the film up to this point: "Me too I fight for my country", Freddy says. "Reward? You think I do this for money? [...] You don't think I do this for me, for my future, for my country, for all these things? Whatever you want here I want more than you want. I want to help my country". Miller, who has been all masculine able-bodied dynamism up to this point, stands confused, speechless and suddenly vulnerable by way of response.

The scene enacts a complex intersection of multiple topics and tropes through its sudden and surprising focus on disability (Freddy has been in several previous scenes with no hint as to his limb loss). The prosthetic limb itself is first an indexical personal and historical marker, a permanent reminder for Freddy of his part in the Iran–Iraq war of the 1980s. But it is also iconic, in that it breaks the logic of Miller's insertion, as a willing combatant, in the military/technological infrastructure of the US presence in Iraq. Instead, he witnesses (as does the audience) a revelation of what is clearly presented as a powerful core humanity, an individual story that forces him to revise his allegiance to his mission. Here, Freddy's prosthesis performs the double movement common to disability signification that this study has noted previously; it signals both *loss*, in that Freddy's body is 'incomplete' and as such stands in for the trauma of the Iran–Iraq war and pity for its victims, but it is also *excessively* human, producing an overflow of emotion encapsulated in Freddy's speech and Miller's arrested response. It is when facing Freddy's disability that Miller is first forced to confront the 'cost' of his participation in what the film, from this scene onwards, will show to be the fruitless search for Iraqi chemical and nuclear weapons. As a consequence, Miller turns from a cog in the military machine to an idealist searcher for the truth, later confronting his superiors with the details of their cover-up and fabrication of evidence. In a time of what Edward Luttwak has called the new 'postheroic war', *Green Zone* seeks to rewrite the soldier as a liberal humanist.[40]

Beyond the immediate context of the narrative, the signifying humanism expressed through Freddy's disability becomes the vehicle for a consideration of the very public foreign policies that led to the catastrophic intervention in Iraq. Miller is a surrogate in the articulation of the liberal view that wishes the 2003 invasion had not taken place; an outlook that, in its imagining of history, seeks to rewrite the events of the war. His humanity, conveyed by a powerful yet fragile body (he is beaten on a number of occasions, including the scene immediately before the conversation with Freddy), counters the post-truth rationale of his Pentagon superiors (encapsulated in the character of Clark Poundstone (Greg Kinnear)) who justify the fiction of WMD. The film's humanism is, in narrative terms, brought to the fore through the sudden startling focus on Freddy's disability and then sanctioned by the actions that flow from this deployment, particularly the overt criticism of government agencies who are represented as being explicit in their cover-up of the truth.

In *Green Zone*, it is crucial that the audience understands Miller's individualism, humanity and the resulting humanist re-membering of the war in Iraq is in opposition to the posthumanist assemblage of the military machine and kill-chain. Damon's acting, and the way in

The thinking soldier as liberal humanist hero: Roy Miller (Matt Damon) in *Green Zone*

which the camera focuses on him, consistently present Miller as a site of *personal* confliction; his facial twitches, explosive physicality and confused anger all express an extended state of constant frustration. Such human characteristics are set against the technology of brutal Special Forces helicopter assaults or depersonalised systems that demand obedience in the perpetuation of state falsehoods. Greengrass' film is achingly liberal in many ways. It ends with Miller emailing a document outlining all the official lies he has discovered to multiple media outlets across the globe, accompanied by a one-line message: "Let's get the story right this time". More widely, Miller's desire for what he perceives as truth and justice saturate the film: in response to his sergeant's assertion that, in following orders to visit potential WMD sites that the army know to be empty, "with all due respect Chief, we're here to do a job; reasons don't matter", Miller counters immediately that "they matter to me". In a similar vein, when asked by CIA operative Martin Brown (Brendan Gleeson) why he thinks he is in Iraq in the first place, he replies, "I came to find weapons and save lives, and I didn't find shit. I want to know why". Miller's individualism and humanism is, ultimately and unsurprisingly, colonial; his actions appear to be directed towards the idea of a benign US rule over Iraq, even though the film's own post-event knowledge and scepticism knows this to be impossible.

Crucially, Freddy's disability and the idea of embodiment it conveys writes an additional layer of complexity into an already chaotic and incoherent narrative. In the narrative denouement, it is Freddy who intervenes and kills General Al-Rawi (Igal Naor), a key figure from the Saddam Hussein regime who has been hunted by US forces for much of the film. Freddy's sudden appearance in this scene, intervening and killing Al-Rawi just as Miller is about to do so, is highly anomalous, given his disability and that all the other characters involved have been involved in a long foot race that has careered through the narrow streets of Baghdad. But narrative consistency is not the point here: what matters is that, as a central touchstone of *Green Zone*'s humanist guilt, Freddy can carry out the murder that the film's complex politics projects as being an act beyond Miller. His actions appear as revenge for the decimation of his country, although it is telling he enacts this against Al-Rawi, while regarding the US Army here (personified by Miller) as a friend and not an invading enemy. *Green Zone* may present a powerful critique of the US in Iraq, but not powerful enough to have a non-combatant Iraqi citizen shoot an American soldier.[41] The US presence in the country is a disaster, but Iraqis still kill each other as a way of providing closure for liberal hand-wringing.

Key to my argument, however, is that it is a *disabled* character that fulfils this role. The trace-like presence of Freddy's absent leg runs (I use the verb deliberately) through the film, operating to provide baseline ideas about embodiment and narrative prosthesis familiar from disability theory. Freddy's body is definitely "complex", fitting the articulation of complex embodiment advanced by Tobin Siebers; it is "vital and chaotic" and explicitly associated with "human mortality and fragility". But whereas Siebers asserts that "Disability gives even greater urgency to the fears and limitations associated with the body", *Green Zone* appropriates the representation of the disabled body to limit the 'fears' of an able-bodied audience, with Freddy functioning as a limping avenger who can assuage both Miller's and the predominantly American audience's guilt.[42] It is possibly more straightforward to see the film in the classic terms of narrative prosthesis advanced by David Mitchell and Sharon Snyder, as both "a stock feature of characterization and [...] opportunistic metaphorical device".[43] The 'one-legged man', with its heritage of metaphorical meaning – Ahab in Herman Melville's *Moby-Dick* or Long John Silver in Robert Louis Stevenson's *Treasure Island* – allows for the mobilisation of Miller's singular, personal, humanist truth in the face of networked posthumanist technologies and government system. In the end, we might feel that *Green Zone* is every much a sham as Frank Baum's Emerald City, but without the self-awareness.

Like *Green Zone*, Kathryn Bigelow's 2008 feature *The Hurt Locker* also examines the nexus of prosthesis, the human and military power; and, on certain levels, it does so to explore similar questions of humanism, posthumanist assemblages and the body. The limits and boundaries of the body are central to the film and, as with Greengrass' feature, are explored in relation to the technologies that surround (but also threaten) the bodies on display. *The Hurt Locker* is, however, a more complex narrative than *Green Zone*, with a storyline that complicates (as opposed to advocates) the singular presence of the heroic male figure. Its representation of disability is subtler as well, eschewing the crude conception of the body signalled by Freddy's missing leg for a nuanced examination of the liminality of the precarious and vulnerable body, as well as issues of mental health that arise as a consequence of war. In Bigelow's film, disability is used to question the power humanism might be expected to express as a response to the trauma created by conflict and 'terror'.

The Hurt Locker's opening scene offers a micro example that encapsulates many of the wider dynamics the film visualises and displays: a US Army bomb disposal team led by Sergeant Matthew Thompson (Guy Pearce) attempts to detonate an improvised explosive device (IED) in a Baghdad street. Following protocol, Thompson and his team deploy a robot carrying explosives to set off the bomb (the film actually opens with footage from a camera mounted on the robot, a small non-human aside in a scene otherwise focused on human limitations), the technology functioning as a prosthetic extension of military capability and the externalising of force beyond the body of the combat soldier. But the trolley the robot is carrying breaks when a wheel falls off and Thompson has to intervene, inserting his own body in a Kevlar protection suit, leaving the protection of the mobile base from which he was controlling the robot, and attempting to manually carry the broken trolley with its explosives to the bomb. The action fails, the device is detonated remotely, and Thompson is killed.

The need for Thompson to use his own body stems from a technological failure that creates a vulnerability that, in turn, leads ultimately to his death. The human, the film's opening makes clear, is a fragile entity, a state that fits an understanding of the Iraq war as a conflict where the rules of engagement lack clarity and definition (the initial scenes are full of quick edits and untidy framing and shots from the soldiers' point of view that replicate fears of the threats posed by unseen civilians). Robert Burgoyne observes that the technical aspects of the film's opening, particularly its music and editing, "emphasize the vulnerability of Thompson's body, a vulnerability that is exaggerated

The fragile human: Matthew Thompson (Guy Pearce) walks to his death in *The Hurt Locker*

by the suit of armour". Encased in his protective suit, Thompson's "laboured breathing, the physical effort of moving, the sensation of paralysing weight" create a precarious humanity that contrasts with the "speed and fluency of the camera work" in the opening scene.[44] But, it should be stressed, Thompson only has to intervene because of faulty technology; the trolley carrying the explosives is so basic in its construction that its inadequacies offer an obvious comment on the poverty of military ordnance ("Did you build that?" Thompson asks fellow team member Specialist Owen Eldridge (Brian Geraghty). "No" Eldridge replies with sarcasm, "the US Army did"). For all the vulnerability of the human then, the complexity of the military machine offers no better protection. Here, US Army engineering appears as exposed and thin as the human body.[45]

Thompson's death is, however, only the prequel for a longer meditation on the qualities and place of the human as seen through the actions of his replacement, Sergeant William James (Jeremy Renner). Where Thompson followed protocols and worked closely with his team, James is a renegade; he ignores orders and the safety of the men he works with, rejects using technology, and deactivates devices through intuition. In place of what should be an efficient and developed technological system, in which danger is externalised through the prosthetic extension of engagement – what Gregory, in his analysis of contemporary drone warfare, terms "optical detachment" – James is the human run riot.[46] His risk-taking is unplanned and beyond programming; it disrupts the logic of assemblage central to the systems of a posthuman war fought at distance. James literally climbs *into* the devices he deactivates: a car in the second mission he undertakes and, in a powerful scene, when extracting explosives from within the body of a dead boy being used as a 'body bomb'. He overpowers the enemy's improvisation with his own, illustrating human capabilities that are victorious over an opponent that would kill by stealth.

As such, within a standard cinematic narrative trajectory of character development and individual achievement James should function as an exemplar of humanism; it is, after all, his maverick *personality* that guides his actions. For Burgoyne, this element of the personal drives the film. "*The Hurt Locker*", he writes, "foregrounds the idea of private experience and pleasure as a somatic engagement that takes place in war, rendering war as a somatic engagement that takes place outside any larger meta-narrative of nation or history".[47] But while this seems to be a potentially valid reading of the film, disability and posthumanist perspectives revise the notion of 'private experience and pleasure', dispersing it from ideas of origin or centred selfhood. For James is clearly disabled, a psychologically damaged figure who is, in fact, completely alienated from the core elements that should, within a humanist narrative, underscore his individual presence. He is distanced from his family and accompanying idea of home or community: he is unable to speak to his wife when he calls her from Iraq, for example, and ultimately rejects his son during a brief visit back to the US before returning to another tour of duty; is incapable of bonding with his peers while serving; and is portrayed as profoundly antisocial. In *The Hurt Locker* then, qualities seen as specifically human, particularly individualism and embodiment, and human*ist*, especially familial/social affiliation, become stripped of accompanying value and, ironically, are projected in terms of emotionless automata. The film's narrative ends not with any homecoming, but rather with the powerful image of James, eyes fixed ahead and expressionless, starting his new year-long tour and striding down a Baghdad street that bears a marked resemblance to that on which the story opened. Unlike *Green Zone, The Hurt Locker*, then, eschews notions of teleology and progression – any sense of an individual 'journey'. In contrast, James is caught in a loop that signifies disconnections, alienation and pathology more than any conventional sense of 'pleasure'.

In addition, James' 'private experience' is still about processes of public memory. Although Burgoyne reiterates that, in *The Hurt Locker*, "the figure of the combat soldier is divorced from any national or social meta-narrative. Instead, a mood of pure visceral excitement prevails", the film's move towards a pattern of repetition more properly constitutes a form of cultural forgetting.[48] If *Green Zone* wants to assert that there are still narratives of ethics and citizenship to which individuals can connect, basically that good is still possible in the world, *The Hurt Locker* – as a posthumanist *narrative* of looping and repetitious assemblages – erases such possibilities. 'Visceral excitement' is in fact more a numbed amnesia, a state that has a powerful connection to a social narrative in which the American public wishes to forget the war in Iraq. For all that disability appears peripheral in Bigelow's film, it actually makes possible a posthumanist argument of prosthetic distance and cultural amnesia that reads both individual and collective in terms of *difference*.

William James has his name for a reason. The film evokes the nineteenth-century American philosopher of the same name and, in doing so, raises a specific model of interpretation provided through a psychological reading. James the philosopher is widely held to be one of the founders of functional psychology, in which an individual mental life finds meaning in terms of a relationship with an environment. *The Hurt Locker* ascribes much of its ideas of the meaning of the conflict in Iraq in such terms. After the death of Thompson, Eldridge is visited by an army psychiatrist (Christian Camargo) as he plays a violent video game. In response to some standard questions about his state of mind and the need "to start thinking about other things", Eldridge repeatedly raises and pretends to fire his weapon. "This is a war" he says, "people die all the time. Why not me?" The scene ends with the psychiatrist unable to comment, and the doctor will later be killed while out on a mission with Eldridge. There is no therapy in this environment, and Eldridge is traumatised throughout each mission he undertakes until he is himself disabled with a serious leg injury near the film's conclusion. As he is evacuated, he screams abuse at James, who has been the cause of his injury. All of the major characters in *The Hurt Locker* are depicted with significant psychological damage.

The representation of trauma *as disability* is central to many films depicting US military involvement in the conflicts in Iraq and Afghanistan. Alexandre Moor's 2017 feature *The Yellow Birds*, adapted from the novel by Kevin Powers (who served in Iraq), is centred on the mental health struggles of its two young combatant protagonists (Alden Ehrenreich and Tye Sheridan) who fail to adapt to deployment in Iraq and the authority of a senior figure (Jack Huston) who is himself traumatised. Nick Broomfield's 2007 *Battle for Haditha* constructs its entire narrative around the extreme violence produced by trauma, reconstructing a 2005 massacre of 24 Iraqi civilians by US Marines in the Western Iraqi city of Haditha. Shot in a semi-documentary style, Broomfield's film portrays the Marines' response to the death of a colleague as a pathological (mis)function of the US mission, in which the logic of murder and the kill-chain become materialised in an act of barbarism.[49] At the same time, the film carefully creates a potentially explanatory context for some of the perpetrators, presenting them as clearly psychologically damaged by the circumstances in which they find themselves.[50] Brian De Palma's *Redacted* (2007) also loosely dramatises an historical event, a rape and subsequent murder of a family that took place in Samarra, in central Iraq, in 2006. Like *Battle for Haditha, Redacted* characterises US soldiers as impaired, disturbed predators and narrativises such a state as a natural consequence of the conflict in Iraq. In De Palma's film, however, there is no representation of any chain of command or wider military context before the atrocity, no connection to what Cooper identifies as the "strategic redefinition of the tenets of U.S. defense" that occurred in the first decade of the twenty-first century, where "full spectrum dominance, counterproliferation and pre-emption" are central.[51] In the absence of this, the depiction of sexual violence as perpetrated by 'traumatised' individuals in the film effectively absolves the broader military and state of any responsibility for the actions that follow. While both *Battle for Haditha* and *Redacted* aim to offer clear critiques of the US presence in Iraq, their concentration on questions of mental health as ultimately being personal and individualist raise troubling questions surrounding the attribution of violence and issues of structural accountability.

Tim Hetherington and Sebastian Junger's 2010 documentary *Restrepo* is far less sensationalist and caricatured than either Broomfield's or DePalma's film, but it still emphasises the centrality of trauma in conflict situations. The film follows a single platoon engaging the Taliban in eastern Afghanistan during a 15-month deployment over 2007–2008, a cycle that, as one soldier (Staff Sergeant Joshua McDonough) notes, was the longest period of sustained combat the US military had undertaken since Vietnam. Interviewed on his journey back to the US after his tour of duty, McDonough anticipates an epidemic of post-traumatic stress disorder that will follow the return of combatants because of a lack of knowledge about the psychological effects of such prolonged fighting: "They're gathering intel right now basically on how to deal with us" he observes, "because there's no real research or intel on how to treat us right now [...] Dealing with guys who are coming back". As is made clear in *Restrespo*, the mental health costs of participating in conflict are considerable. One articulation of the posthumanist version of the military is that of the 'ultimate warrior' whose body is modified through the addition of technology or drugs that allow for 24/7 operation in a permanent war. But it is perfectly possible to read the globalised network of US military power as being a posthumanist assemblage that ultimately disables its protagonists. To make this argument is not to subscribe to some stock concept of the 'contained' humanist individual; soldiers such as McDonough are not stripped of their place in complex bioeconomies and technological operations because of the reality of trauma. Rather it is more instructive to recognise and understand disability trauma as a *product* of the posthumanist connections that the war on terror has produced.

The combination of trauma, disability and a prostheticised, posthumanist military capability intersects in 2014's *American Sniper*, directed by Clint Eastwood and loosely adapted from the memoir written by ex-Navy SEAL Chris Kyle, published in 2012. Kyle served four tours of duty in Iraq and was credited with more confirmed kills than any sniper in US military history. Following his discharge in 2009, Kyle worked with veterans and was killed in 2013 by an ex-Marine with PTSD. Pre-production on *American Sniper* was in process at the time of Kyle's death and the resulting film becomes in effect a memorial to him, a celebration of life and service. At the same time, Eastwood's film evidences the central fragility and posthumanised networks of the military discussed earlier. Its narrative of technical excellence and male capability (Kyle's proficiency as a sniper) is underwritten by a story of vulnerability. On the surface, this is a standard (and therefore masculine) humanist narrative: a man fulfilling his duty is dehumanised by war and made to face a potentially emasculating state of vulnerability, to then be rescued through a re-engagement with family and an acceptance of precarity that is channelled into the public space of help for others. But such a trajectory cannot contain another story, one about ideas of distance, prosthetics, the contextual meaning of war and the hetereonormativity of family, that runs thread-like through the film. It is this latter story that frequently pivots around representations of disability in crucial scenes that underwrite much of the film's narrative power.

As a sniper, Kyle (Bradley Cooper) kills from a distance. In standard cinematic practice viewers are incorporated into the scopic act of this as the camera adopts the sighting position of his rifle, though this does not appear at any point to implicate the audience in the violence and serves more to bolster an understanding of Kyle as an individual. For all his technical excellence, however, the film displays a complex conceptualisation of distance and proximity in which disability and vulnerability are crucial elements. Kyle's killing is presented as an act of singularity; he individualises the power of the US military in the single shot. His rifle is an obvious prosthetic appendage, symbolising and enabling, in micro, the kind of "surgical, sensitive and scrupulous [...] precision-strike capability" Gregory attributes to contemporary warfare.[52] In being an extension of his body, Kyle's rifle and the hybrid self it produces fulfils all of Gregory's terms: it allows for precision-level surgery (he never misses); it is sensitive in its creation of a human/non-human embodiment (Kyle is taught, and we are shown, the importance of regulating his breathing in the acting of firing, while his interaction with his weapon is one of clear conjoinment); and it is scrupulous in that Kyle can always justify his kills, to himself and others, as preventing further deaths (whether American or Iraqi).

Kyle and his rifle are an assembled form of embodiment, created through the kinds of processes Pramod Nayar identifies as a post-humanist "reformatting" of the body. Together, man and weapon materialise the technological, globalising and moral systems of the US military in Iraq, in a process Nayar terms an "evol[ution] with technology and then environment, where identity emerges as a consequence of the layered flows of information across multiple routes and channels". Kyle is networked in exactly these ways: he is physically and environmentally connected to the troops on the ground his sniping protects, while his decision-making is communicated and authorised through various audio command channels, enacting what Nayar terms an "info-flow", a process "materially produced through a mix of human and non-human actors where the possibility of action is embodied as both territory and bodily locations".[53] Kyle's action takes place across and through the technology he uses (these even – improbably – include phoning his wife Taya (Sienna Miller) in the US while he is under fire). For all that he might appear as an individualised, coherent and centred self (and is constructed as such through the film's narrative concentration on his subjectivity), his environment is in fact a matrix often composed of distributed relationships made meaningful through distance.[54]

Up close, things are different. With proximity, the fragility of the body cannot be denied, and technology loses much of its effect. As a sniper, Kyle operates mainly on rooftops, but on the first occasion he joins a house-to-house search in a search for information about suspects, he is confronted with a young girl who has had her arm

Weaponry as prosthesis: Chris Kyle (Bradley Cooper) in *American Sniper*

amputated by Al Qaeda because her family spoke to US troops. His response to the visceral here, a disabled body *right in front of him,* is to be shocked in a manner that echoes Miller's encounter with Freddy in *Green Zone*: the proximity of the young girl and her presence in a small, crowded room reconfigures Kyle's engagement with bodies in conflict. A similar moment comes when Kyle is back in the US on a break between tours and is approached by a young ex-Marine, Mads (Jonathan Groff), who informs him that Kyle saved his life in Iraq in his role as a protector of troops on the ground. In response to Kyle's question about how he is coping, Mads rolls up his trouser leg to reveal a prosthetic leg. Kyle is clearly uncomfortable by the display, especially because it takes place in a confined situation (a small reception area) and is made more so when Mads talks about the soldiers who have returned from Iraq with psychological problems: "they made it back but they're just not right". Mumbling platitudes and unable to properly respond to Mads' invitation to visit a veterans' centre, Kyle leaves. Similarly, when Kyle's friend Biggles (Jake McDorman) is shot in the face and blinded, Kyle's hospital visit again produces an uncomfortable confrontation with the materiality of disability, his awkward support and forced humour symptomatic of a removal from his technologised comfort zone. The untouchable performer with the "long gun" (as one of his fellow combatants terms it) is unnerved and disturbed by the physical difference war produces when he is forced to encounter it.

In the final combat scene in the film (somewhat ridiculously punctuated by his calling Taya to say he is coming home), Kyle is injured and left scrambling to climb aboard a vehicle leaving the conflict scene. As he does so he drops his rifle, and the camera focuses on it in a single, short close-up. The gun, it is clear, is now rejected; it is to be left behind as the militarised killer, having completed his service, refutes his role. There will be no distance following his return. Rather the film's narrative arc then focuses upon Kyle's struggle to accept the dehumanisation he has experienced because of his exposure to conflict. Trapped within memories of Iraq when he is back home, Kyle hears explosions in the closing of every car door and is obsessed with televised news of the conflict. He withdraws into a classic PTSD position, one the film reads in terms of a consequential absence of his individual humanity: "I need you to be human again" Taya says to Kyle when his suppressed trauma is at its worst; "I need you here. If you leave again, I don't think we'll be here when you get back". "Even when you're here, you're not here" she adds, encapsulating the idea of the schizoid veteran unable to adjust to his return.

Kyle's return to wholeness is, however, ultimately utterly predictable. The creation of family dynamic is, in the end, successful, while his selfhood is regained *through* an engagement with disability. Kyle becomes a confidante and lay therapist for returned veterans, the implication being that he can conquer his psychological wounds through an engagement with others with disabilities (real disabled veterans play themselves in these scenes). Now, proximity is positive; it is personal, conversational and supportive. The film, however, can only be destabilised by its final act: the murder of Kyle by an ex-Marine *unable* to process the trauma of the war. And Kyle's death takes place on an average day at home, outside of the geographies of conflict and the distance-killing of Iraq. As such, the carefully constructed narrative of restitution in *American Sniper* cannot contain the excessive complexities that are raised in its deployment of networked and technologised bodies. Human wholeness cannot replace posthumanist dispersal; the successful transition to family is negated by the deadly legacy of traumatic distance.

The three central characters discussed in the films in this section – Miller in *Green Zone*, James in *The Hurt Locker* and Kyle in *American Sniper* – are all examples of Squier's liminal lives and Puar's characterisation of debility and capacity. The intersections between their bodies, selves and the posthumanist militarised technologies they inhabit exemplify the "unstable, porous, and culturally implicated practice" Squier identifies as central to contemporary representations of biotechnological liminality, while Puar's stress on how "prevailing notions of chance, risk, accident, luck and probability" interact with the body to "give rise to a new set of bodily capacities" is captured by the films' complex stories of individualisation.[55] Whatever their narrative resolution, each character is, for the bulk of their stories (and, indeed for the entirety of James' experience in *The Hurt Locker*), positioned on an edge defined by a struggle between a desired singularity and performative distribution. Within this frame, the constant narrative need for disability in the three films performs complex acts of welcome and rejection. Read positively, 'unstable' and 'porous' constitute a set of disability revisions to humanist categories of coherent and centred selfhood, and *Green Zone* and *American Sniper* contain such possible revisions: in the powerful revelation of Freddy's leg and Kyle's acceptance of vulnerability, for example. These are akin to those moments of visualisation identified earlier in *Source Code*, where Stevens' networked body can only function *because* it is disabled and different. They are all instances of a posthumanist disability presence, spaces of a potentially radical reconfiguration of bodies and selves. As we have seen, however, each is closed down through a humanist process of narrative resolution. For its part, *The Hurt Locker* remains precariously balanced on a liminal edge, refusing to commit to any standard conclusion that stresses individual worth. Because of this, its depiction of trauma keeps the possibility of difference open and its representation of one character's exposure to the conflict in Iraq acts to interrogate, rather than endorse, ideas of centred, rational personhood. While it would be wrong to claim it as any kind of showcase for a progressive deployment of posthumanist disability, *The Hurt Locker*'s narrative and aesthetics are suggestive of possible new delineations of technologised bodies. Such suggestions are rare in US films focused on the conflict in Iraq, however, and Bigelow's feature is the exception in a genre otherwise committed to resolution. As we have seen though, while such commitment might be desired it is often undermined and critiqued by the presence of the unruly disabled body that pushes back against easy closures.

Analyses of US films about disability, technology and conflict tell multiple stories of how the messy intersection between posthumanism and humanism inflects the ways in which bodies are written, but it requires an obvious counterpoint. Most disabilities produced by the conflict in Iraq are not American, and they do not allow for the kinds of restitution and renewal central to many Western narratives. This is as much a literal understanding of the workings of situated poverty as it is any heritage about the ways character trajectories work in cinema across cultures; physical restitution through complex medical prostheses, for example, is impossible for nearly all civilians wounded following the US invasion of Iraq in 2003. Rather disability has become everyday and ordinary in the ruined frontiers of those Middle Eastern communities brutalised by the war on terror. Writing on cinema from the region, Karen Lury points to the ways in which film reflects the "conflicted and blurred geography of Iran, Iraq and Afghanistan", and the deployment of disabled bodies is common as part of such confliction and blurring in features that represent the conflict.[56] This does not mean, however, that technology is absent from these portrayals or of course that embodiment is not central to narrative. As opposed to the violent power of US military ordnance as represented in the films discussed above, technology in films from Iraq, Iran, Syria or Afghanistan becomes repurposed and revived, in some cases as a response to disability. The bodies that interact with this technology do so in the specific social and cultural contexts that provide them with meaning. But if disability and technology are plentiful in these films, is the category of the posthuman – used as a description of connected environments or critical approach – in any way useful? Can the relentless and microscopic focus on networked, interfaced and porous assemblages from the global North, so evident in scholarship on posthumanism, have any relevance for films that tell stories of brutality from war-torn communities? In asking these questions I want to make it clear that I am differentiating between a specifically critical *posthumanist* analysis and the recognisable post-structuralist critical humanisms that, at the end of the twentieth century, undid ideas of the rational, centred and autonomous subject and the notions of history that accompanied this. The methodologies share much in common but, as we have seen in previous chapters, processes of posthumanist enquiry increasingly shape readings of the new complexities of a contemporary technologised world. Given that ongoing war across boundaries is a contemporary constant, can posthumanism contribute to reading the storylines and aesthetics of Middle Eastern films that visualise bodily difference in situations where vulnerability and precarity are a constant? In the next section of this chapter, this is one of the questions that will be teased out.

Reformatting and reuse: films from the Middle East

Even before the US invasion in 2003, filmmaking in Iraq, Iran and the surrounding region was a perilous process. Authoritarian regimes and economic sanctions made the establishment or continuation of the necessary structures for filmmaking especially challenging. Iran's production heritage especially, both pre-and post- the 1979 revolution, constitutes a major body of work, though the sanctions of the 1990s curtailed output and productions were still shut down and films were banned for political reasons.[57] In Iraq itself, making dramatic features was more or less impossible after 2003: indeed both Oday Rasheed's 2005 drama *Underexposure* (the first film made in Iraq following the invasion) and Mohamed Al-Daradji's 2008 documentary, *Iraq: War, Love, God & Madness*, are productions explicitly about the difficulties of making films in the context of the American occupation (Al-Daradji's film focuses on the problems encountered making his 2006 feature, *Ahlaam*, discussed below). The majority of the films that have been made are low-budget documentaries aimed at capturing the lived experiences of the social and political transformations the nation has experienced.[58]

Unsurprisingly, given the destruction caused by conflict, depicting and deploying disability has been central to films produced in the region in the contemporary period. In the films discussed here, disability is routine and everyday, rarely charged with the narrative focus on overcoming or achievement typical of much Western commercial filmmaking. Rather, representations of disabled bodies and trauma are often accompanied by imaginings of fractured families, communities and environments and in many of the features characters are forced to be mobile; imperilled, vulnerable or neglected they move across landscapes and between social configurations. In *The Color of Paradise* (1999) a blind boy moves from Tehran to the countryside, to be then passed between family members and strangers before he falls to his death from a bridge across a river. *Tramontane* (2016) also centres on blindness as a blind musician travels across Lebanon in search of his identity following the violence of the civil war. *In My Mother's Arms* (2011) is a drama about a man running an orphanage in Baghdad, providing support for traumatised children across the city who have lost their parents following the 2003 invasion. In the 2000 Iranian/Kurdish feature *A Time for Drunken Horses*, two Kurdish brothers and a sister who have been orphaned through conflict criss-cross the Iran/Iraq border, smuggle goods in an attempt to raise funds for the operation that the younger, severely disabled brother requires in order to prolong his life. In both *Tramontane* and *A Time for Drunken Horses* disabled characters are played by disabled actors (Barakat Jabbour in the former and Madi Ekhtiar-Dini in the latter), though arguably it is wrong to term Ekhtiar-Dini's presence in *A Time for Drunken Horses* as acting. In the film it is clear that Ekhtiar-Dini is himself in constant pain and the story revolves around his actual and viscerally visible disabilities as it portrays the plight of stateless Kurds lost between and across borders. *A Time for Drunken Horses* utilises Ekhtiar-Dini's extraordinary deployment of his disability to underwrite a narrative that eschews metaphor or morality and blurs the line between fiction and documentary in its depiction of embodied personhood. At the close of the film, the two brothers embark on another trip across the border with no end in sight of their hardships and no prospect of accessing medical help.[59]

Unlike the films mentioned above, Mohamed Al-Daradji's 2006 feature *Ahlaam* focuses on the specific impact of the US invasion of Iraq in 2003 and, as such, offers the potential for comparative readings with the US features discussed earlier. As with *Green Zone*, *Ahlaam* opens at the moment of the initial attack on Baghdad. Where Greengrass' film begins with television commentary and generated images of the opening bombardment, *Ahlaam* uses news footage of the bombing of the city. But in contrast to *Green Zone*'s seamless post-credits transition into the US Army search for WMD, Al-Daradji's film juxtaposes the attack with scenes of patients in Baghdad's major psychiatric hospital screaming as the building is rocked by the resulting explosions. The narrative then goes back five years to develop three narrative strands that come to intertwine at the point of the 2003 bombardment: title character Alhaam (Aseel Adil) is traumatised when her fiancé Ahmed (Mortadha Saadi) is arrested by state police on the morning of their wedding day; two soldiers, Ali (Basher Al-Majid) and Hasan (Kaheel Khalid), are sent to occupy border positions as part of their national service; and a medical student Mehdi (Mohamed Hashim) works to become a newly qualified doctor. Alhaam's grief results in her referral to the hospital because of the mental illness it creates; Ali fails to save Hasan's life when their post is attacked by US and UK aircraft as part of Operation Desert Fox in 1998, and is subsequently tried for desertion, sent to military prison and then, heavily traumatised, hospital; and Mehdi is forced to undertake military service before being able to take up a medical position as a new doctor at the psychiatric institution. When the film returns to the 2003 present (using the same news footage as the opening), the audience realises that two of the patients screaming in fear at the start are Ahlaam and Ali.

If *Green Zone* or *The Hurt Locker* portray the immediate world of post-invasion Baghdad as a set of spaces dominated by US military technology, in *Ahlaam* it has become an environment suffused with disability. The bombing destroys much of the hospital and the patients flee to roam through the city. In a series of highly charged shots, Ahlaam walks through the rubble and deserted streets of Baghdad in her wedding dress (it is implied that she has been wearing it for five years), confused and desperately seeking Ahmed. Ali likewise wanders, semi-naked, through the devastation, trying in moments of lucidity to find other patients and help them return to the hospital. Mehdi, who has been beaten during the looting of the hospital, organises people to also help bring to safety any patients that can be found. The film creates the environment of Baghdad's streets in the immediate aftermath of the invasion as a space of trauma and mental illness. City residents flee the emerging chaos of looting and local militias as numerous patients stumble in fear through the devasted remains of abandoned and destroyed buildings. *Ahlaam* portrays the destruction of lives and communities through a disability lens, with social breakdown mirrored by the traumatised presence of individuals broken by the onset of war. Despite the striking imagery, however, the film does not use disability as a metaphor. The Baghdad streets become spaces of embodied experience: fantasising that a man she meets is Ahmed and agreeing to let him help her, Ahlaam is raped, beaten and thrown from a moving car; while Ali is killed by a militia sniper as he attempts to help two fellow patients back towards the hospital.

In *Ahlaam*, Baghdad becomes the space at the end of the 'kill-chain'. The film eviscerates the logic of a military process that purports to create precise and efficient warfare with minimum cost and casualties, or one that (as in *Green Zone*) seeks to search for 'truth'. The destruction of the city in 2003 was enabled by a posthumanist network of command and control of the kind outlined by Gregory and others; orchestrated from distance, the bombardment identified specific targets in a mapped devastation. But Al-Daradji's film shows that the damage created exceeds and breaks down all notions of autonomous precision. In the closing scenes of the film, Ahlaam has become separated from all those searching for her on the streets and is alone at the top of a tall building in the centre of Baghdad. Covered with antennae, it appears to be some centre for communications (though the exact detail of this is not made clear) and offers a panoramic view over the city. Crucially, however, such a vantage point provides no knowledge or further understanding of either Ahlaam's predicament or that of her community. Any authority over space that might be presumed

The end of the kill-chain: Baghdad in *Ahlaam*

by a final position of surveillance is undercut because of the nature of Ahlaam's trauma. The final shots of her alone, lost and confused convey a powerful sense of fragmentation, incoherence and distress. While this lends substance to a reading of disability in the film that stresses standard tropes of lack and loss, this is contextualised by *Ahlaam*'s aesthetics. The film places trauma centrally, particularly in its second half. It figures the bodies of the patients as exemplars of the effects of devasting warfare, and not as peripheral to a broader narrative of overcoming. There is no restitution for Ahlaam, Ali or Mehdi, no recovery from the onslaught that destroys their lives. Destruction and consequential disabilities, it is suggested, will be permanent states in Baghdad for as long as can be imagined.[60]

In the contemporary era US military technology is the product of a vast assemblage of research, manufacture and deployment. As Cooper observes, it drives contemporary revolutions in biotechnology in order to reach into all aspects of health and life sciences, producing bodies in which the interface between individual and machine, and then between the technologised subject and networks of communication and control, become commonplace. Gregory's category of the 'everywhere war' reminds how these bodies and networks are situated across all aspects of US-led conflicts in the contemporary era. The war zones affected by these US invasions cannot escape the extent of this 'everywhere'; they are inevitably subject to its technologies and their lethal consequences, Puar's maiming. But for all of the overwhelming nature of such force, part of a process of resistance produced by the communities affected is the creation of technological meanings of their own. Whether through the co-option of the materials of invasion or the development of everyday objects in newly accentuated forms, the worlds of the dispossessed and displaced furnish alternative ways to tell stories of the relationships between human and non-human, and between bodies and environments.

Bahman Ghobadi's 2004 feature *Turtles Can Fly* is set in the Kurdish village of Kanibo on the Iraqi–Turkish border in the period immediately up to the US invasion in 2003. Like Ghobadi's earlier *A Time for Drunken Horses*, it focuses on children and work, and has a special concentration on disability; and like *Ahlaam* it especially centres on events immediately surrounding the US invasion of 2003. An early scene establishes a subtle play on the meaning and use of technology that subsequently run through the film. 15 men stand on a hillside outside a village, each holding a television antenna that they move slowly in response to shouted orders from children in the houses below. No matter what direction the antennae are turned, however, reception is impossible, and it is left to the resident expert in technology, a young boy appropriately named nicknamed Satellite (Soran Ebrahim), to convince the villagers that they will only be able to gain access to the television news they crave if they come together to buy a satellite that he will then install. Any idea that a technological upgrade – and Satellite needs to trade in all the village's radios to help purchase the new dish – will result in improved information proves illusory, however; when the regional governor and elders meet to watch the newly accessible CNN news, no one is capable of understanding what is being said. Pushed into service as a translator, Satellite's basic English only allows him to surmise that a complex discussion of a possible US invasion is a weather forecast predicting rain. Nothing is gained here from being networked to the world's news; there is no new information as to whether or when the US Army or Iraqi resistance will come to Kanibo, and the moment is rather defined by a grim humour.

Satellite is a dealer and fixer ("all the villages in this area want me" he boasts at one point, in reference to his skills with technology), and the leader of a group of children who work for him collecting deactivated mines and other detritus, to sell and use, left over from various border conflicts.[61] In a number of long shots, the children are pictured uncovering the mines, strung across the landscape in rows and working the fields as if they were farmers, inching forward with wicker baskets as they reap a deadly harvest. This reusing of technology for local ends (it is American and Italian mines that fetch the most money; Iraqi ones are worth nothing) is a constant throughout the narrative; numerous scenes take place against the background of a waste land composed of shell casings and discarded, forgotten military vehicles. In a powerful set of images, used shells are thrown from a trunk and gathered by children who are paid to stack them together. In one shot capturing the process, the camera is positioned on the ground and the empty casings appear to be falling from the sky, a reminder of past conflicts and portend of the violence that awaits the village.

In *The Hurt Locker*, the deactivation of IEDs is central to a narrative that explores questions of individual worth. Bigelow's film interrogates the US presence in Iraq through James' encounters with the technologies of destruction produced by the Iraqi resistance. As each bomb is rendered safe, additional emphasis is placed on the value of individual action set against the US military assemblage and unseen Iraqi assailants. The devices themselves, however, become meaningless once their threat is contained and they are discarded, occupying no further place in the film's storyline. Deactivated mines in *Ahlaam* function differently. They are reworked and recycled as part of a community economy, becoming objects that transcend their technological origins as they become part of the village's social fabric. In Kanibo, access to mines is access to power, but of a wholly different kind than that in US discourses of the conflict's technology.

Even though the contexts are very different, it is possible to see this reimagining and reusing in terms of Louis Bucciarelli's ideas of the "other stories" and "other processes" that can be brought to engineered artefacts. As detailed in the last chapter, Bucciarelli stresses how "other social processes of impacts, of [...] reconstruction, and use" are part of the ways in which the "artefact as object can live again". He continues: "It can become a nexus or icon of social discourse or exchange. In its use it can impose, block, enable, shape social connections and the aspirations of those it meets. There are other object worlds within which the artefact can be seen and used in different ways".[62] This is, in fact, a precise description of the ways in *Turtles Can Fly* that defunct military technology becomes repurposed through transactions within the village. The objects, removed from the matrixes in which they were deployed, are transformed into a local currency that helps structure developing social relations in Kanibo. Hierarchies function through access to technology, as the scene with the village elders shows. It is Satellite, with his knowledge of new communication equipment and (however basic) English, who commands the space in that moment, overriding the authority of the elders and acting as the intermediary between the village and a world beyond its borders.[63]

In addition, Bucciarelli's idea of the artefact/object as 'nexus' also fits what can be seen to be an extension of the film's environments to include posthumanist ideas of networks and boundaries. The fallout of US or Iraqi military assemblages is thrown into encounters with the civilian communities that bear the brunt of invasion or repression. As objects and artefacts become repurposed, they cross spaces of meaning, but the meticulous visualising in *Turtles Can Fly* – its creation of the ordnance as a constant presence in images of the village – ensures that they maintain the trace elements of their origins. There may appear to be an unbridgeable chasm between lives lived in border conflict zones and the workings of posthumanist theorising, but the two can in fact be seen to clearly come together in a powerful representational example of such technology use: the drone strikes that, managed through intercontinental networks of military control, have killed numerous innocent civilians across conflicts in the twenty-first century. These high-profile manifestations of the war on terror exemplify what Gregory terms the "bloody geographies" that are the consequences of posthumanised and technologised warfare.[64] They have a clear and deadly reach into the situated lives of real people and it is worth noting that in *Turtles Can Fly* one of the two trucks unloading the shell casings suddenly (and inexplicably) explodes, killing and wounding several villagers. In light of these examples, a *critical* posthumanist reading becomes a valuable analytic tool, one not simply interested in outlining and describing the manifestations of military networks, but also working – through an emphasis on practices of decentring and deconstructing – to critique the logic behind claims of 'surgical strikes' and precision-based non-human technologies. In Ghobadi's film, lives and bodies are transformed as a direct result of military decisions made thousands of miles away; the vulnerability of a child deactivating a mine is, the viewer comes to realise, part of a pattern that originates in communication channels located elsewhere. But the film also gives the lie to claims that contemporary technologised warfare is somehow made productively *transparent* because of the sophistication of the machinery involved. Rather the narrative presents a chaotic cascade of technology on which meaning *has to be written* and, for all that used military ordnance provides a means of exchange in the village, it is still shown to be unpredictable and lethal.

At one point, about a third of the way through the film, a truck arrives in Kanibo to distribute gasmasks, part of a widening panic

Disability and the detritus of war: Hengaow (Hiresh Feysal Rahman) in *Turtles Can Fly*

as the threat of US invasion becomes more likely. "War doesn't warn of its coming" Satellite says, incongruously framed against the landscape as he stands on one of the trucks wearing a gasmask: "bombardment could start at any time". In fact, the war has already come. The border village has become the site of a refugee camp as people flee from escalating regional conflicts. Following the murder of their parents, brother and sister Hengaow (Hiresh Feysal Rahman) and Agrin (Avaz Latif) have come from Halabjah, a city in Iraqi Kurdistan close to the Iranian border, bringing with them a small boy Riga (Abdol Rahman Karim) who is blind.[65] Hengaow has lost both arms (it is implied through the conflict, but precise detail of this is not given) and is first seen in the film carefully deactivating a mine using his teeth. His disability goes unremarked, part of a pattern in the film in which bodily difference is accepted. Satellite's closest friend Pesheow (Saddam Hossein Feysal) can only use one leg and needs a crutch, but no narrative stress is placed upon this and, unlike the films discussed earlier, there is no use of any prosthetic metaphors to establish an exterior meaning.[66] Instead Pesheow's disability becomes woven into the everyday life of the village, just as Hengaow's and Riga's become part of their wider predicament as refugees. While the camera focuses on their bodies as the narrative requires (as with the striking and powerful scene in which Hengaow deactivates the mine), there is no moment where such visualising becomes a spectacle. In the film's images, the body is pulled away from casual and accepted notions of corporeal integrity.

Thought of in posthumanist terms, bodies in *Turtles Can Fly* become reformatted, particularly in the context of the spaces they inhabit. This is, obviously, not the kind of reformatting through high technology that characterises posthumanism's often breathless emphasis on body morphology but is rather a disability-led reconstitution of embodied and physical space conveyed through the image. To assert this point is not to advocate any apolitical reading of the film, nor does such an approach deny the fact that the story imagines individual and communal identities torn apart by war. But, as this study has tried to show throughout, there is no need to decouple posthumanist critical methods from the understanding of identities and situated ideas of disability futures. In *Turtles Can Fly*, the hardships of refugee life are never denied and are often brutally highlighted, but this does not mean that the events the film portrays cannot be thought of in terms of networks or non-unitary and dispersed subjects.

The film's resistance to orthodox conceptions of character and event can be further seen in its depiction of care. At the start, viewers are led to believe that Riga is the young brother of Hengaow and Agrin (Satellite refers to him as such at one point), but it emerges that he is in fact Agrin's son as a result of her rape during the attack that killed her parents. Throughout the story, Hengaow is a careful and patient carer for Riga, carrying and feeding him (in a powerful scene Hengaow holds a spoon in his mouth as he gives Riga dinner) and looking after him at night. In contrast, Agrin rejects the boy on almost every possible occasion: "Isn't he the child of our parents' killers", she says of Riga to Hengaow, "who did this to me?" As it becomes clear that the US invasion is coming, Agrin suggests to Hengaow that they leave without Riga and at one point takes him away from the camp and abandons him, leaving him tied to a tree before Riga frees himself and returns. There is no conformity to gender roles or family structures in these scenes; rather they have been totally deconstructed by the barbarism of war. And there is no positive resolution or restitution to the story: Agrin drowns Riga in a lake before committing suicide, with both Hengaow and Satellite left inconsolable.

The characters of *Turtles Can Fly* live on a literal border between Iraq and Turkey, but their lives speak of a wider precarious liminality. They enact Squier's identification of the inherent instabilities and volatile convergences created by enforced marginality. The disabled bodies that the film visualises, however, also articulate the second meaning Squier attributes to the 'marginal', as a locus of "rich potential" for the further understanding of liminality. Such potential runs through *Turtles Can Fly*; in Satellite's engagement with the boundaries of technology, for example, or the everyday and accepted nature of disability. It is most apparent, however, in the film's startling revelation that Hengaow is a visionary who can prophecise future events. He sees not only moments of public futures (the arrival of American helicopters and the eventful downfall of Saddam Hussein at the end of the war), but also those that are personal (the deaths of Agrin and Riga). Hengaow is, in fact, a striking example of Squier's precarious and Janus-faced idea of the marginal, in that his visions focus on death and destruction, but their source is (arguably) the most disabled person in the film. Disability is again here difference, with the elusive and quasi-mystical nature of Hengaow's prophecies set against the technology and objects that otherwise form the backdrop to life in Kanibo. It should be stressed that Hengaow's ability is in no way any kind of compensation for his disability; there is in fact no narrative connection between the two and indeed Hengaow's visions (especially that of Agrin and Riga) are tumultuous and disturbing events that only problematise his life. But the potential here is of radical insight (seeing the fall of Baghdad even before the war has commenced, for example) from within the most complex of embodiments.

Close to the end of the film, Satellite is wounded by a landmine and requires crutches to be mobile (it is unclear whether he will have a long-term disability, but the damage done to his leg suggests this might be the case). In the final scene, he stands on a roadside outside Kanibo as US forces drive past as part of their offensive. He is approached by Pesheow, who, mindful of Satellite's enthusiasm for everything American, asks: "Didn't you want to see the Americans coming?" Satellite's face as he looks at his friend reflects the clear trauma he has experienced, and he appears incapable of any response. Without saying anything and awkwardly using his crutches, he turns his back on the convoy before walking out of frame, followed by Pesheow. The final shot is complex: the film ends with two disabled children, their future uncertain, leaving the image as the US invasion continues, but a gap in the procession of trucks and running soldiers means that the fixed camera's focus in the final seconds after the boys have left is on the static, ruined military technology from previous conflicts that litters the road.[67] The ending is a sombre presage of the destruction to come, anticipating that the mobility and capability of US military power will likewise be reduced to wreckage.

Turtles Can Fly was one the first films made in Iraq following the collapse of the Saddam Hussein regime. Its narrative is itself part of a war-torn region in flux and without stability. It speaks to the brutality of history but, unlike the American features discussed earlier, it never resorts to humanist and individualist arguments of restitution and return. Lives, bodies and communities are not made whole again. The film's location in the rawness of the invasion and its grounded specificities might appear to make it impossible to claim that it is in any way a posthumanist text, but a critical posthumanist and disability-led reading illuminates its constant decentring: the grand narratives of history and technology undone by networks of mystical foresight; the power of the military countered by new patterns of reassembling and reuse; and the 'functional' able body reformatted as capable, if fraught and vulnerable, disabled difference.

Conclusion: warfare, disability and 'life'

Melinda Cooper has observed that, for US defence organisations involved in pursuing the war on terror following 9/11, developing technologies in which the "frontier" between warfare and health became "strategically indifferent" became a key goal.[68] It is a telling observation that is articulated through all the films analysed in this chapter. The commercial US features discussed earlier all speak to the 'frontier' between the individual body, immediate environment and enactment of warfare, usually mediated by military technology. In productions from Iran and Iraq, the frontiers are personal, communal and geographical/environmental. In both sets of films, however, warfare and health are collapsed into one another as Cooper suggests. In *Source Code, Green Zone, The Hurt Locker* and *American Sniper* the body becomes vulnerable and fragile, despite the technology that is designed to protect it and expedite a precise and efficient military victory. In *Ahlaam, Turtles Can Fly* and other films from the Middle East, warfare dominates health, with communities destroyed and bodies disabled by the conflict. But whereas the frontier in the US features speaks of a precarity that creates a disabling trauma, undermining the vast assembled power of the military machine, the visceral destruction perpetuated in the frontier war makes disability everyday and ordinary in features originating from those locations targeted by this power. The frantic obsession with individual capability and threats it encounters, so intrinsic to the US features, are absent from films made in Iraq and Iran, where interactions with community feature far more strongly.

Cooper's observation, however, is not one simply expressing conventional ideas about warfare and health, and how one produces changes in the other. Rather her argument is the two come together because of (as the subtitle of her book notes) "biotechnology and capitalism in the neoliberal era". The extension of military technology into the life sciences is, as her book makes clear, partly because of the alignment between biology, capitalism and an aggressive US foreign policy that targeted much of the world as a potential terrorist threat. But her assertion that US organisations promoted a national security platform that wanted a "defense discourse" that would "push further and incorporate *the whole of* life, from the micro- to the eco-systemic level, within its strategic vision" can be applied to the films analysed in this chapter.[69] Embodied, personal and social formations are part of these micro- and eco-systems and, time and again, the features showcase the outcomes of the neoliberal biopolitics that produce the kinds of surplus lives Cooper discusses.

Unsurprisingly, capitalism saturates the US films. The source code programme itself in *Source Code*, the scenes inside the actual Green Zone (with swimming pool parties and takeway food) in *Green Zone*, and the military technologies in *The Hurt Locker* and *American Sniper* are all made possible by particular formations of capital that underwrite US imperialism in the contemporary era. The elements of the films that appear to critique such formations – Stevens' rejection of military/scientific knowledge in *Source Code* or Miller's liberal disdain for the invading regime's lies in *Green Zone* – simply repeat their mechanics through other means, particularly the emphasis on individual success and fulfilment. Capital exchange is central to the films from the Middle East as well, though here it is configured differently. The smuggling in *A Time for Drunken Horses* is part of a process of bare survival, while trade in *Turtles Can Fly* operates in the only economy possible in a border conflict zone. In these examples, health (particularly the prominence of disability in each film), war and economics are folded into one another in exactly the kind of total life experience Cooper outlines.

In her analysis of contemporary conflicts and the ways in which they can be read through a critical posthumanist lens, Rosi Braidotti observes: "New forms of warfare entail simultaneously the breathtaking efficiency of 'intelligent' un-manned, technological weaponry on the one hand, and the rawness of dismembered and humiliated human bodies on the other". This is, she makes clear, "the specifically inhuman edge of the posthuman condition [...] This deployment of technologically mediated violence cannot be adequately described in terms of disciplining the body, fighting the enemy or even as the techniques of a society under control".[70] The films discussed here bear this out. The bodies in the US features are not disciplined; they are precarious and frequently out of control. As we have seen, reading them in terms of disability highlights the often chaotic alignment of vulnerable precarity and violence that unveils cultural fears about the meaning of the 'war on terror'. Equally, it is wrong to call the bodies on show in the films from Iran and Iraq disciplined. They are subject to the crushing impact of war, but – as their own deployments of disability show – they rework embodiment to narrate stories of personhood and community in which disabled selves become normal, part of warfare's social consequences.

Both sets of films articulate Squier's notion of the 'liminal' and Butler's 'precarious life', though the frontiers between technology and health through which they do so differ. Squier observes that "the liminal lives of the twentieth and twenty-first centuries" reveal "biomedicine to be an unstable, porous and culturally implicated practice".[71] We might note that the same is true of technology as well, for all its desire to be autonomous and efficient. What Butler terms "the power of violence" is an intrinsic part of the way such technology functions. As she notes, the mobilisation of post-9/11 military logic came through the recognition that "the national border was more permeable than we thought". As a result, "our general response is anxiety, rage; a radical desire for security; a shoring-up of the borders against what is perceived as alien".[72] When borders are permeable and porous, and lives liminal and surplus, disability is not simply a set of embodied states that arise *as a consequence* of technology and its violence; it also offers a way of analysing and critiquing the processes that form such states. It is precisely because lives lived with disability often occupy porous and liminal frontier spaces that a disability-led critical methodology can unpack the meaning of the technologies and bodies on which this chapter has focuses; and, again, for all that contemporary posthumanist networks are part of the production of such violence, *critical* posthumanist perspectives can align with disability critiques to further extend an understanding of how bodies are produced in contemporary conflicts. The power of the films analysed here is undeniable. In their different ways they visualise and narrate the unstable relationships between technology, individuals and community. Seeing them as disability stories makes reading their power more possible.

Notes

1 Michael Davidson, *Concerto for the Left Hand: Disability and the Defamiliar Body* (Ann Arbor: The University of Michigan Press, 2008), pp. 168 and 172.

2 Clare Barker, '"Radiant Affliction": Disability Narratives in Postcolonial Literature' in Clare Barker and Stuart Murray (eds), *The Cambridge Companion*

to Literature and Disability (Cambridge: Cambridge University Press, 2018), pp. 105–106.

3 Robert McRuer, *Crip Times: Disability, Globalization, and Resistance* (New York: New York University Press, 2018), p. 57. It is important to stress that as well as these practices of disablement, McRuer sees active signs of resistance, aspiration and aesthetic novelty in many instances of disabled global poverty. See also Davidson, *Concerto for the Left Hand*, pp. 170–171 for a series of observations on disability and contemporary global formations.

4 Nirmala Erevelles, *Disability and Difference in Global Contexts: Enabling a Transformative Body Politic* (New York: Palgrave Macmillan, 2011), p. 13.

5 Helen Meekosha, 'Decolonising disability: thinking and acting globally', *Disability and Society* 26, no. 6 (2011), p. 677.

6 Rosemarie Garland-Thomson, *Staring: How We Look* (Oxford: Oxford University Press, 2009), p. 95.

7 Emily Jane O'Dell, 'From leprosy to *The Willow Tree*: decoding disability and Islamic spirituality in Iranian film', *Disability and Society* 30, no. 7 (2015), p. 1126. There are not as many scholarly investigations into disability in Hollywood as might be expected. See Martin F. Norden, *The Cinema of Isolation: A History of Physical Disabilities in the Movies* (New Brunswick, NJ: Rutgers University Press, 1994), although it is dated now; and some of the essays in Marja Evelyn Mogk's more recent edited collection *Different Bodies: Essays on Disability in Film and Television* (Jefferson, NC: McFarland and Company, 2013).

8 Benjamin Fraser, 'Disability studies, world cinema and the cognitive code of reality,' in Fraser (ed.), *Cultures of Representation: Disability in World Cinema Contexts* (New York: Wallflower Press, 2016), pp. 2–3.

9 Fraser, 'Disability studies, world cinema and the cognitive code of reality,' p. 9. Only one of the 18 contributors to the volume is from the global South.

10 Melinda Cooper, *Life as Surplus: Biotechnology and Capitalism in the Neoliberal Era* (Seattle: University of Washington Press, 2008), p. 14.

11 Cooper, *Life as Surplus*, p. 98.

12 See also Kaushik Sunder Rajan's *Biocapital: The Constitution of Postgenomic Life* (Durham, NC and London: Duke University Press, 2006) for a similarly excellent examination of the ways biotech companies construct genes and genomics, on a corporate scale, across global markets.

13 Rosi Braidotti, *The Posthuman* (Cambridge: Polity, 2013), p. 122.

14 Braidotti, *The Posthuman*, pp. 123 and 127. She quotes Mbembe's definition of necro-politics – "the generalized instrumentalization of human existence and the material destruction of human bodies and population" – on p. 122.

15 Braidotti, *The Posthuman*, p. 124.

16 Susan Merrill Squier, *Liminal Lives: Imagining the Human at the Frontiers of Biomedicine* (Durham, NC and London: Duke University Press, 2004), pp. 17 and 9.

17 Judith Butler, *Precarious Life: The Powers of Mourning and Violence* (London and New York: Verso, 2006 [2004]), pp. 65, 29 and 143. Italics in original. The specific 'scenes' Butler is describing in the latter quotation are those of Afghan women published in the US media.

18 Jasbir K. Puar, *The Right to Maim: Debility, Capacity, Disability* (Durham, NC and London: Duke University Press, 2017), pp. xv and xiv.

19 Puar, *The Right to Maim*, pp. 89–92.
20 Squier, *Liminal Lives*, p. 17. Italics in original.
21 Derek Gregory, 'The everywhere war', *The Geographical Journal* 177, no. 3 (2011), p. 239.
22 Zygmunt Bauman, 'Wars of the globalization era', *European Journal of Social Theory* 4, no. 1 (2001), p. 11. For all that Bauman remained a socialist throughout his career, his later work on postmodernism revealed him to have a sure critical sense of ideas such as networks, assemblages or (Bauman's own term) 'liquidity'. An extension of his work to consider posthumanism makes for, I hope, a profitable critical continuity. See *Postmodernity and Its Discontents* (New York: New York University Press, 1997) and *Culture in a Liquid Modern World* (Cambridge: Polity, 2011).
23 Donna Haraway, *Manifestly Haraway* (Minneapolis: University of Minnesota Press, 2016), p. 203.
24 Pramod Nayar, *Posthumanism* (Cambridge: Polity, 2014), p. 8. My use of 'assemblage' in this chapter follows Nayar's articulation, but also includes Margrit Shildrick's Deleuzian formation in which to be 'assembled' means "all distinctions are troubled, whether between self and other, or between the categories of human, animal, and machine". This sense of 'troubling' is evident in many of the films analysed. See Shildrick, '"Why should our bodies end at the skin?": embodiment, boundaries, and somatechnics', *Hypatia* 30, no. 1 (2015), p. 14.
25 Nayar, *Posthumanism*, p. 8.
26 Puar observes: "Maiming thus functions not as an incomplete death or an accidental assault on life, but as the end goal in the dual production of permanent disability via the infliction of harm and the attrition of the life support systems that might allow populations to heal from this harm". As a result, she notes, "Maiming is required" in the practice of war and conflict. *The Right to Maim*, p. 143.
27 Gregory, 'From a view to a kill: drones and late modern war', *Theory, Culture and Society* 28, nos. 7–8 (2011), p. 192. Braidotti reads the use of drones as part of posthumanist patterning: *The Posthuman*, pp. 125–127.
28 Gregory, 'From a view to a kill', p. 196.
29 Chad Harris, 'The omniscient eye: satellite imagery, "battlespace awareness," and the structures of the imperial gaze', *Surveillance & Society* 4, no. 1/2 (2006), p. 102.
30 Harris, 'The omniscient eye', pp. 102–105.
31 Vivian Sobchack, 'A leg to stand on: prosthetics, metaphor and materiality' in Marquand Smith and Joanna Morra (eds), *The Prosthetic Impulse: From a Posthuman Present to a Biocultural Future* (Cambridge, MA and London: MIT Press, 2006), p. 19.
32 Gregory, 'From a view to a kill', p. 190; 'Seeing red: Baghdad and the event-ful city', *Political Geography* 29 (2010), p. 266.
33 Harris, 'The omniscient eye', pp. 101–121.
34 Garland-Thomson, *Staring: How We Look*, p. 15.
35 James Der Derian, *Virtuous War: Mapping the Military–Industrial–Media–Entertainment Network* 2nd ed. (New York: Westview, 2009), p. xxviii. Der Derian's chapter on film is on pp. 151–176.
36 'Source code' is a term used in computing, outlining a broad range of systems

software working. The somewhat vague inclusiveness of the term fits the film's fantasy use of technology: suggestive but lacking technical details.

37 Lambèr Royakkers and Rinie van Est, 'The cubicle warrior: the marionette of digitalized warfare', *Ethics and Information Technology* 12 (2010), p. 291.

38 Anneke Smelik, 'Film' in Bruce Clarke and Manuela Rossini (eds), *The Cambridge Companion to Literature and the Posthuman* (Cambridge: Cambridge University Press, 2017), pp. 115–116. Smelik mentions *Source Code* only in passing, but it is part of a wider argument she advances concerning narratives of "posthuman hybridity" that explore "the relation between the superior memory of the computer and the failing memory of the human being" (p. 114).

39 Cooper, *Life as Surplus*, p. 80.

40 Edward Luttwak, *Strategy: The Logic of War and Peace*, revised ed. (Cambridge, MA: Harvard University Press, 2001), p. xii.

41 "It is not for you to decide what happens here" Freddy tells Miller, explaining why he has killed Al-Rawi. It is an incongruous comment in a conflict (and indeed in a film) where that is exactly what does take place.

42 Tobin Siebers, *Disability Theory* (Ann Arbor: The University of Michigan Press, 2008), p. 26.

43 David T. Mitchell and Sharon L. Snyder, *Narrative Prosthesis: Disability and the Dependencies of Discourse* (Ann Arbor: The University of Michigan Press, 2000), p. 47.

44 Robert Burgoyne, 'Embodiment in the war film: *Paradise Now* and *The Hurt Locker*', *Journal of War & Cultural Studies* 5, no. 1 (2012), p. 14.

45 The idea that the objects of ordnance themselves could be part of posthumanist narration of war is explored in the striking form of Harry Parker's 2016 novel *Anatomy of a Soldier*, in which each chapter is explored from the point of view of a different item involved in the war in Afghanistan, from the materials carried by the soldiers to possessions belonging to the Afghan resistance.

46 Gregory, 'From a view to a kill', p. 191. James refuses to use the robot on his first mission. On his second, he removes his protective suit while defusing a bomb: "If I'm gonna die" he tells Eldrige, "I wanna die comfortable". In response to his actions and the information that up to that point he has disarmed 873 bombs, his senior officer approvingly terms him a "wild man".

47 Burgoyne, 'Embodiment in the war film', p. 13.

48 Burgoyne, 'Embodiment in the war film', p. 13.

49 The Marines are constantly represented as being hysterical, screaming at one another in preparation for action, eyes wide in an overt fanaticism: "You're a fucking machine and you act like a machine" one Marine officer (Andrew McLaren) says to his platoon before they venture out into the city from their base, adding "that's why we train, train, train; to kill, kill, kill".

50 One soldier involved in the massacre, Corporal Ramirez (Elliot Ruiz), admits to an officer before the atrocity that he feels psychologically disturbed and asks to see a doctor, to be told that because of "Marine policy" such help is only available at the end of a tour of duty. Ramirez instigates the massacre when he executes five unarmed Iraqi men shortly after the request. In the final scene of the film, Ramirez imagines again entering the house where the majority of civilians were killed, but this time he creates a fictional alternative in which

no shots are fired, and he rescues a young Iraqi girl. His voice over comments: "We've all seen a lot of action at a young age. I'm 20 years old and this is my third tour of duty. We've all seen things that will haunt us for the rest of our lives. And I guess that after a while you just get hardened. You become numb".

51 Cooper, *Life as Surplus*, p. 75.

52 Gregory, 'From a view to a kill', p. 188.

53 Nayar, *Posthumanism*, pp. 56 and 66.

54 It is instructive to juxtapose *American Sniper* with the 2017 feature *Insyriated*, made by Belgian director Phillipe van Leeuw and set in Damascus during the Syrian civil war. The first word of the film is "sniper" as a group of individuals are fired on in the street. The narrative follows the story of Oum Yazan (Hiam Abbas) and three generations of her family trapped inside her apartment because of the danger outside. *Insyriated* is expressly about space: the claustrophobia and fear of those in the apartment and the unseen (the sniper is never revealed) threat in the public space outside. If *American Sniper* legitimises the killing point of view, *Insyriated* dramatises the space of not knowing where the killing originates.

55 Puar, *The Right to Maim*, p. 19.

56 Karen Lury, 'Children in an open world: mobility as ontology in new Iranian and Turkish cinema', *Feminist Theory* 11, no. 3 (2010), p. 285. *Turtles Can Fly* is one of the films Lury examines in her article. She notes that films that come from Iran, Iraq and Afghanistan "are often categorized as New Iranian Cinema" (p. 285). Although she observes that this category is "elastic" (p. 286), I avoid the phrase in this chapter as some of the films I discuss come from other Middle Eastern countries.

57 Mohsen Makhmalbaf's 1990 feature *Time of Love* was made in Turkey because of political opposition in Iran. It was banned in Iran itself.

58 See, for example, *The Dreams of Sparrows* (d. Hayder Mousa Daffar, 2005).

59 Although it does not explicitly feature disability, Mohamed Al-Daradji's 2010 feature *Son of Babylon* follows a narrative trajectory similar to those films mentioned here. Three weeks after the overthrow of Saddam Hussein's regime, Um-Ibrahim (Shehzad Hussein) and her grandson Ahmed (Yassir Talib) begin a 600-mile journey from northern Iraq to the south of the country to search for their missing son/father Ibrahim, who vanished during the fighting against US and UK forces in the Gulf War of the early 1990s. As with the points made about other Kurdish/Iraqi/Iranian films in this chapter, however, there is no resolution to the quest. Ibrahim is not found (his body is almost certainly in one of the unmarked graves Um-Ibrahim and Ahmed visit) and the grandmother dies from grief, leaving Ahmed alone.

60 For more on the making of the film, its screening in Baghdad and comments from Al-Daradji, see 'New films throw light on the Arab world', *The National*, www.thenational.ae/arts-culture/new-films-throw-light-on-the-arab-world-1.632583#full. Accessed September 17, 2018.

61 Lury's focus in her article is children and she writes on what she calls "the political implications emerging from the representation of the child and its interaction with the land", p. 284.

62 Louis L. Bucciarelli, *Designing Engineers* (Cambridge, MA and London: MIT Press, 1994), p. 195.

63 In the midst of all the recycling and complex relationships between the

villagers and their technology, it is, however, Satellite's bicycle that remains the most constant object in the film. With multiple mirrors and festooned with brightly coloured ribbons, the bicycle is an aesthetic object but also a symbol of power (no other child in Kanibo has one). Satellite uses it to transport refugees and fellow villagers, but also to carry water, the satellite he buys for the village and the automatic weapons he purchases following the US invasion (the market selling communication technology early in the film has been transformed into a space only selling weapons and armaments by the end). The bicycle's utility is straightforward and part of a world in which technology is valued for its use value, but it stands in contrast to other objects because of the degree to which it is personal. Satellite despairs when he thinks he has lost it, and generally his status as an unofficial village leader is enhanced by his possession of it.

64 Gregory, 'The everywhere war', p. 242. On the same page Gregory gives an example of one such drone strike, on a village in Pakistan in 2011.

65 Halabjah is the site of a 1988 chemical attack by Saddam Hussein's army during the Iran–Iran war in which thousands of Kurdish civilians were killed in a genocidal massacre.

66 In one scene next to a fence that marks the Iraqi/Turkish border, Pesheow raises his disabled leg like a gun and pretends to shoot a Turkish border guard in a tower on the other side. It is the one 'prosthetic' use of his body in the whole film, and a grim reminder of the material of killing rather than any moral or humanist meaning.

67 Pehseow brings Satellite one final message from Hengaow, that "in 275 days something else will happen in this area", though it is not made clear what this event will be or if the boys will still be in the village.

68 Cooper, *Life as Surplus*, p. 75.

69 Cooper, *Life as Surplus*, p. 80 (italics in original).

70 Braidotti, *The Posthuman*, pp. 122 and 124.

71 Squier, *Liminal Lives*, p. 274.

72 Butler, *Precarious Life*, p. 39.

CHAPTER FOUR

Reading Disability in a Time of Posthuman Work: Speed, Sleep and Embodiment

Introduction: coming at you

In preparation for writing this book I spent a lot of time looking for media stories about robots. Robots catching the public's attention is nothing new as a phenomenon of course: social fascination with technology has always fixated on robots and automata as strong signifiers of a technologised future and, as such, they have become arguably the most visible manifestation of a broad idea of 'the posthuman' as it functions across a wide cultural consciousness, especially in the twenty-first century. Between 2016 and 2019 it was notable that one storyline about robots appeared to dominate the ways this fascination was articulated, namely the focus on the danger of the 'inhuman' nature of robots and the threat posed to humanity by the accelerated pace of their development. Such a scenario was repeated regularly in news editorial and opinion media, with the same social activity nearly always invoked each time as the clearest example of the supposed coming catastrophe: work, labour and employment. 'The robots are coming to take our jobs' appears as one of the most consistent refrains of the very contemporary period, with faceless and soulless technologised units seemingly poised to replace workers across a whole range of employment sectors; not only the mechanical and labour-intensive realm of production, but also middle-class professions and sections of the service industry. In the ways in which they are characterised in these narratives, these robots are always, it appears, mobile: in a series of ableist metaphors they are moving upwards or forwards, always on a remorseless trajectory of 'conquest' or 'coming', persistently threatening.[1] Robots are not "moral actors and they have no feelings" worried an editorial in the *Guardian* in March 2016: "What they have is power, but this power is growing at a rate that should frighten us all". The very title of the opinion piece – 'The Guardian view on robots and humanity' – struck an air of portentous concern, as if having a 'view' met a need for clear-sighted comment amid a whirl of technological overload.[2]

Shuttling between the fear of replacement and the seduction of enhancement is, as Minsoo Kang has shown, a central part of the long history of automata. "Artificial beings", Kang notes, "were seen from the beginning as inherently unstable", with "the image of the mechanized man" oscillating between "that of a superhuman and a god or a slave and a monster".[3] The first use of the word 'robot' – in Karel Čapek's 1921 play *R.U.R. (Rossum's Universal Robots)* – connected the idea of the automaton to modern labour: 'robota' means 'forced labour' in Czech and Čapek's drama, set in a robot production plant, is an allegorical and satirical investigation of a modern work culture in which robots are created to replace 'imperfect' humans and increase productivity.[4] But the *Guardian*'s concerns update these older narratives, particularly their negative visions, into the contemporary world of global economics. "Their power", the paper continued in its discussions of robots and the networks in which they are situated, "will be used to make money for the firms that finance their development, and then for others quick and clever enough to take advantage of the new world. It's hard to imagine them being used to dent inequality of either wealth or power, globally or within countries". Instead, the editorial continues, "it is far more likely that they will increase inequality and still further hollow out the middle classes as we move towards an hourglass society in which everyone is either very rich or very poor and likely indebted".

What nearly every such editorial, appearing as they did across media and technology outlets globally, had in common (apart from a frequent misunderstanding of much of the work being undertaken in robot technologies) was a strong evocation of a set of core humanist principles. It was implied that, by all accounts, humanity is to be 'lost' in a robot-dominated employment future. "Machines can't feel or do many of the things that make us human" ran the byline under the title of the *Guardian*'s piece; "Sadly that doesn't dispel the concerns about them putting people out of business", evidencing a neat fit between 'machine', 'human' and 'business' that speaks volumes about how the three are, for many, connected. Equally, an article on the idea of taxing robots in the same newspaper from March 2017 asserts:

> Robots won't just take our jobs – they'll make the rich even richer [...] the real threat posed by robots isn't that they will become evil and kill us all [...] it's that they will amplify economic disparities to such an extreme that life will become, quite literally, unliveable for the vast majority [...] What's different this time is the possibility that technology will become so sophisticated that there won't be anything left for humans to do.[5]

The idea of 'our' central humanity (a notion critiqued so effectively by both disability and posthumanist scholarship) being engaged in a battle with automated opponents might appear to belong more to the pages of science fiction than news media, but it is intriguing that the spectre of the robot here leads to such crude generalisations about that which supposedly constitutes its opposite: the human. The reality that robotics technology is being developed to aid people (for example those with disabilities or the elderly) is simply not entertained by a thesis that envisages defenceless humans crushed by an onslaught of robots purely functioning as the tech wing of a global neoliberal economy.[6]

Martin Ford's 2016 book *The Rise of the Robots: Technology and the Threat of Mass Unemployment* crystallises such arguments. Ford makes it clear that the threat robots embody is especially connected to, and meaningful in relation with, work. "We are in all likelihood at the leading edge of an explosive wave of innovation that will ultimately produce robots geared toward nearly conceivable commercial, industrial and consumer task", he observes. Not only, Ford argues, will robot technologies replace low-wage service and industrial jobs (he cites numerous instances, such as the fast food industry, where this is happening already), but "the machines are coming for the high-wage, high-skill jobs as well".[7] The technologies will transform higher education and healthcare, Ford argues, as well as future patterns of consumer behaviour and the development of industry.

There is an element of breathless drama in Ford's survey of the contemporary world of work and technology. While he is in no doubt that an increased use of A.I. and technology could result in positive benefits in some work sectors, the image of lines of unemployed workers nevertheless looms throughout the book, deployed to always undercut the idea that the posthuman future of which he writes might contain a progressive dimension. Given his concentration on business models, I am not best placed to comment on Ford's vision and arguments, but it is noticeable that the approach he takes focuses almost exclusively on the development of technology and automated networks and he has little or nothing to say about the economic and social systems that will *use* robots. The neoliberalism of these networks is taken as a given in the book, overriding any sense that robots and assistive technologies could be made to *work* in any other way, or that there might be alternatives. Kathi Weeks notes in *The Problem With Work* (2011), for example, that faced with the powerful orthodoxies of work cultures, it is important to "insist that there are other ways to organise and distribute that activity" and that it is "possible to be creative outside of the boundaries of work", because "there might be a variety of ways to experience the pleasure that we may now find in work, as well as other pleasures that we may wish to discover, cultivate and enjoy".[8] A specific argument about technology and alternative work environments is made by Nick Srnicek and Alex Williams in their 2015 book *Inventing the Future: Postcapitalism and a World Without Work*, where they assert that full automation should be seen as a desirable 'post-work imaginary'. "The tendencies towards full automation and the replacement of human labour" they note, "should be enthusiastically accelerated and targeted as a political project of the left".[9] While Srnicek and Williams' vision differs radically from Ford's, it is arguable that those with disabilities have little to gain from either scenario given that a persistent exclusion from many economic spaces (whether market- or state-derived) makes access to the potential of new technologies frequently prohibitive. So, when Ford details how developments of autonomous care robots for the elderly will result in the loss of healthcare and nursing jobs, it should be observed that it is already the case that many ageing people who require daily care simply lack the money that can cover the costs involved.[10] For all that there are repeated worries that using robot carers might seem 'inhuman', it is hardly the case that current situations exemplify dignity and respect.[11]

The suggestion of a new technological 'wave' that will see humans supplanted by robots and software is one example of what we might understand as a space of posthuman work.[12] Such a space is one where notions of extension and enhancement play out in terms of productivity, immediacy and efficiency, and are characterised by time and speed as these are changed by developing technologies. Posthuman work creates economies and consumerism, but also produces bodies and subjectivities that operate within and across these spaces. Even if it does not appear immediately obvious, all are affected by, and speak to, disability in the ways in which they create ideas of embodiment, particularly in terms of 'capacity' or 'function'. In this chapter I will explore a range of texts that represent disability within ideas of work, speed and time, and will analyse the bodies, minds and selves that are produced within such contexts. I will concentrate on representations of mobility and speed, body augmentations that allow for more 'efficient' work, and sleep, an experience frequently being eroded given perceptions that it obstructs productivity. While reading sleep in conjunction with disability might seem unusual, I argue that it is an example of the wider argument of this book; namely the productive use of critical disability logics to allow for the investigation of non-disability states. There are disabilities associated with sleep of course – including narcolepsy and fatal familial insomnia – but the combination of reading disability and work opens up new ways to understand sleep and its place in the contemporary world more generally.

The first half of the chapter will focus on ideas of time, how they suffuse contemporary understandings of work, and how within them disability is read in terms of a constructed 'efficiency'. It will also, however, show how the *time* of a disabled body at work challenges the assumptions such constructions produce. Time is foundational in thinking about health and disability. Susan Wendell's work has shown how notions of 'chronic' health revolve almost exclusively around temporality; the problem of 'now' or 'soon', or the potential cure that always belongs to the future.[13] Alison Kafer, Robert McRuer and Margaret Price all articulate the idea of 'crip time', what Kafer calls "a challenge to normative and normalizing expectations of pace and scheduling", and I will use their work throughout the remainder of this chapter, especially in establishing the terms of how, to cite Kafer again, "crip time bends the clock to meet disabled minds and bodies".[14] The bent clock is a marker of the processes through which disability changes the terms of debates around contemporary practices of work. In the chapter's second half the analysis will specifically consider questions of bodies, speed, movement and space in relation to labour, and the ways in which the difference of disability affects norms about mobility and productivity texts. Ultimately, I will argue that disability aesthetics unlock what can appear to be the remorseless logic of work cultures and their seemingly inevitable insistence on greater productivity, and that in so doing they reconfigure the standard notions of lack and absence with which disability conditions are so often associated. As we shall see, disability not only adds to what we know, but the work that we undertake to know it.

The pace of posthuman work and the time of disability

The twenty-first century has seen the consolidation of a neoliberal, post-industrial conception of work that, as many commentators have noted, increasingly revolves around ideas of speed, function, productivity and efficiency. What Jonathan Crary in *24/7*, his 2013 essay on the workings of late capitalism, terms the "expanding, non-stop life-world" of contemporary life is increasingly dominated by a search for perfect, endless production and consumption, or what Crary calls "a generalized inscription of human life into duration without breaks, defined by a principle of continuous functioning".[15] Similarly, Robert Hassan notes in his 2019 study *The Empire of Speed: Time and the Acceleration of Politics and Society*: "We have never experienced such a world where rapidity – *speed* – is at the very core of our collective and individual experience". Contemporary social formations, he goes on, are marked by an "open-ended form of speed, which means that the rate at which humans communicate and the rates of increase in productivity and efficiency can never be fast enough. In this postmodern economy the rate at which we do things has become the defining factor".[16] Likewise, John Tomlinson, exploring speed in terms of an idea of *immediacy* in his 2007 book *The Culture of Speed: The Coming of Immediacy*, maps out the contexts of technology, the media, institutionalisation, regulation and the everyday that have combined to produce "a broad condition of immediacy" that establishes "cultural assumptions and expectations of effortlessness, ubiquity and endless delivery in a fast-paced, technologically-replete and telemediated world".[17] As all three writers show, effortless efficiency, delivered constantly, has become the expectation in many contemporary spheres of activity.[18]

I will use Crary's work, especially his focus on sleep, later in this chapter, but it is worth noting here that his writing offers a searing critique of the processes of neoliberal economics as they impact upon workers. These processes create, he notes, a "24/7 environment that has the semblance of a social world, but [...] is actually a non-social model of machinic performance and a suspension of living that does not disclose the human costs required to sustain its effectiveness".[19] This is not so much Ford's 'rise' of technology and the deployment of actual robots, but rather a wider idea of atomisation and the creation of machine-like, non-human, systems as a consequence of economic demands.[20]

For their part, both Hassan and Tomlinson write in the wake of Paul Virilio, whose work since his ground-breaking 1986 text *Speed and Politics* has connected speed to questions of power and violence and an idea of 'hypermodernism'.[21] For Virilio, interviewed in 2012, speed's "damage is its success" and "its success is also its damage".[22] His writings outline a world where speed has been at the heart of social and (especially) technological development; but in the contemporary period we have hit what he has termed a "wall of acceleration" where such 'progress' and linearity is no longer possible.[23] Virilio's work allows for the connection of ideas of speed to the emerging space of the posthuman; his claims about the current critical point of society chart currents of spatial and technological transformation that align with the kinds of landscapes described in the writings of Donna Haraway, Katherine Hayles, Rosi Braidotti and other writers at the vanguard of critical posthumanism. Virilio's exploration of ideas of "lost dimensions", "tele-presence" and "visual machines" maps on to the kinds of post-anthropocentric formations central to what Braidotti has termed "the Posthuman as Becoming-machine", the processes through which the human and non-human interact.[24] In particular, Virilio paints such moments as being constituted of fear and panic; a loss of logic as speed, in effect, becomes impossibly fast.

Virilio's stress on speed's relationship with power and contemporary manifestations of space, like Hassan's characterisation of its inherently *imperial* nature, speaks to its connection to work, given it is an obvious space of power configurations. It is in structures specific to work environments and practices that ideas of efficiency and the speed of productivity in particular accrue vital meaning. In virtual work cultures especially, what Virilio calls the "direct perception of objects, surfaces and volumes" becomes lost, replaced with an "indirect and mediatized reception" that, precisely because of its lack of presence, can be accelerated to produce the kinds of contemporary speed, with the consequent emphasis on immediate efficiency, explored by Hasan and Tomlinson.[25] Hasan cites, for example, working in the realm of computer-based temporality as the perfect exemplar of such a notion, where it is "seen as a badge of honor to speak of one's life as existing in the 24/7 society", while Tomlinson cites what he terms the "weak demarcation between 'work' and 'life'" that results because of "the reach of capitalist (or capitalist-inflected) work relations into private life".[26] The speed of contemporary work, both writers stress, influences and indeed often regulates core notions of how we have come to define individuals, families, community and society.

In *Exits to the Posthuman Future* (2014), Arthur Kroker sees a time of the posthuman specifically in terms of acceleration. In an echo of Hans Moravec's ideas on the inescapable velocity of technological futures, Kroker notes:

> All our lives have been spent as crash victims of violent, but deeply seductive, technologies of acceleration – speed technologies that move bodies, our bodies of earth and fire and water, to escape velocity [...] When events move at the speed of light, traditional frameworks of

> interpretation are themselves destabilized, weakened in detail and definition as useful indicators of what a future of technological innovation entails.[27]

Such a culture of acceleration, with its crashes and weaknesses, leads not only to the social consequences charted by Hassan and Tomlinson, but extends Virilio's ideas that the mechanisms by which these are assessed are also brought to a point of fracture. Kroker characterises this as 'drift', namely the "the quintessential sign of twenty-first culture" and, as he sees it, the paradigmatic state of posthumanism: "the essence of the data storm that engulfs us" and "ontological foundation of the posthuman axiomatic". Within such drifting he observes, "something fundamental has just happened", processes by which "bodies, metals and AI recombine into new species-forms".[28] Whether thought of as code, history, archives, screen or media (Kroker's examples of drift culture case studies), the posthuman is characterised by constant and perpetual motion.

Within such a context, disability occupies what is an all too often familiar and stereotypical position. In Kroker's theorising, 'bodies' rarely means specific bodies and certainly not the grounded complex embodiment inherent to disabled bodies; as is common with much writing on posthumanism, disabled experience is simply omitted. In turn, for all that the insight displayed by Hassan and Tomlinson allows us to see how disability is read as 'lack' and 'inefficiency' in terms of the contemporary time of work, their analyses give no recognition to work undertaken in the private and domestic spheres. As with women's labour, much disability productivity takes place in the home, where (crucially) it makes time frames of its own. Such difference is one example of crip time, where disability works through subversion and critique to reorient the normalcy of 'progression' through which it is often framed. Wendell observes that "when the pace of life in a society increases [...] fewer people can meet expectations of 'normal' performance; the physical (and mental) limitations of those who cannot meet the new pace become conspicuous and disabling"; but, as Kafer asserts, cripping these expectations of normalcy revises the way time can be conceptualised: "Crip time is flex time not just expanded but exploded; it requires reimagining our notions of what can and should happen in time, or recognising how expectations of 'how long things take' are based on very particular minds and bodies".[29] In a similar vein, David Mitchell and Sharon Snyder argue for the positive "reworking" of "non-productive bodies", a process they see as an "insurrectional force" created by the "definitively multiple forms of nonnormative embodiment". Such embodiment reconfigures the time of labour and "challenges productivity as a basis for an adequate measure of human worth".[30]

This chapter will work through a number of imaginations and fictions where these processes takes place, but it needs to be admitted that cripping work and valuing non-normative bodies takes place in challenging contexts, particularly in times of austerity. McRuer observes that "crip times [...] can and will only end with an aspiration to the outward-looking vision proffered by the indignant ones", and indignancy is a fine concept and position in which to situate disability resistance to contemporary work structure.[31] But 'outward-looking' visions need to work through ever-more complex and restrictive practices of employment, where ideas of time and speed work to characterise disability as a problem that it is easier to jettison than accommodate. McRuer is right to couch indignation within aspiration, but even aspiring can be daunting when circumstances are consistently exclusionary.

In the introduction to the 'Work and Employment' section of the 2011 World Health Organization *World Report on Disability*, the authors note that "working age persons with disabilities experience significantly lower employment rates and much higher unemployment rates than persons without disabilities".[32] In exploring this, they go on to outline the misconceptions and processes of discrimination that surround people with disabilities when being considered for work, observing that "such attitudes may stem from prejudice or from the belief that people with disabilities are less productive than their non-disabled counterparts".[33] In recommending that social attitudes, as much as laws and regulations, are changed, the WHO report identifies a need to "instil a belief among the public that people with disabilities can work, given the proper support".[34] The somewhat patronising idea of 'support' notwithstanding (might not *all* those striving to work need support?), it identifies the intersection between the kinds of speed economies as outlined by Hassan and Tomlinson and the public perception of the extent to which those with disabilities are seen as 'productive' or 'efficient'. As Katherine Quarmby puts in bluntly in *Scapegoat: Why We Are Failing Disabled People* (2011), a study in which she recounts numerous accounts of hate crimes and violence towards disabled people: "Disabled people are not seen as equal citizens. They are seen as a useless burden", and in the context of work 'burden' takes on a specific dimension.[35] It connects the perception of lack and absence, common to many social views of individuals with disabilities, to levels of productivity that they are understood never to be able to meet; and it then reads the necessity to 'make up' the 'shortfall' that such under-productivity produces, in terms of benefits and allowances that society has to pay to support people deemed unable to contribute effectively.

An idea of the 'deserving poor' is, of course, nothing new. But I want to claim here that it is the particular *character* of speed and efficiency in the workplace that lends the contemporary moment its power. Such characterisation is a unique constellation in which ideas of the human, and increasingly the non-human and posthuman, form complex patterns of deployment and meaning – especially in relation to embodiment and cognition – that increasingly shape both disabled lives and the perception of the people who live them, frequently in pejorative terms. And, I want to assert, this character and the meanings it accrues are thrown into sharp vision by contemporary cultural narratives that explore how disability and work interact. As we have noted before in this book through references to the work of Tobin Siebers and Michael Davidson, there is both a disability aesthetic, produced from within an understanding of disability experience, and an aesthetics of disability, symptomatic of wider expressions of disability representations, that come to the fore in texts that self-consciously seek to explore the nature of human difference.

In this chapter I want to place my arguments within the lines of these positions and will do so by looking at a range of fiction – concentrating on the novels *The Unnamed* (2010) by Joshua Ferris, *Under the Skin* (2000) by Michael Faber, and *Fight Club* (1996) by Chuck Palahniuk, as well as Hauraki Murakami's short story 'Sleep' (1993) – that situate issues of disability and posthuman difference within (very different) work settings. As we will see, *The Unnamed* investigates work in urban contexts of speed living and the corporate 'hypereconomy' of the legal profession, while *Under the Skin* explores ideas of a slower cycle of harvesting and production, in which an alien posthuman seeks to define subjectivity and belonging through work centred around bodily difference. In both texts, ideas of a singular and coherent body or self, a humanist 'proveable identity', are critiqued through a creative disability lens and its interrogation of the constitution and consequences of work. Palahniuk and Murakami both focus on sleep, using it to read altered states of consciousness that impact directly on work. As I will show, a critical disability reading of the consequences of work and sleep, as deployed across these texts, produces exactly the kinds of enrichment and complication of which Siebers and Davidson write. Within this we can see again the central thesis of this book, an intersection of productive disability and posthumanist perspectives and the ways they illuminate a range of social and cultural moments.

While work is a much discussed and central category in understanding social experiences of disability, the ways in which it is represented through fictional narratives has received far less attention. This is almost certainly because the link between work and quality of life has been, and continues to be, so important across the disability rights agenda and is rightly the focus of much disability advocacy. But a concentration on the social consequences of disability, employment and the nature of work should not be at the expense of our understanding of the ways in which cultural representations of disability change how we see work, and what this might mean. As we shall see, the fiction examined here offers powerful insight into work environments precisely because of its disability *focus* and the power of the aesthetics that extend from this.

Throughout history, those with disabilities have been seen as being unable to contribute to work as effectively as those without. Such perception has usually been read in terms of a 'limiting' physical difference or cognitive deficiency and frequently codified within law and public policy.[36] But the kinds of speed economies Hassan and Tomlinson outline present new contexts for our understanding of disability and work. In an internet-based, connected, workplace for example, physical impairments may not be as much of a limitation as they were during a period of machine and engineering domination. Indeed, a culture of work acceleration and multiple-project multitasking or, conversely, sustained concentration and single tasking, might seem to welcome the forms of cognitive *variation* inherent in some neurobehavioural conditions. Extending this, the kinds of networked assemblages identified by scholars of posthumanism, with their focus on non-linear, symbiotic and co-evolving existences, also appear to lend themselves towards the inclusion of those with different bodies and minds. When Pramod Nayar speaks of "the human as a dynamic hybrid", for example, focused "not on borders but on conduits and pathways, not on containment but on leakages, not on stasis but on movements of bodies, information and particles all located within a wider system", there is an apparently easy move to see how such plasticity can incorporate the divergent states disability brings with it, and to claim that work might be one of the locations within which an enabling hybridity might flourish.[37] But for the most part the kinds of immediacy demanded by contemporary employment regimes lack this broad view of systems. Hassan stresses that it is "*constant* acceleration" (my emphasis) that is "the defining process of our postmodern, post-Fordist and post-industrial age", and this stress on the constant, the need to *always* be mobile, responsive and flexible, in fact produces work cultures that – as the bare statistics of the WHO report testify – are not designed for those with disabilities.[38]

Indeed, it is intriguing to note the ways in which the language that frequently describes contemporary work cultures contains multiple metaphors that invoke disabled states of being. When Hassan notes that, for proponents of neoliberalism, acceleration equates to 'efficiency', he goes on to observe that within this logic:

> To be efficient is also necessarily to be flexible – to be physically, cognitively, psychologically and metaphorically able to 'move fast' when the time comes [...] To be efficient and flexible is to be able to move rapidly in response to 'outside' economic influences that constantly demand our attention. To be willing and able to move fast means that you can be 'successful' in your life, be able to 'synchronize' with fast-changing scenarios and rapidly unfolding events, staying 'ahead of the game' and hopefully out of trouble [...] In the opening decade of the twenty-first century, we find the pursuit of purported efficiency through speed almost everywhere. To be outside the network is to be cut off from the spaces and times of economic opportunity.[39]

Here, the language of speed explicitly connects to physical mobility, with 'flexibility' and its connection to 'success' employing a particularly overt reference to bodies and norms. One can *only* be successful it seems if one is not simply able-bodied (the kind of 'compulsory' able-bodiedness articulated by McRuer), but rather, in addition, athletic and fast. In what follows I will ask how disability interacts with ideas of 'slow' or 'weak' time and strength in the context of hyperaccelerated work, set against what Thomas Hylland Eriksen, examining the concept of 'slow time', has called "the tyranny of the moment", where the very idea of the *speed* of the present moment is subject to change.[40] For now, however, we might focus on how we can better understand the seemingly pervasive ubiquity of the immediate and accelerated in work cultures of the present.

The ways in which we might all *make* our bodies and minds faster are part of the characterisation of work speed and efficiency, and its consequences for our physical and cognitive selves, which flood contemporary media networks. Traditional diet, workout and meditation regimes have been supplemented by ideas – from mindfulness to biohacking – that specifically aim not simply at well-being but also, in language that often borrows from posthumanism, at *enhancement*. To take one example, the team behind Nootrobox, a pharma/

tech start-up firm based in Silicon Valley, market Nootropics, products presented as "a broad classification of cognition enhancement compounds" designed to accentuate the augmentation of creativity, memory and concentration. According to Nootrobox's publicity, those who take Nootropics are engaged in an explicit process of "hacking your biology" to produce "optimal cognition" and the direct development of their neurophysiology.[41] "Humans are the next platform", Nootrobox's co-founder and CEO Geoffrey Woo observes in an October 2016 interview, using the classic contemporary start-up mix of science and business language that saturates everything the company does. (Fellow co-founder Michael Brandt adds at one point in the interview: "The way Nike owns physical performance [...] we want to own mental performance".)[42] But if it seems that Nootropics might appear to promote a general improving of health, it is clear many of its products are in actuality aimed at enhancing work performance. One of its four major product groups, for example, SPRINT, is essentially a compound of caffeine, L-Theanine and various Vitamin B complexes, to be taken when needed in order to produce greater productivity. SPRINT can (as the website puts it) "help improve attention, provide jitter-free energy and decrease fatigue" and thus create "the ideal mental flow state to get the job done".[43] Nootrobox's website is full of links to articles and 'critical studies' that purport to give a scientific basis to its materials, but its "cornucopia of self-actualization", as journalist Alex Morris puts it in his interview with Woo and Brandt, seems more interested in the assumption that, more than anything else, we all want to work harder and faster.[44]

Whether through enhanced cognition or optimised physicality then, contemporary employment environments seek to produce workers set on pursuing the ever-disappearing horizon of 'efficiency' in ways that have changed dramatically in the last ten years. In a time of posthumanist work, the idea of the worker as a unit challenges the idea of a self-contained and autonomously rational human agent. Faster and more flexible threatens to go beyond the characteristics that supposedly make the human being knowable and expressible. But while such processes enact revisions of humanist conceptions of the self, various states of disability have long been sites of embodiment difference in the time and spaces of work. Even as evolving practices of employment were central to the production of disability categories during a developing modernity, the extent "to which the body becomes thinkable when its totality can no longer be taken for granted" (to again cite Davidson's phrase used earlier) allows us to see the limitations and boundaries of work cultures, however sweeping their effects.[45] And this new thinking suggests a different pace, an alternative texture and experience of labour that exemplifies crip time. Making meaning of disabled ontologies in a time of accelerated immediacies is no simple task, but we might start with a narrative of the body in motion.

Not being able to stop

It is precisely ideas of speed, mobility, work and their connection to achievement and success (and to concomitant topics such as family and community), that are critiqued in Joshua Ferris' 2010 novel *The Unnamed*. Ferris' work overall is strongly focused on work practices and environments: his 2007 novel, *Then We Came to the End*, takes place almost exclusively within the offices of a Chicago advertising agency; while *To Rise Again at a Decent Hour*, his most recent (2014) novel, revolves around a New York dentist, again with much of the narrative set in the workplace. For Ferris, work is one of the ways in which the contemporary moment is most clearly defined and is the context for many of the major themes of his writing.

The Unnamed centres on Tim Farnsworth, a successful Manhattan lawyer, who suddenly develops a condition that causes him, against his will, to have to walk without stopping. Farnsworth's walks take him through and out of New York, often only stopping when, exhausted, he falls asleep. His walking literally embodies the idea of a self out of control: "He looked down at his legs. It was like watching footage of legs walking from the point of view of the walker. This was the helplessness, this was the terror: the brakes are gone, the steering wheel has locked, I am at the mercy of this wayward machine".[46] Farnsworth can be read in a number of ways: as a contemporary flâneur, a mechanised automaton, a self lost in an existential, absurdist universe, or as a man experiencing a crisis of masculinity for example; while the novel itself obviously links his walking to ideas of narrative progression.[47] It is a disability reading, however, that enriches these perspectives and provides a productive and incisive way to unpick the complexities of his embodiment and environment. Stressing Farnsworth as a disabled character, and his presence as a disability presence, points both to the place of affect and embodied difference central to his mobility, as well as the cultural and social networks through which these operate.

Because of his inability to stop moving, Farnsworth is thrown into a disability that functions both as grounded actuality and metaphorical extension. The condition's origins baffle clinical expertise, while Farnsworth himself can only describe its manifestations and sensations in "nonmedical and not very useful ways"; he talks of feeling "jangly, hyperslogged, all bunched up", noting that "he spoke a language only he understood".[48] In a clever analysis of the poverty of medical knowledge surrounding many neurobehavioral conditions, Ferris has Farnsworth subjected to multiple opinions from different medical specialists: he is, varyingly, referred to neurologists, psychiatrists, and environmental psychologists; is subjected to multiple MRI scans; has group therapy suggested because of possible problems with compulsion; given a list of urban toxins as a possible cause; prescribed muscle relaxants; and has rebirthing recommended. One clinician tells him that, given that there is "no laboratory examination to confirm the presence or absence of the condition" it might not "even exist at all"; while another diagnosis "benign idiopathic perambulation", is a nod to the idea that, in a world governed by new neurological knowledge, any unusual activity can be seen as a syndrome.[49] Although "the health professionals suggested clinical delusion, hallucinations, even multiple personality disorder" Farnsworth is sceptical of their expertise. Echoing the Cartesian emphasis on the superiority of the mind over the 'base' elements of the body, he believes that "his mind was intact, his mind was unimpeachable. If he could not gain dominion over his body, that was not 'his' doing. Not an occult possession but a hijacking of some obscure order of the body".[50] For Farnsworth, the possibility that such an "obscure order", affecting the body but located in the brain, is the cause of the walking allows him to admit to a disability while preserving the sense that, psychologically, his mind is intact. As the above description of the walking makes clear, he understands his self to be at the 'mercy' of mechanical control.

If *The Unnamed* presents a clever spin on the mind/brain conundrum, much of the force of Ferris' presentation of Farnsworth's syndrome lies in the ways in which it offers a specific critique of the culture of work. As a trial lawyer, Farnsworth's world is the detailed preparation of cases that involve endless late nights in the office, or the total commitment to work that demands travel all over the country. The financial rewards are considerable but, Ferris makes clear, it is the work itself that drives Farnsworth:

> The point was Houston, Seattle, Pittsburgh, Orlando, Charleston, Manhattan – wherever the trial was. The trial, that was the point. The clients. The casework. The war room [...] And he worked in midtown amid the electricity and the movement. And his view of Central Park was amazing. And he liked the people. And the money was great. And

> the success was addictive. And the pursuit was all-consuming, And the rightness of his place was never in doubt.

On one occasion when he is remembering working into the dark of another late night, Farnsworth observes simply: "That was happiness".[51]

But his condition destroys this capacity for work. Unable to physically stay in his office, attend meetings and see clients, Farnsworth becomes desperate. In an environment that demands immediate expertise and continuous productivity, and ironically given his own mobility, he cannot *keep up*. Having to explain his multiple absences, he falsely claims that his wife Jane has cancer and ultimately fails in his duty to defend a high-profile client, who is (wrongfully) convicted of murder. When he does attempt to attend the trial in a frantic attempt to intervene, Farnsworth experiences a walking episode, leaving the Manhattan courthouse and finally waking up "in a booth in a KFC in Queens [...] a crazy man possessed".[52] This change in location, from smart midtown to working-class suburb, and Farnsworth's shedding his bespoke work suit as he walks, serve as a marker of the change (here, the literal *journey*) his disability produces.[53] He is sacked, and while he is rehired as a lowly staff attorney following an excruciating interview ("Oh please, please take me back!" his internal monologue recounts; "Grant me the full measure of life again [...] I will be good, will do as told. No more breakdowns, promise, promise"), he again fails to hold down this job.[54]

Farnsworth's walking not only stops him from working, but in an ironic twist it undermines the very idea of work. He is in constant motion and always active, but the results of this are completely unproductive. When he walks, Farnsworth is continually 'doing', and his activity should be understood in gendered terms as a critique of the ideas of male stamina and capability in terms of work culture; but, crucially, such labour produces nothing. Rather his body renders its own physical activity as something mysterious, illegible and ultimately pointless, all of which are anathema to notions of work driven by concepts of endless driven efficiencies. Here, embodied alterity returns as an uncanny obliteration of capitalist management and discipline; for all its effort, the body that cannot stop produces no returns.

Farnsworth's commitment to work means he is frequently absent from his wife Jane and daughter Becka. Ferris presents this as an all-too-common deal in the world of high-pressure employment, supposedly justifiable because of the remuneration. But in the same way as Farnsworth's walking destroys his ability to function as a

24/7 employee, it also totally reorders his relations with his family. "I've always felt a strong sense of duty to provide for you and your mom. I've worked hard so that you would never have to work hard for anything", Farnsworth says to his daughter, in a rare moment when they are in the house together, only to be met with the retort: "I don't really think that's why you worked hard". But Farnsworth is, in fact, working up to a confession: "Point is [...] I hid behind my duty. I used work as my excuse to avoid you".[55] Despite such seeming self-knowledge, Farnsworth cannot process this to produce greater insight into his closest relations: Becka's response – "The only reason you're apologising is because you're sick again. If you weren't, you wouldn't even have thought about it. You could have been stoned on crack since I started high school, nothing would have been different" – is withering in its summation and contempt.[56] Farnsworth's failure as father, unable to help Becka through her teenage anxiety about her appearance, is matched by his being powerless to stop Jane's drinking or understand her version of living with his illness, while his condition changes the literal space of the family home. In a desperate attempt to prevent the destructive consequences of his walks he is restrained in his bedroom, tied to a bed while his legs move constantly and with either Jane or Becka watching over him.

The novel also connects Farnsworth's condition to wider narratives of American individualism and success: "Before he got sick, he was under the illusion that he needed only to seek help from the medical community, and then all that American ingenuity, all that researched enlightenment, would bring about his alienable right to good health".[57] But, as Ferris makes clear, a humanist language of rights, enlightenment and scientific knowledge constitutes an illusion when disability effectively casts Farnsworth into the world of another America, one of unemployment, homelessness and despair; a space governed by what Andrew Tate, in his reading of the novel, terms "a pre-apocalyptic mood". Tate observes that Farnworth's "aimless journeys by foot [...] separate the protagonist from a secure, suburban domestic life and propel him into the wilds of an America tainted by environment ruin; these abandoned edgelands suggest that a wealthy nation is in the midst of a catastrophe".[58]

Farnsworth believes in his 'right' to offset such catastrophe, to be successful at work through study and application, and then consequentially develop self-knowledge, achievement and the qualities that allow for earned advancement. It is precisely such logic that his condition unpicks. Disability here counters the speed of the efficient and immediate workplace, the endless drive of casework and trials, with the different, embodied, pace of Farnsworth's walking. His body's motion and mobility destroy not only the possibility of his work (and indeed work itself), but the sense of self and the meanings he derives from it. In the end, Farnsworth literally walks out of the narrative of his work self and his place in his family. As Jane becomes genuinely sick with cancer and Becka's adult life continues with her wedding, Farnsworth is estranged from them both. He follows a loop of continuous walking until, by the novel's end, he lies down in a tent in a snowstorm, apparently to die, feeling that, "He never had to rise again [...] Never had to walk".[59]

Crucially, Ferris presents Farnsworth as a figure who learns little or nothing from his walking. He barely registers the details of the environments through which he passes, nor is he prompted to reflection by them. *The Unnamed* is not a disability narrative that resolves itself through a protagonist finding 'human' meaning because of their condition. "Try your best that he doesn't forget what it means to be human" a doctor tells Jane after another failed medical intervention.[60] But it is precisely this forgetting and failure the novel charts. Exiled from posthumanist spaces of work, Farnsworth has become non-human by the story's end, animal-like in his roving across the landscape at the mercy of nature. *The Unnamed* refutes the notion, integral to a long tradition in American writing, that there is individual or social insight to be gained from a flight from the complexities of society back to nature.[61]

But if Farnsworth fails to understand the effects his disability has on his life, this is certainly not true for the novel's readers. Ferris' central conceit – a pace that cannot be controlled in a world moving ever faster – presents a masterful destabilising of the world of contemporary work. The disability optic the novel utilises operates the kinds of aesthetics outlined by Davidson: the idea that 'the body can no longer be taken for granted' and that the social and cultural meanings associated with it can no longer 'be assumed' fit *The Unnamed* perfectly. It is precisely because Farnsworth's body rebels, through its excessiveness, that the meanings it produces, especially those related to work, are thrown into relief and challenged. With a body that cannot be won over by casework, or long hours in the office – indeed, one that is in fact immune to any attempt to establish argument through precedent – Farnsworth is projected into a realm for which he has no expression. Instead, Ferris unmasks the extent to which 'success' is constituted through many vectors of ableism: the compliant body; the idea of a unified self; the internalisation of the need for competition; and the heteronormativity of family. As Farnsworth's disability highlights the collapse of boundaries between the different states that he assumes made up his self, these all fall away, one step at a time.

Work was the cure

The Unnamed explores the relationship between work, speed and the body through a concentration on contemporary ideas of time and pressure. What Tate observes as Farnsworth's "loneliness [...] estrangement from family [...] and any sense of community" tells a story of a present that readers may recognise and connect with.[62] Other fictions explore these topics in other ways. In Michael Faber's novel *Under the Skin*, published in 2000, a very different kind of work serves as the focus for an exploration of ideas of difference, the body and selfhood. The central character, Isserley, is an alien sent to Earth by her employers, Vess Incorporated, to trap and kill humans who are then processed into exotic food products (voddissin) for consumption by the elite of her home planet. Isolated apart from a few colleagues who work in the production and packaging of the human meat for transportation, she drives back and forth across the often deserted roads of the far north of Scotland, luring male hitchhikers into her car, which is specially adapted to anaesthetise passengers using a sedative called icpathua delivered through needles in the seats. Isserley takes the bodies to a farm that serves as a cover for the processing of the human meat, which is transported home through a regular delivery schedule. In a clever twist that informs much of the novel's politics of embodiment and physical difference, the aliens refer to themselves as human and the humans on Earth as 'vodsels'.

The novel situates the idea and practice of work as the context for a series of questions about subjectivity and agency. Isserley is solely on Earth to gather bodies because she is an employee, and only agreed to take the job because refusal would have meant being condemned to the 'New Estates' back on her home planet. The Estates are an underground housing complex composed of an "unmistakable ugliness" where "decay and disfigurement were [...] par for the course", and where overcrowding, poor diet and sanitation, and a lack of medical care, produce what she terms "an almost subhuman taint".[63] But the price Isserley pays to avoid this future is her own disfigurement, as to work on Earth requires radical surgery that renders her alien features unrecognisable to vodsels. It is in the subtleties of this presentation of bodily change that the novel can be read within a set of disability aesthetics, as Isserley's frequent reflections on what she sees as her 'enfreakment' punctuate her developing psychological awareness of the alien race she is encountering and her place on their planet. Isserley has had a series of major operations to prepare her for work on Earth. She has "had half [her] backbone amputated, and metal pins inserted into what was left" in order to remove a tail and, because of this, has had to relearn how to walk – on two legs as opposed to her normal four – and balance.[64] In addition, she has had "strange humps grafted onto" her body, her "breasts removed" to be replaced by vodsel breasts based on those of a glamour model, and her "fur shaved off".[65] Her "once-beautiful body" has become, in her eyes, that of a "mutilated cripple" with "scarred flesh", while her face "was the only bit she could look at nowadays without self-loathing, the only bit that had been left alone".[66] The gender implications of the changes, and their interactions with ideas of work, are subtle: Isserley does not associate her previous 'beauty' with any model of the feminine, and her new breasts fundamentally serve a work purpose, creating an attraction that lures hitchhikers into her car. As such, even though she does not consider herself a sexual being and although the work she is doing involves the capture and processing of food, Isserley's labour here offers clear parallels to that of a sex worker, with her driving being a form of reverse kerb crawling. Faber's skill is to write this grounded gender narrative, with all its associations, while at the same time maintaining the genuinely 'alien' subjectivity of the novel's central protagonist.[67]

Ultimately Isserley is, she feels, "a freak", someone who has been made into a "hideous animal" by the transitions necessary for her to take up her new job.[68] In the face of such difficulties of self-image, she initially falls back on the routine and detail of work to provide her with stability. "To stop herself thinking about the more embittering specifics of her sacrifice, Isserley abruptly decided to get back to work [...] Work was the cure" she asserts.[69] But unlike the ideas of corporate efficiency and urban speed explored in *The Unnamed*, work in *Under the Skin* is less a process of continual 24/7 engagement. Although Isserley's drives across the Scottish roads are a constant, finding vodsels is frequently occasional and random. As such, work prompts a more a more reflective state, and its time functions in a different way: "Nothing happened", the narrative notes at one point while Isserley waits in her car for a vodsel to appear, "and time stubbornly refused to pass".[70] Isserley is still subject to the demands of Vess Incorporated's business model and its need for product and has to work to timetabled requirements surrounding delivery and quantity, but she is left to herself for the majority of the time and decides upon her own driving routes and methods of vodsel capture. As such her reflection on her own perceived disabilities, a process that becomes integral to her sense of self as she realises the extent to which she is alienated from a sense of home, takes place in a slow time of contemplation and learning, what Tomlinson has termed "slow values".[71] Central to this is a realisation that work, in fact, is *not* a cure for the complexities of her position. Upon learning that the price of voddissin is so prohibitively expensive back home that almost no-one can afford it, Isserley is also informed that there are moves to make a synthetic, substandard, replacement. "Do me out of a job?" she responds, laconically, fully realising that in all likelihood such circumstances will leave her 'mutilated' self useless and with no possibility of return.[72]

Isserley's selfhood is a careful construction of a subjectivity that sees itself *as human* and vodsels as alien. In one passage, Faber astutely reveals Isserley's value system through a description of vodsel limitations:

> In the end, though, vodsels couldn't do any of the things that really defined a human being. They couldn't siuwil, they couldn't meshnistil, they had no concept of slan. In their brutishness, they'd never evolved to use hunshur; their communities were so rudimentary that hississins did not exist; nor did these creatures seem to see any need for chail, or even chailsinn.[73]

While this is a powerful statement of the contempt Isserley feels for the inhabitants of Earth, at no point in the novel are any of the non-English words explained, so there is no possibility of the reader identifying with Isserley's own core 'definitions' of human agency and community. Seeing herself as human but 'crippled' by the violence produced by her surgery, Isserley is posthuman only within the context of our *reading*; her embodied difference working through the refraction created by our apprehension of our own 'humanity'. Such a process illuminates the ways in which the novel's inversions enact numerous processes of critique. As well as the points noted above about gender, for example the treatment of the vodsels after capture, in which they are "shaved, castrated, fattened, intestinally modified [and] chemically purified" during their processing, works as a clear comment on the nature of contemporary meat industries.[74]

If Farnsworth's walking in *The Unnamed* raised the possibility of posthumanising processes in which human becomes machine, then *Under the Skin* suggests a parallel process of becoming-animal, a critical exploration central to much recent scholarship on posthumanism.[75]

As Sarah Dillon has shown, the novel is full of inversions that tease out questions of species identification, particularly through linguistic transformations.[76] Dillon notes how Isserley replaces possible empathic connections to vodsels with a more focused "animation of the inanimate", particularly (though Dillon does not stress this) in relation to the objects that are central to her work: "While the vodsels are drained of life, cars, road networks, tractors, steering wheels, factories, icpathua needles, machines, shower nozzles, windows and chocolates are all imbued with an uncanny vitality. Isserley seems strangely capable or more empathy with, and care of, her car, than with the vodsels".[77] But such identification is not strange if we understand that Isserley is seeking to 'cure' her sense of her own freakishness through a concentration on work. Though *Under the Skin* is full of material for the kind of human/non-human animal comparisons in which Dillon is interested, the use of a disability optic to read the novel in terms of its presentation of embodied work alters the terms in which we might read Isserley as a character invested in 'becoming'. While Isserley can be read in terms of 'becoming-animal', she is clearly – in her own terms – attempting a process of self-identification through which her attitudes to work might reclaim her 'human' self from the mutilated, disabled subject she feels she has become.

But Faber makes it clear that cure and, concomitantly, Isserley's self-identity as a productive and respected worker, are not possible. Crucially, Isserley is *working* at the end of the novel when a car accident leaves her trapped and bleeding to death. The narrative concludes with Isserley at the point of committing suicide, about to detonate hidden explosives rather than allow herself to be identified by a woman who comes to her aid. Work has not saved her, and it is rather an idea of connections to the natural world that appear as her last thoughts: "When it snowed, she would be part of it, falling softly to earth, rising up again with the snow's evaporation. When it rained, she would be there in the spectral arch that spanned firth to ground. She would help to wreathe the fields in mists, and yet would always be transparent to the stars. She would live forever".[78] In place of trying to negotiate the complexities of a disabled body through the detail of work, Isserley finally appears to reject embodiment altogether. The ending is, however, ambiguous: in her desire to become "part of the sky" through her death, Isserley rejects both her adapted body and the terms of the employment that have defined her, but the novel offers little evidence that such abstraction is anything other than a final fantasy.[79] Isserley exits the vodsel world, probably blown "into the smallest conceivable particles", with the same absence of full meaning with which she arrived.[80] During the interval of her stay, however, her narrative enables a highly perceptive account of the nature of embodied work.

The disability aesthetics at work in *The Unnamed* and *Under the Skin* create powerful reworkings of time and the body as they are inflected through work. If Ferris' novel articulates the complexities of speed and immediacy when read as determinants of efficiency and productivity, it is important to stress that the 'slow time' of Faber's narrative does not suggest a more enabling counter-discourse. The (apparent) death of both protagonists shows that slow time (and slow work) is no antidote to the destructive properties of the ever-increasing speed of contemporary labour; it is rather its own space of restrictions and pejorative codifications. Any expectation that disability experiences might somehow constitute a preferred 'slow' mode of work is, in fact, just part of the same logic that assumes those with disabilities cannot be efficient or productive because they lack some attribute that qualifies all those without disabilities to work 'normally'. As Tomlinson argues: "The slow movement [...] is congruent with the condition of immediacy, matching both its mood of fluid complexity and over-determination, and the individualizing effects of both telemediatization and the shaping of consumption towards delivery" (this last point rings especially true for the work practices explored in *Under the Skin*).[81] In fact, advocates of slow time, and those who write on the topic, often invoke an idea of a collective 'us' in their discussions of how 'we' operate in the modern information age, a mode of writing essentially humanist in its assumptions around rationality, agency and individual action.[82] As *Under the Skin* shows, Isserley's slow time does not allow for any such comforting affiliations.

It is more productive to read both novels in terms of the way they articulate moves away from the various categories – fast/slow, human/alien, identified self/erased self, embedded/dislocated – that at first seem central to the representations of their protagonists and environments. In each, work identities fall away because of the messy embodied nature of disability, which proves to be beyond either institutional structures of control or any idea of self-will that might change the body back into some 'preferred' mode. It is important to stress that, although both Farnsworth and Isserley are frequently at war with their newly disabled bodies, neither novel posits disability experience itself as negative. Both authors refuse to indulge in the standard narrative moves – sentimentality, melodrama, or overcoming/restitution – that traditionally create sympathy for the disabled protagonist when a character is understood to be 'suffering'. Rather each novel uses the *clarity* provided by a disability perspective to unpick the network of assumptions that underwrite ableist work environments and subjectivities. At the same time, these disability perspectives do not suggest that there is a simplistic process by which one mode of identity, the self as defined through work, is replaced by another, that of the disabled outsider. There are no "fantasies of identification" in either text, to adapt Ellen Samuels' useful phrase, no straightforward labels of belonging that offer restoration to some more 'authentic' subject position.[83] Instead, disability functions in both novels to stress the non-normative nature of the body and its connections *across* objects and locations, as opposed to any iteration of an essentialising mastery. Whatever Farnsworth and Isserley might wish for their *selves*, their bodies refuse to submit to the centrifugal forces that might convey wholeness or some sense of unified being-in-the-world.

In this way, both *The Unnamed* and *Under the Skin* portray disability as a set of anormative positions and experiences that rewrite assumptions about 'being human' or dehumanisation. Because of their disabilities, Farnsworth and Isserley are seemingly caught on the wrong side of a boundary, that of class in *The Unnamed* and species in *Under the Skin*. But through highlighting the disabled body, each text demonstrates the fictional nature of enforcing such boundaries. The building blocks of – respectively – prosperity and human/non-human identification are shown to be fragile entities rather than secure foundations. Here, then, we find a space of interaction between the relational, plural and unsettling productivities of disability critique and the positive energies of a critical posthumanism as envisaged by writers such as Hayles, Braidotti, Nayar and others. What Kafer asserts as the "collective affinities" of disability, and its status as "a site of questions rather than firm definitions" (here understood through crip time in particular), are matched by Hayles' claims for the posthuman as being a condition that marks "the end of a certain conception of the human".[84] As Hayles adds, in terms that speak to the processes of critique at work in Ferris' and Faber's novels: "Located within the dialectic of pattern/randomness and grounded in embodied rather than disembodied information, the posthuman offers resources for rethinking the articulations of humans".[85] The combination of these two positions frames what I hope has been the articulation of my central concerns here and indeed with this book as a whole, that the aesthetics of disability representation not only engage with such 'site of questions' and 'rethinking', but indeed go further: mobilising critical insight into human activities that further reveals the differences of, within and between bodies as they engage with the world.

I am thus drawing a distinction between the nature of posthumanist *work*, which we can characterise in the kinds of terms of neoliberal demands discussed at the start of this chapter, and the acuity of a critical posthumanist *studies*, which serves as an assembly of disciplines that functions to read the terms of contemporary bodies, cultures and societies. Disability is only one part of this assembly, but its place in intersectional arguments that also welcome discussions of gender, race and forms of the non-human is vital. To focus the power of this critical investigation upon employment and work is especially fruitful, given their ubiquity across multiple and various manifestations within global societies. Stereotypes abound when constructions of the body are aligned with ideas of work but, as Ferris and Faber demonstrate, disability reformats this relationship.

Sleeping is for losers

There is a huge literature covering the cultural, philosophical and social meanings of sleep and its relationship to wakefulness. If being awake is, as Jonathan Crary puts it in *24/7,* a state of "self-awareness in which one has the ability to evaluate events and information as a rationale and objective participant in public or civic life", then sleep retains the capacity of an often indescribable unknown or vacancy and is usually seen as inherently private.[86] Representations of an *absence* of sleep, as opposed to a comparison between the two states, insert a further complex variable into such categorising, frequently accentuating notions of the mysterious and non-rational in understanding the sleep deprived. Mathias Énard's 2017 novel *Compass* takes place over a single sleepless night, with a protagonist lost in doubt and vulnerability as he is forced to revisit and evaluate recollections and feelings over the key relationships in his life. In Stephen King's 1994 novel *Insomnia,* the lack of sleep experienced by the two central characters becomes central to an exploration of different states of embodied consciousness and, indeed, the apprehension of a coming apocalypse. In Christopher Nolan's 2002 film, also called *Insomnia,* the white nights of an Alaskan summer and subsequent lack of sleep force police detective Will Dormer (Al Pacino) to confront personal guilt and corruption during a murder investigation after he shoots and kills his partner.[87] Each morning, staggering from an angst-ridden night into work, Dormer becomes progressively emotionally incoherent and desperate. His death at the end of the narrative is presented by the film as a release from the torment that an absence of sleep has created.

For its part, science and speculative fiction frequently explores the relationship between sleep and labour. Possible most famously, Gabriel Garcia Marquez's visionary *One Hundred Years of Solitude* (1967) recounts how an insomnia plague descends upon the town of Macondo, with the result that the inhabitants develop acute memory loss and objects need to have labels placed on them to remind people what they are and how they must be used. Nancy Kress' 1991 novella *Beggars in Spain* revolves around the idea that rich parents can genetically engineer their children so that they become 'Sleepless', with a specific view that, as the children become adults, they will achieve more in terms of education and work than their sleeping peers. As a result, the book suggests, the Sleepless will pioneer an idea of "mutual cooperation" and "beneficial trade" through a form of benign capitalism based around notions of complete efficiency.[88] In a dark twist, 'Sleepers' turn on the Sleepless because of their difference, passing ordinances and regulations that block many of their civic rights – to rent apartments or serve on juries for example – and even banning them from operating 24-hour businesses because such activities create "unfair competition".[89] In *Beggars in Spain*, the Sleepless become a feared and outlawed community, despite what appear to be their manifest advantages. In its representation of prejudice and persecution, Kress' fiction raises clear parallels with disability and the extent to which difference is excluded. In a more contemporary moment, Karen Russell's 2014 novella *Sleep Donation*, possibly inspired by Garcia Marquez, centres on an insomnia plague that sweeps across the US, killing much of the population through suppressing the production of the neuropeptide orexin. It is countered by a process of 'sleep donation' or transfusion, in which healthy volunteers donate to a 'sleep bank' that is then used to treat the most chronically afflicted. Russell's narrative introduces the conceit of making the sleep of babies the most powerful and 'pure', thereby investigating the ethical, legal and social consequences of medical practices through the dilemmas faced by the protagonist, Trish Edgewater. Trish advises on the donations following the death of her own sister ("she died awake, after twenty days, eleven hours, and fourteen minutes without sleep. Locked flightlessly inside her skull") from the plague.[90]

Similar in its exploration of the social meanings of sleep, Lionel Shriver's 2016 novel *The Mandibles* is an excoriating presentation of the US as it undergoes an economic disaster in the mid twenty-first century. In a world of hyperinflation and the crash of property prices, rich characters can sleep in induced comas as a way to avoid any need to work. With citizens forced to work multiple jobs simply to reach barely minimal living standards, and drugs having been legalised (so that they can be heavily taxed), such 'slumbering' emerges as the "ultimate narcotic". That sleep does not involve costs is additionally part of its attraction: "A pharmaceutical nudge into an indefinite coma was cheap, and a light steady dose allowed for repeated dream cycles. Inert bodies expended negligible energy, so the drips for nutrition and hydration had seldom to be replenished". Given that "the regular turning to prevent pressure sores provided welcome employment for the low skilled", sleep actually becomes a job creator. In Shriver's caustically imagined future, 'rest homes' are now simply "warehouses of the somnambulant, who were only roused and kicked out when their pre-payments were extinguished". Where before the rich saved for pensions, they now hoard their money "with an eye to dozing away as many years of their lives as the savings could buy" in order to avoid the demands of employment in a catastrophic recession.[91]

Kress, Russell and Shriver examine issues of sleep in connection to the private world of family (*The Mandibles* has the subtitle 'A Family 2029–2047', and Mandible is the surname of the dynasty at the centre of the story) and the public world of economics and social (in)cohesion. Crary, reading Emmanuel Levinas' work on insomnia, notes that, for Levinas, insomnia is "neither in public or fully private" and "always hovers between self-absorption and a radical depersonalization", and it is this space of 'hovering' between states, and the physical and cognitive changes that accompany it, that most fit pluralist conceptions of posthumanist states.[92] It is the in-between nature of sleep deprivation that those, like the Nootropics team with their stress on greater work efficiency, want to eradicate. Crary laments the culture of 24/7 work precisely because it seeks to erase what he terms the "shadows and obscurity [...] of alternative temporalities". He continues: "A 24/7 world [...] is a world identical to itself, a world without the shallowest of pasts, and thus in principle without specters. But the homogeneity of the present is an effect of the fraudulent brightness that presumes to extend everywhere and to preempt any mystery or unknowability".[93]

By way of contrast, Crary argues that, "in the context of our own present, sleep can stand for the durability of the social", and that, as such, it "might be analogous to other thresholds at which society could define or protect itself".[94] If, as Crary suggests, contemporary formations of posthumanist work want to negate sleep (as he observes, the "stunning, inconceivable reality is that nothing of value can be extracted from it [...] within the globalist neoliberal paradigm, sleeping is for losers") might disability be one of these social 'thresholds' in which we can reconfigure embodied experience and, as a consequence, the boundaries of selfhood?[95] Within disability, we can read states of embodied difference that exemplify the kind of 'durability' Crary identifies here, understood as social in the broadest sense. What, then, might a disability-inflected reading of sleep and work look like?[96]

A productive disability reading of sleep, and its relation to posthumanist constructions of work, might emerge around axes of reciprocity that Crary identifies, namely "between vulnerability and trust [and] between exposure and care".[97] All four words suggest concepts in which disability is central, both in terms of links to lived experience and as potential points of *critical* departure. A culture of posthumanist work oriented around the pursuit of endless immediacy and efficiency has no place for vulnerability, or the possible selflessness (but also the unpaid labour) inherent in care. What Crary terms the "weakness and inadequacy of human time, with its blurred, meandering textures" is scorned in configurations of work that see the human body as a biohackable platform.[98] But such meanderings can be claimed as critical disability tools, in the ways in which they emphasise the distinctiveness that different bodies and minds produce. The seeming straightforward nature of the Nootrobox team's approach to cognition, noted earlier, namely that it is in effect a process of identifiable physiological function, masks a reality in which many consumers of 'smart' drugs do so for reasons of mental ill health or psychological 'exposure'. An appreciation of the solicitude and interdependencies that surround sleep – watching others sleep, caring about them as this takes place, placing trust in others to watch over us – is another of those activities made richer through its disability connotations.

Though it is rarely read as such, Chuck Palahniuk's iconic 1996 novel *Fight Club* is a narrative about sleep, work and disability, and a text that can productively be read through the terms of Crary's critical axes noted above. In a 2014 article entitled 'Insomnia and Me', Palahniuk spoke both of his own insomnia and its place in the genesis of his most well-known work:

> In 1993, I found myself stranded in Reno, Nevada, with no money and nowhere to stay. At night I wandered sleepless through the empty all-night casinos and restaurants, exhausted, delirious, and inventing a story about a man who thought he had insomnia but was actually living a double life: whenever he thought he was asleep, his alter ego would venture forth to have all the adventures he, himself, could never consciously dare. As the sun rose over the "biggest little city in the world", I had the basic novel written in my head.[99]

For Palahniuk, imagining fights (especially *losing* fights) became a way into sleep: "My long, imaginary fights would be wordless and brutal, and then I'd lose and fall asleep".[100] And while much criticism of the novel has focused on its deployment of ideas of bodies, masculinity and violence, there has been much less on the idea that it is a disability narrative centred around the absence of sleep and the exposure and vulnerabilities that arise from this. Yet sleep is central to the story: "The first time I met Tyler, I was asleep", the narrator says as he attempts to piece together the reality of his self following the novel's central revelation, that "Tyler is a projection. He's a dissociative personality disorder. He's a psychogenic fugue state. Tyler Durden is my hallucination".[101] Continuing, he remembers: "I took a vacation, I fell asleep on the beach and when I woke up there was Tyler Durden", except – as he now realises – "When I fall asleep, I don't really sleep".[102] What appeared as a narrative of insomnia is, in fact, a novel centred on the combination between schizoid disassociation and a lack of sleep.[103] That such a position renders the narrator vulnerable and exposed is clear. While placing his body in the way of violence is a deliberate act, the mechanics and consequences of such actions are unknown. Not knowing the truth of his disassociated, disabled self leaves him in an exposed state of partial understanding, but it is an exposure that we, *as readers*, can use as a lens through which to see a critique of embodied wholeness and the demands of neoliberal work. It is when the narrator is most disassociated that the practices of work cultures he encounters – the exploitation and deception, the lack of opportunities for empowerment – are most laid bare.

Fight Club is also rooted in the idea that the participants in the clubs and their extension, the anarchic 'Project Mayhem', are reconfiguring their identities as *workers*. The forgettable "kid who works in the copy center" becomes memorable when he "kick[s] the air out of an accountant representative twice his size [...] and pound[s] him until the kid had to stop".[104] As the fight clubs develop and spread throughout the US, the narrator finds himself coming across fellow fighters, but almost exclusively in work settings: "Now I go to meetings and conferences and see faces at conference tables, accountants and junior executives or attorneys with broken noses spreading out like an eggplant under the edges of bandages or they have a couple of stitches under an eye or a jaw wired shut".[105] Here, it is the individuals conceived of in terms of *the jobs they do* that is striking; the copy centre kids, accountants, junior executives and attorneys are the host identities, we are told, of the "quiet young men" who eschew sleep to meet and fight in the early hours of the morning. And the looks they exchange ("we nod to each other"), the shared bond of fight club 'membership', articulates an idea of care that, Palahniuk suggests, possesses real value despite its genesis in the splitting of the narrator's consciousness.[106]

Much has been made of *Fight Club*'s representations of bodies and violence as stemming from ultimately fascistic world views. The many variations of this argument can be encapsulated in Robert T. Schultz's assertion that the narrator "is like a Nazi leader" and Tyler "an egotistical maniac who sees himself as a god"; but there are other ways to read the differences of the body that the novel portrays.[107] While I do not agree completely with Olivia Burgess' argument that the novel presents positive possibilities for utopian change, I do think that her assertion that Palahniuk's narrative advances the "body as a marker of possibility" is enabling.[108] Burgess notes that "exhausted bodies [...] *are* the opportunities for change", while she perceptively observes that the Narrator's attempts to combat his chronic insomnia – attending support groups for cancer survivors and the terminally ill – all "revolve around the body in some way: testicular cancer, parasites, brain dysfunction, degenerative bone disease, leukemia".[109] Equally, the stories Tyler Durden tells of his early acts of public disruption – urinating in soups when working as a waiter in high-end restaurants; splicing split-second shots of erect penises and vaginas into films when employed as a projectionist – involve what Burgess calls "the abject lower body" with its "rejected and unwanted waste and excess".[110] Similarly, Marla Singer, the novel's central female protagonist, possesses a body that appears to be always on the point of disintegration. Emaciated, animal-like and with burned, scabbed and cracked skin, Marla states proudly "I embrace my own festering diseased corruption" as she deliberately burns herself in front of the narrator.[111] A character who "never has any fat of her own", Marla imports her mother's collagen to sell on, only for the narrator to then steal it in an anarchist soap-making venture.[112] Whether broken and beaten in the fights themselves, or as represented in associated states of abjection, bodies in *Fight Club* diverge from normative notions of the able-bodied and the values that accompany them. The labour of the bodies in the novel can be read as being inherently a process of disability.

Seen in this way, *Fight Club*'s bodies become a perfect example of Tobin Siebers' theories of complex embodiment. For Siebers, the disabled body not only speaks of an understanding of "the effects of disabling environments on people's lived experience of the body", it also stresses "that some factors affecting disability, such as chronic pain, secondary health effects, and aging, derive from the body".[113]

The complexity here, then, is to see the situated locations of the social processes that produce disabled bodies *and* the physical, somatic bodily difference that arises from human variation. A consequence of this, Siebers notes, is that "complex embodiment theorizes the body and its representations as mutually transformative".[114] As such, the working bodies of *Fight Club,* battered and broken in protest at a capitalistic system against which they rebel, are at one and the same time disabled bodies, marked by physical limitations and a chronic absence of sleep. The combination of the two produces versions of work, masculinity, embodiment and mental health that are more complex than are the case if we leave disability out of the critical frame. The novel's world of work, understood as a *location and culture* of disablement, is opened up through such a reading, and the representation of the narrator's mental health is seen in a more critically informed light as a consequence.

Siebers almost appears to be talking about Palahniuk's novel when, in noting how straightforward it can be to pass from being abled-bodied to being disabled, he notes: "The disabled confront the intolerance of society on a daily basis. In nearly no other sphere of existence, however, do people risk waking up one morning having become the persons [*sic*] whom they hated the day before".[115] The narrator of *Fight Club* does not, in fact, wake to find himself in such a position and Tyler appears as a hero/role model for that section of the narrative when the two identities appear separate; but the realisation that he is *not* waking, but rather that Tyler is the pathological extension of his self, begins the process by which the narrator starts to disassociate himself from Tyler and his 'terrorist' project. It is not 'hatred' maybe, but it is a violent rejection.

In assessing the politics of *Fight Club* as a text it is, however, the terms of this that require scrutiny. The narrator's rejection of Tyler in fact represents a twist away from the kinds of embodied possibilities described above. Upon realising that Tyler is not a separate entity, but rather an extension of his self, the narrator immediately comes to view Tyler's actions as problematic and dangerous: "The second I fall asleep", he observes, "Tyler takes over and something terrible will happen". His subsequent need to "undo the damage" Tyler is seen to cause rewrites the kinds of complex difference as described by Siebers. The narrator's frantic search for the architects of Project Mayhem, to stop their actions, reins in the productive potential suggested in the bodies up to this point in the novel. All of a sudden, the novel's representation of sleep changes. "For years now, I've wanted to fall asleep", the narrator observes, "the sort of slipping off, the giving up, the falling part of sleep. Now sleeping is the last thing I want to do".[116] In needing to "do something to get rid of Tyler", the narrator moves from a disassociated state of sleep-deprived disability to one where the lack of sleep becomes refigured in terms of productivity and action, mobility and knowledge.[117] Where before the novel's bodies and minds suggested possibilities of reconfigured selfhoods, now the need to halt all of Tyler's actions signals a return to ideas of wholeness: "I think fight club has served its purpose", the narrator tells the assembled men at one club meeting, adding "Project Mayhem is canceled [...] This game is over".[118] As it approaches its conclusion, the novel takes a turn towards an ending in which the abject, the deranged and the different body are disavowed. For all that he ends the narrative institutionalised and on medication, the narrator is clear that his excising of Tyler is a rational act that prevents further violence.

Fight Club's turn to restitution keeps its complex and unruly bodies at bay. Although the narrator ends the novel (presumably) in an altered mental state, the drive of the last quarter of the story is towards completion and the resolution of a difference that is ultimately seen to be problematic. As the narrator's desire to shut down Project Mayhem makes clear, such resolution is equally applied to the representation of work. The anarchic work spaces that dominate the majority of the novel are dismantled, replaced by a dramatic finale in which the narrator and Tyler tussle on the roof of a skyscraper as police helicopters hover overhead and Marla appears with "all the people from the support group" to try to prevent the narrator from what appears as suicide.[119] It is a twist on the cliff-hanger ending, with the fight between hero and villain actually the final confrontation of the halves of a schizoid self. Ideas of fracture, splitting or liminality here cannot, however, disguise the novel's wider move towards the attempted reformulation of coherence

If *Fight Club* resorts to (even partial) resolution in its final chapters, Haruki Murakami's short story 'Sleep', from his 1993 collection *The Elephant Vanishes*, refuses such closure. The story begins with the unnamed female narrator stating: "This is my seventeenth straight day without sleep".[120] What she has though, she stresses, is "nothing at all" like insomnia: "I just can't sleep. Not for one second. Aside from that simple fact, I'm perfectly normal. I don't feel sleepy, and my mind is as clear as ever. Clearer, if anything".[121] The narrator lives in a Japanese household in many ways defined by work: her husband is a dentist who is "serious" and "works hard", and her role as wife, mother and homekeeper is presented in terms of work responsibilities: "you've been working too hard", her husband tells her at one point when he notices her behaviour changing.[122] Murakami places his narrator's life (her own and that within her family) firmly within the context of a contemporary Japanese demand for work immediacy and efficiency.

'Sleep' critiques this demand in a number of ways, utilising the language of disability and norms surrounding the idea of the 'working self' to do so. In contrast to the narratives described so far in this chapter, Murakami's story reclaims the ostensibly 'private' world of home as a space of work that it then transforms. As such, it illuminates the limitations of conceptions of work (such as Tomlinson's, noted earlier) that set private against public constructions of labour, revealing especially the ways in which these fail to capture the complexities of gender. The home has, as Silvia Federici has shown, always been a place of women's work, not least of reproduction.[123] Murakami's story captures this, with the narrator gradually withdrawing from her regular work routine and the attention she pays to her husband to rather obsessively read. She reads and rereads *Anna Karenina* ("as many times as I could"), an engagement with a famous narrative of marital conflict that illuminates her growing awareness of the restrictions of her own relationship, before moving on to Dostoyevsky, and all the time "I could read book after book with utter concentration and never tire. I could understand the most difficult passages without effort. And I responded with deep emotion".[124] Rather than these total levels of concentration, undisturbed by sleep, being evidence for some kind of biohacking perfection, however, the narrator begins to understand her housework as "chores I perform day after day like an unfeeling machine [...] Push the buttons. Pull the levers. Pretty soon, reality just flows off and away. The same physical movements over and over".[125] Here it is reading, the consuming desire for which is produced by the absence of sleep, which causes the narrator to recognise the 'non-human' manner of her daily work. But within a context of normalised capitalism and the pattern of work the story otherwise reproduces, reading is, of course, an activity that is unproductive. The narrator's reading transforms her sense of herself but adds nothing to the sense of her marriage and family being a (conventionally understood) *working* unit.

While such a critique of gendered work is a subtle unpicking of some of the core constituents of Japanese society, it is the story's associated concentration on bodily difference that provides a specific link between sleep, work and disability. A striking feature of the narrative is the way in which, as her time without sleep develops, the narrator becomes absorbed by the idea that her body is transforming. She finds that she has broken "the connection between my mind and my body [...] While my body went about its business, my mind floated in its own inner space. I ran the house without a thought in my head, feeding snacks to my son, chatting to my husband". Increasingly, this mind/body division leads her to revise her notion of her own reality as a worker:

> After I gave up sleeping, it occurred to me what a simple thing reality is, how easy it is to make it work. It's just reality. Just housework. Just a home. Like running a simple machine. Once you learn to run it, it's just a matter of repetition. You push this button and pull that lever. You adjust the gauge, put on the lid, set the timer. The same thing, over and over.[126]

Intriguingly, this process of becoming-machine ("No matter how mechanically I worked", she observes, "no one noticed that I had changed") is matched by a growing obsession the narrator has with the uncanny nature of bodies, and especially faces.[127] While walking around her home at night she finds herself staring at her reflection in the bathroom: "I would look at my face in the bathroom mirror – just look at it for fifteen minutes at a time, my mind a total blank. I'd stare at my face purely as a physical object, and gradually it would disconnect from the rest of me, becoming just some thing that happened to exist at the same time as myself".[128] This body dysmorphia intensifies as the narrator continues to go without sleep. She finds herself frozen in a dream, unable to move her limbs, and then focuses on a "mistlike something, hung there inside my body like a certain kind of potential", before asserting that "I wanted to purge my body of something by exercising it to the limit" but adding: "Purge it – of what?"[129] Finally, another encounter with her reflected self in front of the mirror leads her to "discover that my body appeared to be almost bursting with vitality" without "the slightest hint of excess flesh". Following this surprise, she "sat down and looked at my face for a good thirty minutes. I studied it from all angles, objectively [...] What was happening to me?"[130] Without sleep, and with a transforming attitude towards the patterns of work that have come to define her sense of self, the narrator enters a space where bodies, and the meanings applied to them, appear to shift.[131] For Murakami's narrator, any number of totalities – especially those connected to family, responsibility and self-image can no longer be taken for granted. 'Sleep' is very much a narrative in which assumed meanings and values can be seen to lose their attachment to the norms through which they might be understood to operate.

In the story, the narrator's dysmorphic gaze extends to her immediate family. She finds herself unable to apprehend her husband's body: "How long had it been – years? – since the last time I had studied his face as he slept?" she asks one night while watching her husband; and continues:

> So there I stood, looking at him sleeping as soundly as always. One bare foot stuck out from under the covers at a strange angle – so strange that the foot could have belonged to someone else. It was a big, chunky foot. My husband's mouth hung open, the lower lip drooping [...] There was something vulgar about the way his eyes were closed, the lids slack, covers made of faded human flesh. He looked like an absolute fool! [...] How incredibly ugly! He sleeps with such an ugly face! It's just too gruesome, I thought.[132]

This slippage of affection extends to her son – "something about my son's face annoyed me" she observes at one point, before noting: "And then it hit me. What bothered me about my son's sleeping face was that it looked exactly like my husband's [...] Stubborn, self-satisfied". The revelation is, it appears, conclusive: "This little boy is a stranger to me, finally. Even after he grows up, he'll never be able to understand me, just as my husband can hardly understand what I feel now".[133] The blank, posthumanised faces that appear at the start of the story become signifiers of strange alienation by the end. The intersection of an absence of sleep, a revision of notions of work, and the perception of body-as-machine/body-as-other, makes for a haunting narrative in which any concept of self is highly unstable.

Murakami ends 'Sleep' in a manner that appears to point to the idea of sleep as a mysterious, unknowable entity. Wearing her husband's cap and performing yet another body shift through her choice of clothes – "I look like a boy" – the narrator goes out for a night drive. She sees the road full of people on their way to work, "Those guys don't sleep at night. They sleep in the daytime and work at night for greater efficiency", and feels she has joined their ranks, her new state meaning she has moved beyond biology and nature: "I'm beyond that. A priori. An evolutionary leap. A woman who never sleeps. An expansion of consciousness".[134] But this seeming connection to a state of 'greater efficiency' is destroyed when her stationary car comes under attack from a crowd of men. Unable to get out, the narrator finishes the story "locked inside this little box, I can't go anywhere. It's the middle of the night. The men keep rocking the car back and forth. They're going to turn it over".[135] The ambiguity is challenging. Is this a reminder of the brutal power of conventional gender roles and a reversion to a former state (the 'little box')? Is it punishment for hubris? The product of a sleep-deprived mind? A reminder of the inherent precariousness that comes with difference? Whichever way the ending is read, it appears that, ultimately, the belief that sleeplessness is indeed some form of posthumanist evolutionary leap, or indeed any coherent activity, is a delusion. Murakami challenges us to configure precisely what sleep, and its absence, might mean.

The complexities of 'Sleep' present the non-sleeping state as a space of blurred boundaries, thresholds and ambiguities. Murakami's unstable bodies, wild spaces and the threats to the recognition of the familiar that the story presents can all be understood as the workings of a creative aesthetic that match the hovering indistinctness that Crary finds and celebrates in Levinas. The narrator of 'Sleep' is in many ways empowered by the world she finds when she fails to sleep, but – as the end of the story displays – she is also rendered acutely vulnerable. When Crary outlines the reciprocities of the vulnerability/trust and exposure/care axes he notes that they articulate "the cohesion of social relationships [that] come together around the issue of sleep".[136] 'Sleep' functions in precisely such terms of the troubled reciprocity surrounding relationships and cohesion. The story's critique of a rigid and gendered culture of work comes in the shifting uncertainties of bodies and minds that fill the narrator's waking nights. Crucially, the story ends in such a vulnerable and exposed space, unlike *Fight Club* with its desire for an individual-centred (however split) resolution. Its aesthetics stress the provisional nature of both sleeping *and* wakefulness; what the body or mind means, and what it might do, hover in a liminal difference.

Conclusion: mundane work

2017 and 2018 saw the publication of a slew of publications that showcased an ongoing obsession with how people sleep. The most prominent of these was neuroscientist Matthew Walker's book *Why We Sleep: The New Science of Sleep and Dreams*. For Walker, sleep is first and foremost about embodiment. A 24-hour circadian rhythm, the nightly release of melatonin and growth hormone, and the extent of blood sugar levels, brain cell regeneration and structures of memory are only some of the ways in which the body and sleep interact. Equally, Walker shows how type 2 diabetes, Alzheimer's disease, heart attacks and cancer are all more likely in individuals who are sleep deprived.

At every turn, *Why We Sleep* returns to the body, foregoing discussions of psychology and lifestyle for detailed analysis of brain activity and bodily response.[137]

Walker's study is also one focused on time. It is the different times within sleep, particularly the relationship between REM and NREM, that regulate health. Understanding this allows for a consideration of sleep as a way in which different bodies pace themselves – how disability and sleep are linked. The sleep experienced by many people with autism for example, works to different rhythms than those who are not autistic, while research into sleep disorders in both adults and children with cystic fibrosis shows that obstructive sleep apnea is common. There are numerous other disabilities that necessitate different patterns of sleep across the 24 hours of the day.

The promise of an automated work future is that it will provide 24/7 productivity; robots, after all, do not sleep. In this dizzying imagining of a hyper-efficient future, compliant technologies simply respond to commands and create employment environments of desirable monotony (it is noticeable that such visions rarely consider the limitations of such technologies or their inability to perform functions). At the end of *24/7*, Crary posits that sleep can be the condition that counters the overwhelming acceleration and intensification of technological labour. Sleep harbours the promise of what he terms a "radical interruption [...] a refusal of the unsparing weight of our global present". This might, he notes, look towards a "future other than barbarism or the post-human".[138] Crary's equation of these two states is telling: the posthuman is, he feels, a danger, potentially a carrier of those processes of technological change that will irreparably alter humanity. Within his humanism, however, there is a disability logic. Crary even uses the word "disabled" to describe those last moments before sleep: "the lying awake in quasi-darkness, waiting indefinitely for the desired loss of consciousness". He continues: "During this suspended time, there is a recovery of perceptual capacities that are disabled or disregarded during the day".[139] The word 'disabled' here is positive; a process of accessing a liminal space in which norms, both those of the body and the pressures of societies that shape those bodies, do not apply. Within this state, we access "the most mundane level of every experience", a level that "can always rehearse the outlines of what more consequential renewals and beginnings might be".[140]

It is only a partial against-the-grain reading that can characterise Crary's vision of the future as a space of disability. As this book has argued all along, the mundane and ordinary are sites of disability presence, and often critique. The mundane levels of the everyday are the spaces where experiences take place, both those of disability and not. They are the grounded actuations of what Mitchell, Antebi and Snyder term the *matter* of disability, locations of materiality and affect that provide "evidence of embodiment's shifting, kaleidoscopic, dynamically unfolding agency".[141] These include work in all its manifestations, from the banal to the profound, but as we are reminded here, the disabled body in particular calls into question, through its nonnormative agency, the 'naturalness' of late capitalism's creation of work cultures. What Mitchell and Snyder elsewhere term the "social relationships indicative of an evolving society of control" are pivotal in the establishment of contemporary labour formations, but the "strategic fluidity" of disability presence, both individual and collective, allows for the "disability countercultural formations" that challenge the seemingly inevitability of such worlds.[142]

This chapter has shown how a certain posthumanist idea of work threatens to eclipse difference and extend the boundaries that limit employment for many people with disabilities. But it has also promoted disability as a disruption of these process, a pushing back against practices of technological uniformity. The texts examined here unpick assumptions in which technology 'marches' into the future. They suggest a derailing, a pulling off the tracks or the change of the beat that guides such a march. Disability work will continue and the pace it creates will be within a time of its own making.

Notes

1 See, for example, a leader in *The Economist* in June 2016: 'March of the machines: what history tells us about the future of artificial intelligence – and how society should respond', www.economist.com/leaders/2016/06/25/march-of-the-machines. Accessed January 6, 2017. The metaphors are used more widely across other forms of publications. See, for example, Martin Ford, *The Rise of the Robots: Technology and the Threat of Mass Unemployment* (London: Oneworld, 2015) and Thomas Rid, *Rise of the Machines: The Lost History of Cybernetics* (Melbourne and London: Scribe, 2016).

2 'The Guardian view on robots and humanity: passing Go'. March 9, 2016, www.theguardian.com/commentisfree/2016/mar/09/the-guardian-view-on-robots-and-humanity-passing-go. Accessed March 27, 2016.

3 Minsoo Kang, *Sublime Dreams of Living Machines: The Automaton in the European Imagination* (Cambridge, MA: Harvard University Press, 2011), pp. 21 and 13.

4 See Despina Kakoudaki, *Anatomy of a Robot: Literature, Cinema and the Cultural Work of Artificial People* (New Brunswick, NJ and London: Rutgers University Press, 2014), pp. 134–140 for a specific discussion of robots and work in Čapek's play.

5 Ben Tarnoff, 'Robots won't just take our jobs – they'll make the rich even richer', *The Guardian*, March 2, 2017, www.theguardian.com/technology/2017/mar/02/robot-tax-job-elimination-livable-wage. Accessed March 4, 2017. A more balanced and less dramatic account of technology in the development of twenty-first century work can be found in Ryan Avent, *The Wealth of Humans: Work and its Absence in the Twenty-First Century* (London: Penguin, 2017), though Avent still frames his arguments within the "belief in the capacity of humanity" to oversee the development of new worlds of work (p. 241).

6 A standard narrative of human superiority over robots and A.I. is common in contemporary fictional explorations of the interaction between the two, whether humans overcoming a global robot uprising in Daniel H. Wilson's 2011 novel *Robopocalypse*, or the more mundane exploration of robots, relationships and society in Ian McEwan's 2019 *Machines Like Me*. The novels are very different, both in terms of content and style, but united by a core humanist conviction in human superiority manifested in both the nature of human actions and (crucially) the ability of humans alone to control the meaning of the story that emerges from the engagement with emerging technologies. (In relation to the above note, it is worth observing that McEwan's novel touches briefly on the idea of taxing robots when central character Charlie has Adam, his robot, take over his stock market speculation and, through knowledge of A.I. systems, substantially increase Charlie's income.)

7 Ford, *The Rise of the Robots*, pp. 6 and 27.

8 Kathi Weeks, *The Problem with Work: Feminism, Marxism, Antiwork Politics, and Postwork Imaginaries* (Durham, NC and London, 2011), p. 12.

9 Nick Srnicek and Alex Williams, *Inventing the Future: Postcapitalism and a World Without Work*, revised ed. (London: Verso, 2016), p. 109.

10 Ford, *The Rise of the Robots*, pp. 161–165.

11 Stewart Dakers, 'A robot carer? No thanks – we still need the human touch', www.theguardian.com/society/2015/sep/01/robot-carer-human-paro-seal. Accessed February 27, 2017.

12 See Illah Reza Nourbakhsh's *Robot Futures* for a thoughtful assessment of the topic from a roboticist's point of view. In a powerful metaphor, Nourbakhsh describes a "robot smog" that will descend on contemporary societies driven by technological change. "Whether or not the mass of robots that comprose our robot smog will be members of a single megacolony is open to debate", he observes. "But what is certain is that our robot smog will have massive connectivity with itself and with the information superstructure of the digital world". Nourbakhsh, *Robot Futures* (Cambridge, MA: MIT Press, 2013), p. 42.

13 Susan Wendell, *The Rejected Body* (New York: Routledge, 1996), pp. 35–38; and 'Unhealthy disabled: treating chronic illnesses as disabilities', *Hypatia* 16, no. 4 (2001).

14 Alison Kafer, *Feminist, Queer, Crip* (Bloomington and Indianapolis: Indiana University Press, 2013), p. 27. See also Margaret Price, 'The bodymind problem and the possibilities of pain', *Hypatia* 30, no. 1 (2015), pp. 268–284.

15 Jonathan Crary, *24/7: Late Capitalism and the Ends of Sleep* (Cambridge: Verso, 2014), p. 8.

16 Robert Hassan, *Empires of Speed: Time and the Acceleration of Politics and Society* (Leiden and Boston, MA: Brill, 2009), pp. 7–8 and 17.

17 John Tomlinson, *The Culture of Speed: The Coming of Immediacy* (London: Sage, 2007), p. 158.
18 For an idiosyncratically personal and conservatively humanist analysis of the speed of contemporary life at the end of the twentieth century, see Stephen Bertram's *Hyperculture: The Human Cost of Speed* (Westport, CT: Praeger, 1998). For Bertram, "the explosion of technology" is part of a "warp speed [that] disengages us from the past" and "plunges us towards the future". It transforms (as Bertram's chapter titles attest) the individual, the family, social, democracy, the environment and international relations. Bertram's concerns about the future echo those of Francis Fukuyama, *Our Posthuman Future* (analysed in Chapter 1). "We must", Bertram asserts, "reassert control over technology [and] look beyond the artificiality and impermanence we have created to recapture a sense of what is natural, enduring and true". Bertram, *Hyperculture*, pp. 2–3 and 194.
19 Crary, *24/7*, p. 9.
20 Such a world is critiqued in the biting satire of Douglas Coupland's 1995 novel *Microserfs*, in which a group of Microsoft employees largely fail to avoid work dominating their lives through the kind of feudal relationship suggested by the book's title. Coupland's novel, set in the early 1990s, is one of the first to anticipate the kind of posthuman work environment that has developed with the digital age. Coupland returned to the idea (and form – both novels intersperse chunks of code, emails, lists and data readings with 'standard' prose; both are written on the central characters' laptops) of the novel in the 2006 *JPod*, which follows a group of video game programmers brought together within an intense and dominating work culture.
21 See Ian James, *Paul Virilio* (London and New York: Routledge), pp. 29–44.
22 Paul Virilio, *The Administration of Fear*, with Bertrand Richard, trans Ames Hodges (Los Angeles, CA: Semiotext(e), 2012), p. 69.
23 John Armitage (ed.), *Virilio Live: Selected Interviews* (London: Sage, 2001), pp. 97–98.
24 See Paul Virilio, *The Lost Dimension*, trans. D. Moshenburg (New York: Semiotext(e), 1991) and *The Vision Machine*, trans J. Rose (London: British Film Institute, 1994); Rosi Braidotti, *The Posthuman* (Cambridge: Polity, 2013), pp. 89–95.
25 Virilio, *The Lost Dimension*, p. 84.
26 Hassan, *Empires of Speed*, p. 23; Tomlinson, *The Culture of Speed*, p. 88.
27 Arthur Kroker, *Exits to the Posthuman Future* (Cambridge: Polity, 2014), pp. 11–12.
28 Kroker, *Exits to the Posthuman Future*, pp. 15–16.
29 Wendell, *The Rejected Body*, p. 37; Kafer, *Feminist, Queer, Crip*, p. 27.
30 David T. Mitchell with Sharon L. Snyder, *The Biopolitics of Disability: Neoliberalism, Ablenationalism, and Peripheral Embodiment* (Ann Arbor: University of Michigan Press, 2015), pp. 211, 214 and 216. The authors outline that: "Nonproductive bodies are those inhabitants of the planet who, largely by virtue of (in)capacity, aesthetic nonconformity, and/or nonnormative labor patterns, have gone invisible due to the inflexibility of traditional classifications of labor (both economical and political. They represent the nonlaboring populations – not merely excluded from, but also resistant to, standardized labor demands of productivity particular to neoliberalism" (p. 211).

31 Robert McRuer, *Crip Times: Disability, Globalization, and Resistance* (New York: New York University Press, 2018), p. 54.
32 World Health Organisation, *World Report on Disability* (WHO, 2011), p. 235.
33 *World Report on Disability*, p. 240.
34 *World Report on Disability*, p. 251.
35 Katharine Quarmby, *Scapegoat: Why We Are Failing Disabled People* (London: Portobello Books), p. 226.
36 There are many histories of the development of disability through patterns of employment, but Sarah F. Rose's *No Right to Be Idle: The Invention of Disability, 1840s–1930s* (Chapel Hill: The University of North Carolina Press, 2017) is a stand-out text. Though focused on the US, its examination of the ways in which those constructed as 'disabled' became separated from the category of 'worker' during the development of industrial modernity has wide applicability. As Rose observes, a "perfect storm" of "changes in family capacity, the rapidly evolving labor market, public policies that sought to deter dependency, and the mutability and complexity of disability itself" resulted in bodies that "were now deemed unproductive, or insufficiently productive, by employers and lawmakers". A result, she notes, is that "the common twentieth-century notion of equating 'disability' with unproductivity, poor citizenship, and dependency on public or charitable assistance was, truly, an invention" (p. 13).
37 Pramod Nayar, *Posthumanism* (Cambridge: Polity, 2014), p. 10.
38 Hassan, *Empires of Speed*, p. 19.
39 Hassan, *Empires of Speed*, pp. 19–20.
40 Thomas Hylland Eriksen, *Tyranny of the Moment: Fast and Slow Time in the Information Age* (London: Pluto, 2011).
41 Nootrobox, 'The Complete Full Stack' and 'The Biohacker's Guide', https://nootrobox.com. Accessed January 23, 2017.
42 Alex Morris, 'The pill freaks of Silicon Valley', *New York Magazine*, October 19, 2016, https://www.scribd.com/article/327687787/The-Pill-Freaks-Of-Silicon-Valley. Accessed December 6, 2016.
43 See https://hvmn.com/sprint (accessed November 12, 2018). An earlier 2017 description of SPRINT asserted that it produced "higher-order cognitive work", though this term has now disappeared from the product description.
44 Morris, 'The pill freaks of Silicon Valley'.
45 Michael Davidson, *Concerto for the Left Hand: Disability and the Defamiliar Body* (Ann Arbor: The University of Michigan Press, 2008), p. 4.
46 Joshua Ferris, *The Unnamed* (London: Penguin, 2010), p. 33.
47 Peter Ferry writes on Ferris' novel in terms of masculinity, New York and the tradition of the flâneur (which he terms "the definitive figure of the post-modern age") in 'Reading Manhattan. Reading masculinity. Reintroducing the flaneur in E.B. White's *Here is New York* and Joshua Ferris' *The Unnamed*', *Culture, Society and Masculinities* 3, no. 1 (2011), pp. 49–61. The idea of Farnsworth lost in an unknowable and unnameable crisis surely owes much to the link between Ferris' title and Samuel Beckett's 1953 novel *The Unnameable*. Beckett's famous ending – "I can't go on, you must go on [...] you must go on, I can't go one, I'll go on" – frames ideas not only of Farnworth's walking, but also the contested meaning attached to it. Samuel Beckett, *Three Novels: Molloy, Malone Dies, The Unnameable* (New York: Grove Press, 2009),

p. 407. For Marina Ludwigs, "Tim's uncontrollable leg and [...] resisting mind" enact a mind-body division that "taps into the heart of narrativity [...] the text's metanarrative emphasis throws light on the captivating and irresistible nature of narrative desire". Ludwigs, 'Walking as a metaphor for narrativity', *Studia Neophilologica* 87 (2015), p. 116.

48 Ferris, *The Unnamed*, p. 126.
49 Ferris, *The Unnamed*, p. 41.
50 Ferris, *The Unnamed*, p. 24.
51 Ferris, *The Unnamed*, p. 37.
52 Ferris, *The Unnamed*, p. 103.
53 In an interview he gave the week before *The Unnamed* was published, Ferris reflected on New York not only as an environment for his fiction but as a place itself for his own work. The city, he says, is "a very nurturing place, but the work itself is at odds with that impulse because the work itself requires so much time and attention". And, in an interesting link between his own working practice and an explicit disability frame of reference, he goes on: "The city is a guarantor of ADD, and you have to be steeled against your worst impulses". See Tara Atkinson with Joshua Ferris, 'Vacuuming the Whole House and Where Do We Go Now: A conversation with Joshua Ferris', *The Iowa Review* 40, no. 2 (2010), p. 127.
54 Ferris, *The Unnamed*, p. 129.
55 Ferris, *The Unnamed*, pp. 34–35.
56 Ferris, *The Unnamed*, p. 36.
57 Ferris, *The Unnamed*, p. 63.
58 Andrew Tate, *Apocalyptic Fiction* (London: Bloomsbury, 2017), p. 88.
59 Ferris, *The Unnamed*, p. 310.
60 Ferris, *The Unnamed*, p. 117.
61 For more on ideas of 'the national' in Ferris' work more generally, see Ruth Maxey, 'National stories and narrative voice in the fiction of Joshua Ferris', *Critique: Studies in Contemporary Fiction* 57, no. 2 (2016), pp. 208–216.
62 Tate, *Apocalyptic Fiction*, p. 88.
63 Michael Faber, *Under the Skin* (Edinburgh: Canongate, 2014), p. 64.
64 Faber, *Under the Skin*, p. 127.
65 Faber, *Under the Skin*, p. 232.
66 Faber, *Under the Skin*, pp. 64, 284, and 88.
67 There is not sufficient space here to properly analyse *Under the Skin* as much as I would have liked in terms of either gender or (thinking through the resonances of 'alien') race. It is clear that there is a process of 'becoming-woman' in Faber's novel, as it is only in the scene of the car crash at the end that a vodsel is noticeably and continually described as "female" and "a woman", in a move that suggests that Isserley's slow learning has reached at a point where she identifies – through the woman who comes to her aid – a possible emerging gender of her own. Equally, the novel's many descriptions of skin, fur and bodily difference invite a critical race reading that offers more evidence of its productive aesthetic strategies.
68 Faber, *Under the Skin*, p. 75.
69 Faber, *Under the Skin*, p. 65.
70 Faber, *Under the Skin*, p. 88.
71 Tomlinson, *The Culture of Speed*, p. 147.

72 Faber, *Under the Skin*, p. 234.
73 Faber, *Under the Skin*, p. 174.
74 Faber, *Under the Skin*, p. 97.
75 See Mel Chen, *Animacies: Biopolitics, Racial Mattering, and Queer Affect* (Durham, NC and London: Duke University Press, 2012); Pramod Nayar, *Posthumanism* (Cambridge: Polity, 2014), pp. 77–99; Cary Wolfe, *What is Posthumanism?* (Minneapolis and London: Minnesota University of Minnesota Press, 2010), pp. 99–144; and Wolfe, *Animal Rites: American Culture, the Discourse of Species, and Posthumanist Theory* (Chicago, IL: University of Chicago Press, 2013).
76 Sarah Dillon, '"It's a question of words, therefore": becoming-animal in Michael Faber's *Under the Skin*', *Science Fiction Studies* 38, no. 1 (2011), pp. 134–154. Dillon characterises the novel as being 'science fiction', although Faber has expressed reservations about the label. For more on the relationship between posthumanism, science fiction and disability, see Elaine Graham, *Representations of the Post/human: Monsters, Aliens and Others in Popular Culture* (Manchester: University of Manchester Press, 2002); Neil Badmington, *Alien Chic: Posthumanism and the Other Within* (London and New York: Routledge, 2004); Kathryn Allan (ed.), *Disability in Science Fiction: Representations of Technology as Cure* (New York: Palgrave Macmillan, 2013): Lars Schmeink, *Biopunk Dystopias: Genetic Engineering, Society and Science Fiction* (Liverpool: Liverpool University Press, 2016); as well as my analyses of Becky Chambers' writing in Chapter 2.
77 Dillon, 'It's a question of words', p. 143.
78 Faber, *Under the Skin*, p. 296.
79 Faber, *Under the Skin*, p. 296.
80 Faber, *Under the Skin*, p. 295.
81 Tomlinson, *The Culture of Speed*, p. 149.
82 See Eriksen, *Tyranny of the Moment* pp. 147–164; and Bertram, *Hyperculture*.
83 Ellen Samuels, *Fantasies of Identification: Disability, Gender, Race* (New York: New York University Press, 2014).
84 Alison Kafer, *Feminist, Queer, Crip* (Bloomington and Indianapolis: Indiana University Press, 2013), p. 11; N. Katherine Hayles, *How We Became Posthuman: Virtual Bodies in Cybernetics, Literature and Informatics* (Chicago, IL: The University of Chicago Press, 1999), p. 286.
85 Hayles, *How We Became Posthuman*, p. 287.
86 Crary, *24/7*, p. 23.
87 Nolan's film has fun with names. As well as that of Pacino's character, the Alaskan town at the heart of the narrative is called Nightmute.
88 Nancy Kress, *Beggars in Spain* (Rockville, MD: Phoenix Pick/Arc Manor, 1991), p. 92. Kress' story was originally published, in 1991, in *Isaac Asimov's Science Fiction Magazine*. Kress subsequently revised the text and published it as a stand-alone text in 1993 as well as producing two sequels: *Beggars and Choosers* (1994) and *Beggars Ride* (1996).
89 Kress, *Beggars in Spain*, p. 113.
90 Karen Russell, *Sleep Donation* (Atavist Books, 2014, Kindle. EBook).
91 Lionel Shriver, *The Mandibles: A Family, 2029–2047* (London: Borough Press, 2017), p. 418.
92 Crary, *24/7*, p. 19.

93 Crary, *24/7*, p. 19.
94 Crary, *24/7*, p. 25.
95 Crary, *24/7*, pp. 11 and 14.
96 It has to be noted that Crary's withering critique of contemporary constructions of sleep maintains a degree of nostalgia for an analogue age. He observes that "the uncertain status of sleep has to be understood in relation to the particular dynamic of modernity which has invalidated any organization of reality into binary complementaries" and that "sleep is now an experience cut loose from notions of necessity or nature". For the most part, the book presupposes a coherent self that has lost meaning as sleep has been eroded and for all of the sharp insight, especially around the development of global technologies, there are humanist structures to his arguments. Even with his use of cultural theorists who are central to much posthumanist thinking, such as Deleuze, Crary is pulled towards the idea of a more 'natural' time for sleep and notion of health, for all that such time contained innumerable other health hazards (pp. 12–13).
97 Crary, *24/7*, p. 28.
98 Crary, *24/7*, p. 29.
99 Chuck Palahniuk, 'Insomnia and me', *The Guardian*, April 19, 2014, www.theguardian.com/lifeandstyle/2014/apr/19/chuck-palahniuk-struggles-insomnia. Accessed March 27, 2015.
100 Palahniuk, 'Insomnia and me'.
101 Chuck Palahniuk, *Fight Club* (London: Vintage, 2006), pp. 172 and 168.
102 Palahniuk, *Fight Club*, p. 173.
103 David Fincher's 1999 film version of *Fight Club* prioritises the question of sleep at the outset of the narrative, with the narrator remarking "For 6 months I couldn't sleep" in the film's first few minutes. He then visits a doctor seeking medication, only to be told "you need healthy, natural sleep".
104 Palahniuk, *Fight Club*, pp. 48–49.
105 Palahniuk, *Fight Club*, p. 54.
106 Palahniuk, *Fight Club*, both p. 54.
107 Robert T. Schultz, 'White guys who prefer not to: from passive resistance ("Bartleby") to terrorist acts (*Fight Club*)', *The Journal of Popular Culture* 44, no. 3 (2011), pp. 593–594.
108 Olivia Burgess, 'Revolutionary bodies in Chuck Palahniuk's *Fight Club*', *Utopian Studies* 23, no. 1 (2012), p. 271.
109 Burgess, 'Revolutionary bodies', p. 267 (emphasis in original) and pp. 270–271.
110 Burgess, 'Revolutionary bodies', pp. 271–272.
111 Palahniuk, *Fight Club*, p. 65.
112 Palahniuk, *Fight Club*, p. 91.
113 Tobin Siebers, *Disability Theory* (Ann Arbor: University of Michigan Press, 2008), p. 25.
114 Siebers, *Disability Theory*, p. 25.
115 Siebers, *Disability Theory*, p. 26.
116 Palahniuk, *Fight Club*, all p. 181.
117 Palahniuk, *Fight Club*, p. 182.
118 Palahniuk, *Fight Club*, p. 178.
119 Palahniuk, *Fight Club*, p. 204.

120 Haruki Murakami, 'Sleep' in *The Elephant Vanishes* (London: Vintage, 2003), p. 74.
121 Murakami, 'Sleep', p. 76.
122 Murakami, 'Sleep', pp. 105 and 93.
123 Silvia Federici, *Revolution at Point Zero: Housework, Reproduction and Feminist Struggle* (Oakland, CA: PM Press, 2012). Federici's analysis is particularly astute in its exploration of the sexual division of labour and its place in developing global practices. Her focus on care work and the elderly is especially pertinent to Murakami's story and to disability readings more widely: see 'On Elder Care Work and the Limits of Marxism', pp. 115–125.
124 Murakami, 'Sleep', p. 101.
125 Murakami, 'Sleep', p. 99.
126 Murakami, 'Sleep', p. 96.
127 Murakami, 'Sleep', p. 96.
128 Murakami, 'Sleep', p. 81.
129 Murakami, 'Sleep', p. 93.
130 Murakami, 'Sleep', p. 97.
131 Murakami's narrator can here be seen to link to Isserley's views on her body in *Under the Skin*. As both characters come to increasingly inhabit similar solitary spaces, they experience a change in how they see their bodies in relation to the new parameters of their work environments.
132 Murakami, 'Sleep', pp. 102–103.
133 Murakami, 'Sleep', pp. 104 and 105.
134 Murakami, 'Sleep', pp. 106–107.
135 Murakami, 'Sleep', p. 109.
136 Crary, *24/7*, p. 28.
137 Matthew Walker, *Why We Sleep: The New Science of Sleep and Dreams* (London: Penguin, 2017). See pp. 109–111, 114–115, 157–163, 169–171 and 183–186.
138 Crary, *24/7*, p. 128.
139 Crary, *24/7*, p. 126.
140 Crary, *24/7*, pp. 12, 8.
141 David T. Mitchell, Susan Antebi and Sharon L. Snyder, 'Introduction' in Mitchell, Antebi and Snyder (eds), *The Matter of Disability: Materiality, Biopolitics, Crip Affect* (Ann Arbor: University of Michigan Press, 2019), p. 2.
142 Mitchell and Snyder, *The Biopolitics of Disability*, p. 216.

Conclusion: On Not Wanting to End

The theoretical physicist Stephen Hawking died in March 2018. Later that year a collection of his essays, entitled *Brief Answers to the Big Questions*, was published.[1] The topics covered in the book ranged from the theological to the cosmological, exploring issues relating to – among others – technology, philosophy and the environment. It seemed somehow fitting that a visionary scientist whose life's work involved considering the nature of the universe should be able to speak from beyond the grave; and not only speak, but consider the future of artificial intelligence, life on earth and the very trajectory of humanity. Here was an intelligence – a "rare genius" as proclaimed on the back of the book – evidencing one last example of its precocity.

Hawking was, of course, a disability icon, possibly the most effective public figure in rebutting the idea that to have a disability was to be all-pervasively associated with loss or lack. Hawking's disabled body was so *obvious*, so visceral. His story appeared to be primarily one of physical decline, from his diagnosis with amyotrophic lateral sclerosis aged 21 in 1963 to the recognisable later figure in a wheelchair communicating through voice-assisted communication technology. But the disability went hand in hand with and did not restrict the intelligence and achievement, something felt by a public that would self-admittedly never understand Hawking's research. Later, Hawking became a celebrated figure, featuring in *The Simpsons* and *The Big Bang Theory* as an emblematic representation of scientific capabilities, while his life was dramatised in the 2014 feature *The Theory of Everything*. The voice produced by his speech technology became his own voice, owned in the same way as his body was clearly *his* body. Hawking's combination of technology and selfhood was an exemplary disability narrative in terms of his embodiment, first and foremost about everyday life; but it was revelatory in the way it carried the presence of that embodiment into recognition of his intellectual achievement. His body became the site in which disability met 'rare genius'.

To call Hawking a cyborg or posthuman figure during his life seemed almost diminishing, an objectifying gaze that lacks recognition of his intelligence, possibly even a dehumanising process.[2] While this might be true, much of his experience as an adult was that of an interaction between human and technology, involving personal and intimate acts, and the kinds of issues surrounding access and mobility common to millions of people with disability. If a term such as cyborg can have the breathless excitement stripped away from it, then there is much to see in Hawking's life as evidence of the intersection between disability and emerging technology, an experiential articulation of something that might correctly be identified as 'posthuman'. If such a view is contentious, however, it does not take much of a critical twist or linguistic sleight-of-hand to see the posthumous publication of *Brief Answers to the Big Questions* as an obviously posthumanist event: Hawking pontificating on the 'big questions' from an after-human position, new knowledge still evident despite his death.

The book's essay on whether artificial intelligence will "outsmart us" rehearses a familiar rewards vs risks argument about a future increasingly shaped by A.I. There may well be, Hawking observes, "no physical law precluding particles from being organised in ways that perform even more advanced computations than the arrangement of particles in human brains", while he also notes that "AI can augment our existing intelligence to open up advances in every area of science and society". But, he goes on, "the concern is that AI would take off on its own and redesign itself at an ever-increasing rate. Humans, who are limited by slow biological evolution, couldn't compete and would be superseded".[3] There are few details of future technologies in the essay (in one Hawking says he believes that "the future of communication is brain–computer interfaces" and he observes that his disabilities mean that he finds "appealing" the possibility of "creating realistic digital surrogates of ourselves") and it concludes with an appeal to generic wisdom: "Our future is a race between the growing power of our technology and the wisdom with which we use it. Let's make sure that wisdom wins".[4]

For all that *Brief Answers to the Big Questions* is a posthumous publication, Hawking's writing skirts around the idea of endings, possibly sensibly given his knowledge of an expanding universe. His view of the future is that it is to be approached with caution, that humanity needs to trust in science and should be guided by appropriate competence and the best capacity of human judgment. To those transhumanists eager for technologies that counter ageing, boost intelligence or create hyperable bodies, Hawking is perhaps a disappointment, especially because his intelligence is exactly the kind of quality they would wish to preserve and subsequently learn from. The transhumanist strand of posthumanism abhors endings, unless they are the ending of what they consider to be the ignorance of the present.

Such perspectives on the problematic ending of life appear to be increasingly common. In *To Be A Machine,* Mark O'Connell travels to the Alcor Life Extension Foundation in the Sonoran Desert in Arizona to meet Max and Natasha More. Max More is Alcor's president and CEO and oversees the foundation's cryopreservation facility. The facility takes the recently dead bodies of clients who have paid to have their bodies preserved in anticipation of future scientific developments that will allow for physical and cognitive regeneration. O'Connell notes that Alcor's mission "is presented as a humanitarian one" but is nevertheless driven by core business concerns and the need "to expand their customer base"; for all the talk of preserving life, the frame of its activities is fundamentally and foundationally capitalistic.[5] He also cannot contain other senses he experiences as he walks through the facility's corridors: that the place has the air of suggested religious redemption; that it enacts a strange contemporary version of American Manifest Destiny – "boundless national potential and individual fulfilment"; or that its "morbid ritual" feels like a "B-movie dismemberment".[6] The people stored at the facility, O'Connell notes, will never be brought back to life, but this fact seems to have no effect, indeed is not recognised, on More's transhumanist vision of transcendence.

It is in conversation with Natasha More that O'Connell encounters the most succinct version of this vision. She dreams of what she terms "a platform diverse body", where – as O'Connell summarises – "the human form itself was entirely replaced by a sleekly anthropomorphic device [...] which would be inhabited and controlled by an uploaded, substrate independent mind". But, O'Connell wonders, "wasn't Natasha's vision of a wholly mechanized body, of an impenetrable shell of technology, also a dream self-portrait – a creative denial of her own fragility and mortality?" More's response evidences a pure transhumanism: "'If this body fails', she said, 'we have to have another one. You could die at any moment, and that's unnecessary and unacceptable. As a transhumanist, I have no regard for death. I'm impatient with it, annoyed. We're a neurotic species – because of our mortality, because death is always breathing down our necks'". For O'Connell, such comments "reminded me of what I had always found so disturbing about transhumanism. There was the truth of its premise, that we were all of us trapped, bleeding, marked for death. And there was the strangeness, that technology could redeem us, release us from that state [...] None of it was remotely plausible, as far as I was concerned, and yet here we were".[7]

Transhumanism is explicit in seeing biological death as a state that can eventually be avoided. In so doing, it obviously wishes to eradicate disability. Within its own logic, this is a humanitarian good: if *all* bodies can be changed, augmented and enhanced, then an end to disabilities is simply part of a wider process through which humanity as a species improves and betters itself. Such a position masks more insidious thinking of course. Inherent in transhumanism's fear of death is a hatred of the ageing body and the disabilities that come with this. In turn, this is a hatred of the body that is seen to be failing, so that even before old age the disabled body is seen to be a signifier of something gone wrong, a malfunction or error. This is a contemporary retelling of humanism's hatred of disability. Its appeal to technological knowledge is simply an updated version of an old story that in its ultimate form leads to genocide and the characterisation of a 'life not worth living'. Every transhumanist would deny this vehemently and yet running through most transhumanist thinking is a desire to change bodies, and that desire is not limited to the wish to preserve life.

Given transhumanism's vision of the future, it might appear counterintuitive to suggest that fundamentally it lacks imagination. But this is the case. It articulates a sometimes ferocious logic of perfection and betterment but ignores everything that does not come within its tunnel vision. As O'Connell walks with Max More through the Alcor facility, he is struck as much by what is *not* there, what goes unacknowledged, as by the various assertions of profundity uttered by More, so that, for example, More's excitement at the prospect of potentially preserving brain activity in cryonically suspended heads "deflected attention away from the fact that what we were talking about was severed heads", a move that O'Connell drily notes was "not entirely successful".[8] The technical language of the processes – vitrification, cephalon, patient care, dewars – literally fails to *see*, and indeed masks, the versions of embodiment it produces.

There are uncanny similarities between O'Connell's visit to Alcor and Don DeLillo's 2016 novel *Zero K*. The novel focuses on exactly the kind of facility overseen by the Mores, even with similarities as to the location. O'Connell talks of encountering "a squat gray block of a building" as he arrives at Alcor, in "a landscape reclaimed from the radiant emptiness" of its desert setting.[9] *Zero K* starts with its protagonist, Jeffrey Lockhart, arriving "following a marathon journey" in a desert of "salt flats and stone rubble", to find "several low structures, possibly interconnected, barely separable from the bleached landscape".[10] But where Alcor appears resolutely American in its mission, the facility in DeLillo's novel (called the Convergence) is transnational, located somewhere (it is never precisely named) between Kyrgyzstan and Kazakhstan. Where Alcor is a product of a peculiarly American ideas of the self, the Convergence is made by global capital; its no-space status is a tribute to the lack of borders in the international bioeconomy. It erases its location because it has the power to do so, eradicating the possibility of other spaces; there is no question that the technology the facility has at its disposal might be available to anyone outside.

Lockhart has been summoned to the Convergence by his father, Ross, who wants him to be present at the moment his stepmother Artis is taken for cryogenic suspension. Ross is a billionaire hedge fund manager and investor in the facility's transhumanist project, and the novel is full of proclamations of what is promised in its vision of a "future beyond imagining".[11] Jeffrey listens while Ben-Ezra, the mysterious figure who runs the Convergence, outlines its aims:

> We understand that the idea of life extension will generate methods that attempt to improve upon the freezing of human bodies. To re-engineer the aging process, to reverse the biochemistry of progressive diseases. We fully expect to be in the forefront of any genuine innovation. Our tech centres in Europe are examining strategies for change. Ideas adaptable to our format. We're getting ahead of ourselves. This is where we want to be.

"Those of us who are here don't belong anywhere else", Ben-Ezra continues, "We've fallen out of history. We've abandoned who we were and where we were to be here [...] Those who eventually emerge from the capsules will be ahistorical humans. They will be free of the flatlines of the past, the attenuated minute and hour".[12]

While Jeffrey wants to respect the feelings of his family, like O'Connell he is drawn to everything that is not said or shown at the

Convergence. "Did such a man have a family?", he wonders of Ben-Ezra, "Did he brush his teeth, see a dentist when he had a toothache".[13] The facility building itself is featureless, a series of levels containing empty hallways and basic, utilitarian rooms: "Blank walls, no windows, doors widely spaced, all doors shut". The doors themselves are "painted in gradations of muted blue" and when Jeffrey knocks on them he receives no answer.[14] The only objects at the Convergence that deflect from the logic of its mission are mysterious screens that randomly descend when Jeffrey walks the silent halls and show images of disaster: tsunamis and earthquakes destroying buildings, or people being consumed by fire.

In the face of such a seemingly pristine transhumanism, DeLillo inserts two corrections: language and the complexities of embodied difference. The idea of a new language is central to the Convergence project: Ben-Ezra asserts that it will be "a language isolate, beyond all affiliation with other languages [...] To be taught to some, implanted in others, those already in cryopreservation", a language that "will approximate the logic and beauty of pure mathematics in everyday speech. No similes, metaphors, analogies".[15] But Jeffrey becomes the vehicle for the novel's critique of this; he displays an obsession with linguistic meaning, telling stories of how, in his past, he found himself forced to look up words in dictionaries, only then to follow word chains as the referents escaped him. DeLillo notes that to try to limit language is impossible. Jeffrey narrates how he discovered his father changed his name from Nicholas Satterswaite to Ross Lockhart (predictably more masculine but, of course, more revealing in the choice of surname). He reacts to this recognition of "Names. Fake names" by inventing names for people he knows, turning words over as he imagines whether they fit the characters in question.[16] He also brings such creativity to his thinking about his own self, observing that "certain words seemed to be located in the air ahead of me, within arm's reach. *Bessarabium, penetralia, pellucid, falafel*. I saw myself in these words".[17] Language swirls around Jeffrey, and it is exactly this sense of a sliding difference that he brings to his reading of the Convergence project and its quest for everlasting life.

Language and the imagination, DeLillo asserts, are what transhumanism lacks in its articulation of technological renewal, and it is the messy, inexact language of fiction – always relative and slipping away – that *Zero K* gives its readers. The novel as a whole is a strange and shimmering text, narrated and described as if, no matter the effort, words cannot fully name the acts, emotions or objects they encounter. It is full of inexplicable moments that appear to defy definition: mannequins appear in the facility's corridors and suggest links to the real naked, shaved bodies that are preserved; Jeffrey debates if the images on the screen are real footage or computer-generated, only then to be shocked as what appear to be real people come out of the screen and run down the corridor towards him. "Do I ask the question or do I accept the situation passively?" he says to his father early in the novel; "I want to know the rules".[18] But it turns out that this is Jeffrey trying to talk to his father in the elder's terms. His own actual apprehension of 'the rules' is not something that can be answered in such a clear and deterministic fashion.

DeLillo makes it clear that the difference of language is inherently connected to the difference of the body. It is as Jeffrey chases words following the discovery of his father's real name, for example, that he develops a fake limp: "The limp was my faith [...] something to cling to, a circular way to recognize myself, step by step, as the person who was doing this. Define *person*, I tell myself. Define *human*, define *animal*".[19] It is important to stress here that fake does not mean unreal. It is precisely this *imagining* of himself within these shifting definitions that allows Jeffrey not to submit to the monotonous logic of the novel's transhumanism. This is emphasised by those moments when he encounters people with disabilities, whether *inside* the Convergence or beyond its walls. When, early in the novel, he meets a boy in a motorised wheelchair in a corridor he is surprised and "didn't know what to say". As a locater of his identity and to break the silence, Jeffrey says his own name:

> Then he began to speak, or to produce what sounded like a random noise, a series of indistinct sounds that were not mumbled or stuttered but only, somehow, broken. He was expressing his thoughts but I wasn't able to detect a trace of any known language, or a nuance of meaning, and he showed no awareness that he could be understood.

Fixated on the idea of the boy being 'broken', he takes his hand and conjectures on "how much time remained to him. In his physical impairment, the nonalignment of upper and lower body, in this awful twistedness I found myself thinking of the new technologies that would be one day applied to his body and brain, allowing him to return to the world as a runner, a jumper, a public speaker".[20] Jeffrey's immediate reaction to the boy is to see absence and loss, and to conjecture on a technology-as-cure narrative that will save him from his disability.

But Jeffrey's encounters with bodies as the novel progresses change this. His lack of conviction in the justification the Convergence makes for the trajectories its bodies take, and the supposedly straightforward act of transcendence that underpins the journey, opens up a more complex version of embodied difference. Through his girlfriend, a teacher at a school for disabled children, Jeffrey meets a group of children with a range of disabilities, "from speech disorders to emotional problems". "All these disorders had their respective acronyms", he observes, "but she [his girlfriend] said that she did not use them". He then notices a boy who, though Jeffrey does not comment on this, appears to be a version of the boy he had seen at the Convergence:

> There is the boy at the end of the table who can't produce the specific motor movements that would allow him to speak words that others might understand. Nothing is natural. Phonemes, syllables, muscle tone, action of tongue, lips, jaw, palate. The acronym is CAS, she said, but did not translate the term. It seemed to her a symptom of the condition itself.[21]

'Nothing is natural'. At this moment, DeLillo makes clear the embodiment of language. Jeffrey connects the body to the physical production of language but notes that the issue here is whether the other has 'words that others might understand'. The words Jeffrey has heard at the Convergence are often incomprehensible, a babble of technospeak that he likens to a cult or the speech of religious prophecy. This moment of speaking/not speaking with the disabled boy is, however, of a piece with the way DeLillo stresses that language actually works. The two differences converge. The force of this is confirmed when the boy (still unnamed but again apparently connected to the previous depictions) appears at the end of the novel, on a bus with Jeffrey in New York, and at that rare Manhattan moment when the sun aligns with the city's street grid. "His hands were curled at this chest", Jeffrey observes, "half fists, soft and trembling [...] The boy bounced slightly in accord with [his] cries and they were unceasing and also exhilarating, they were prelinguistic grunts. I hated to think that he was impaired in some way, macrocephalic, mentally deficient, but these howls of awe were far more suitable than words".[22] The boy's disabled difference produces a version of presence that is superior to any fixed version of language. Rather than the obsession with the 'end' that consumes the transhumanist project of the Convergence, the boy's joy at seeing the sun on a cross-town bus emphasises diversity and difference in the stress on the 'suitability' of language. And, crucially, it does so in the imagined world of fiction, created through DeLillo's language and with a sliding, contradictory and impressionistic method that match the complexities of the bodies it depicts.

There is no grand gesture towards the future with which to conclude this book, although there is a series of hopes. One is that an understanding of the interaction between disability and posthumanism can become more global, and especially that the formations this interaction take outside of Euro-American locations can drive new theories, grounded in local specifics, of how bodies find meaning in technological networks. I hope that the analyses of race and cultural texts from the Middle East and Japan in this study have moved towards this, but it is obvious that more work needs to be done.[23] Another is straightforward: that there might be greater clarity of perception that allows the recognition of the foundational position disability holds in any consideration of how the nexus of bodies and technologies work. Scholarship on posthumanism needs to look in even as is looks out; to consider the everyday and ordinary as much as the allure of brave new worlds of the beyond. As ever with disability, this involves greater *listening*: to the ways disabled lives and experiences are told and to how these can ground theories of technological futures. A third hope is that more attention is paid to fiction's vital place in the formation of the cultural imaginaries that express, shape and contain posthumanist bodies. In a world where biotechnologies hold such power in the articulation of disability it can be easy to forget the power of stories; yet stories (of all kinds: narrative, episodic, critical, tenuous, evanescent) are how senses of worlds are made. Ignoring their power and reach is a failure of imagination, be that personal, civic or political. Particularly when it is the potentially blank canvas of *futures* that is under discussion, the shapes stories make of what bodies might be are more necessary than ever.

I do not foresee any moment of singularity or the possibility of shared hyperabilities producing any sudden technological transformations of lives. I have no great knowledge on this topic, but it is clear that for all that modernity, whether analogue or digital, has revolutionised how all of us live over the last 150 years, even the most profound changes have been incremental and multifaceted, and there is no reason to suppose that this will not be the case in the future. In developing these ideas, I am drawn towards Nikolas Rose's subtle formation of the question in *The Politics of Life Itself*:

> As with our own present, our future will emerge from the intersection of a number of contingent pathways that, as they intertwine,

> might create something new. This, I suspect, will be no radical transformation, no shift into a world 'after nature' or a 'posthuman future.' Perhaps it will not even constitute an 'event.' But I think, in all manner of small ways, most of which will soon be routinized and taken for granted, things will not be quite the same again.[24]

Rose's suggestion here that there may be no posthuman future will disappoint those ardent advocates of posthumanism that foresee amalgamations and networks of person, machines and environments that cross the boundaries of human and non-human, whether technological or species. But this does not mean that these crossings will not take place, rather that they will not announce their presence with banners, fireworks and the full ceremony of a radical emergence.

This observation, I would argue, can be understood to be a disability statement. As I hope this book has shown, interactions between the human and non-human take place all the time in disability lives and do so in everyday 'taken for granted' ways. Technology, embodiment and disability have been connected for as long as humans have made interventions in health or responded to congenital physical differences. This is bound to continue and, as ever, it will be transformative. But disability transformations are not the same as those that herald the comings of (some) posthuman futures. As part of the schemata of the body, disability is the base for extraordinary theory, versions and visions of embodiment, cognitive states, selfhoods and communities that are rich and complex; but this theory is, at its, best grounded in material experience. It is philosophical and situated, abstract and local. It finds, as I hope I have displayed, common cause with those critical posthumanist expressions that seek to do justice to the emerging technologised bodies of the present and to do so through connections to the ways in which those bodies live. Rose's 'contingent pathways' are many things and the site of many moments in which complexities come together: these include not only disabled bodies, properly configured, but also the narratives and stories that are told about them and their futures. Representations and deployments will continue to be among the most important ways through which we make sense of the ever-moving horizon of the present as it takes us, with all our body shapes, towards whatever the next version of technologised embodiment may be. As much as ever, we need them to help explain to (all of) us who we are, and who we might be.

Rose's pathways are also, of course, the yellow brick roads of Oz and, in seeing them as such, this book comes full circle. For all the advice to, as the song puts it, "follow the yellow brick road", it should be noted that in both books and film there is more than one such road in Oz. There are in fact numerous crossroads and intersections where decisions need to be made about which directions to follow and which paths to take. There is no singular or coherent route and, even then, as we saw in the preface, there is no guarantee that the Emerald City will be what it seems when and if there is any arrival: it may well not be an 'event' or promise of a passage home. "The disability to come", Robert McRuer observes, "will and should always belong to the time of the promise", a promise to "comprehend disability otherwise" and "collectively, somehow access other worlds and futures".[25] If a passage along roads becomes both a journey of all types of people, in all forms, as well as a time of future promise, then it is towards a world worth making.

Notes

1 Stephen Hawking, *Brief Answers to the Big Questions* (London: John Murray, 2018).
2 This did not stop some people from trying of course. The question was a favourite in internet forums and on question platforms.
3 Hawking, *Brief Answers to the Big Questions*, pp. 187 and 186.
4 Hawking, *Brief Answers to the Big Questions*, pp. 194, 191 and 196.
5 Mark O'Connell, *To Be a Machine: Adventures Among Cyborgs, Utopians, Hackers, and the Futurists Solving the Modest Problem of Death* (London: Granta, 2017), p. 31.
6 O'Connell, *To Be a Machine*, pp. 31 and 27.
7 O'Connell, *To Be a Machine*, pp. 39–40.
8 O'Connell, *To Be a Machine*, p. 27.
9 O'Connell, *To Be a Machine*, p. 21.
10 Don DeLillo, *Zero K* (London: Picador, 2017), p. 4.
11 DeLillo, *Zero K*, p. 15.
12 DeLillo, *Zero K*, pp. 126 and 129–130.
13 DeLillo, *Zero K*, p. 126.
14 DeLillo, *Zero K*, pp. 10 and 23.
15 DeLillo, *Zero K*, p. 130.
16 DeLillo, *Zero K*, p. 104. I considered inserting another mention of the Tin Woodman, from *The Wonderful Wizard of Oz*, here in relation to the clear resonances of 'Lockhart' but thought that those who have read this far will have worked this out for themselves. It is also worth noting that Artis, a Celtic name meaning 'noble strength' is of course only a single letter away from 'artist'. Max More also changed his surname, from O'Connor to More, to signal the promise of the world he wishes to enter.
17 DeLillo, *Zero K*, p. 107; italics in original.
18 DeLillo, *Zero K*, p. 29.

19 DeLillo, *Zero K*, p. 103.
20 DeLillo, *Zero K*, p. 94.
21 DeLillo, *Zero K*, pp. 189–190.
22 DeLillo, *Zero K*, p. 274.
23 In 2006 Julie Livingston noted that "while four-fifths of the world's disabled persons live in developing countries, there is a relative dearth of humanities and social science scholarship exploring disability in non-Western contexts". While the situation has improved, it is clear that this imbalance is still a significant problem, especially given, as Jasbir Puar and Kaushik Sunder Rajan have noted, one manifestation of a capitalistic posthumanism's claim on the makeup of bodies and health is precisely that it can control the availability of medical technologies in the global South. See Livingston, 'Insights from an African history of disability', *Radical History Review* 94 (Winter 2006), p. 125, n. 16; as well as the discussion of the problematic relationship between disability and critical postcolonial scholarship in Clare Barker and Stuart Murray, 'Disabling postcolonialism: global disability cultures and democratic criticism', *Journal of Literary and Cultural Disability Studies* 4, no. 3 (2010), pp. 219–236.
24 Nikolas Rose, *The Politics of Life Itself* (Princeton, NJ: Princeton University Press, 2006), p. 5.
25 Robert McRuer, *Crip Theory: Cultural Signs of Queerness and Disability* (New York: New York University Press, 2006), p. 208.

Bibliography

A Time for Drunken Horses. Film. Iraq/Kurdistan: Bahman Ghobadi, 2000.

Adam, Alison. *Artificial Knowing: Gender and the Thinking Machine*. London and New York: Routledge, 1998.

Agar, Nicholas. *Humanity's End: Why We Should Reject Radical Enhancement*. Cambridge, MA and London: MIT Press, 2010.

Ahlaam. Film. Iraq: Mohamed Al-Daradji, 2006.

Ahmed, Sara. *The Cultural Politics of Emotion*. 2nd Ed. Edinburgh: Edinburgh University Press, 2014.

A.I.: Artificial Intelligence. Film. United States: Stephen Spielberg, 2001.

Allan, Kathryn. 'Reading disability in science fiction.' In *Disability in Science Fiction: Representations of Technology as Cure*, edited by Kathryn Allan, 1–15. Basingstoke: Palgrave Macmillan, 2013.

American Sniper. Film. United States: Clint Eastwood, 2014.

Armitage, John. *Virilio Live: Selected Interviews*. London: Sage, 2001.

Atkinson, Tara with Joshua Ferris. 'Vacuuming the Whole House and Where Do We Go Now: A conversation with Joshua Ferris.' *The Iowa Review* 40, no. 2 (2010): 125–131.

Avent, Ryan. *The Wealth of Humans: Work and its Absence in the Twenty-First Century*. London: Penguin, 2017.

Backpacker. Nike print advert. October 2000.

Badmington, Neil. *Alien Chic: Posthumanism and the Other Within*. Abingdon: Routledge, 2004.

Badmington, Neil. 'Introduction: approaching posthumanism.' In *Posthumanism*, edited by Neil Badmington, 1–10. Basingstoke: Palgrave Macmillan, 2000.

Balsamo, Anne. *Technologies of the Gendered Body: Reading Cyborg Women*. Durham, NC and London: Duke University Press, 1996.

Barker, Clare. '"Radiant affliction", disability narratives in postcolonial literature.' In *The Cambridge Companion to Literature and Disability*, edited by Clare Barker and Stuart Murray, 104–119. Cambridge: Cambridge University Press, 2018.

Barker, Clare and Stuart Murray. 'Disabling postcolonialism: global disability cultures and democratic criticism.' *Journal of Literary and Cultural Disability Studies* 4, no. 3 (2010): 219–236.

Battle for Haditha. Film. United States: Nick Broomfield, 2007.
Baum, L. Frank. *The Patchwork Girl of Oz, The Complete Collection*. Vol. 3. London: Simon & Schuster, 2013.
Baum, L. Frank. *The Tin Woodman of Oz. Oz, The Complete Collection*. Vol. 4. London: Simon & Schuster, 2013.
Baum, L. Frank. *The Wonderful Wizard of Oz*. London: Penguin, 1995.
Bauman, Zygmunt. *Culture in a Liquid Modern World*. Cambridge: Polity, 2011.
Bauman, Zygmunt. *Postmodernity and Its Discontents*. New York: New York University Press, 1997.
Bauman, Zygmunt. 'Wars of the globalization era.' *European Journal of Social Theory* 4, no. 1 (2001).
Beckett, Samuel. *Krapp's Last Tape and Other Shorter Plays*. London: Faber, 2009.
Beckett, Samuel. *Three Novels: Molloy, Malone Dies, The Unnameable*. New York: Grove Press, 2009.
Berger, James. *The Disarticulate: Language, Disability, and the Narratives of Modernity*. New York: New York University Press, 2014.
Berger, Thomas. *Adventures of the Artificial Woman*. New York: Simon & Schuster, 2005.
Bertman, Stephen. *Hyperculture: The Human Cost of Speed*. Westport, CT and London: Praeger, 1998.
Bérubé, Michael. 'Afterword.' In *Disability Studies: Enabling the Humanities*, edited by Sharon L. Snyder, Brenda Jo Brueggemann, and Rosemarie Garland-Thomson, 337–343. New York: Modern Language Association of America, 2002.
Bérubé, Michael. *The Secret Life of Stories: From Don Quixote to Harry Potter, How Understanding Intellectual Disability Transforms the Way We Read*. New York: New York University Press, 2016.
Betcher, Sharon. 'Putting my foot (prosthesis, crutches, phantom) down: considering technology as transcendence in the writings of Donna Haraway.' *Women's Studies Quarterly* 29, no. 3/4 (Fall 2001): 35–53.
Bioglio, Livio and Ruggero G. Pensa. 'Identification of key films and personalities in the history of cinema from a Western perspective.' *Applied Network Science* 3, no. 50 (2018). https://doi.org/10.1007/s41109–018–0105-0.
Blackford, Russell. 'The great transition: ideas and anxieties.' In *The Transhumanist Reader*, edited by Max More and Natasha Vita-More, 421–429. Chichester: Wiley-Blackwell, 2013.
Blade Runner. Film. United States: Ridley Scott, 1982.
Blade Runner 2049. Film. United States: Denis Villeneuve, 2017.
Bostrom, Nick. *Superintelligence: Paths, Dangers, Strategies*. Oxford: Oxford University Press, 2014.
Braidotti, Rosi. *Metamorphoses: Towards a Materialist Theory of Becoming*. Cambridge: Polity, 2002.
Braidotti, Rosi. *Nomadic Subjects: Embodiment and Sexual Difference in Contemporary Feminist Theory*. New York: Columbia University Press, 1994.
Braidotti, Rosi. *Posthuman Knowledge*. Cambridge: Polity, 2019.
Braidotti, Rosi. *The Posthuman*. Cambridge: Polity, 2013.
Braidotti, Rosi and Nina Lykke, Eds. *Between Monsters, Goddesses and Cyborgs: Feminist Confrontations with Science, Medicine and Cyberspace*. London: Zed Books, 1996.

Breen, Jonathon S. 'The exoskeleton generation – disability redux.' *Disability and Society* 30, no. 10 (2015): 1568–1572.

Brown, Steven T. 'Machinic desire: Hans Bellmer's dolls and the technological uncanny in *Ghost in the Shell 2: Innocence*.' *Mechademia* 3 (2008): 222–251.

Bucciarelli, Louis L. 'Between thought and object in engineering design.' *Design Studies* 23, no. 3 (2002): 219–231.

Bucciarelli, Louis L. *Designing Engineers*. Cambridge, MA and London: MIT Press, 1994.

Burgess, Olivia. 'Revolutionary bodies in Chuck Palahniuk's *Fight Club*.' *Utopian Studies* 23, no. 1 (2012): 263–280.

Burgoyne, Robert. 'Embodiment in the war film: *Paradise Now* and *The Hurt Locker*.' *Journal of War & Cultural Studies* 5, no. 1 (2012): 7–19.

Butler, Judith. *Bodies That Matter: On the Discursive Limits of "Sex"*. New York and London: Routledge, 1993.

Butler, Judith. *Precarious Life: The Powers of Mourning and Violence*. London and New York: Verso, 2006.

Butler, Octavia E. *Xenogenesis*. New York: Doubleday, 1989.

Caidan, Martin. *Cyborg*. New York: HarperCollins, 1975.

Carrigan, Anthony. 'Postcolonial disaster, Pacific nuclearization, and disabling environments.' *Journal of Literary and Cultural Disability Studies* 4, no. 3 (2010): 255–272.

Chambers, Becky. *A Closed and Common Orbit*. London: Hodder & Stoughton, 2016.

Chambers, Becky. *Record of a Spaceborn Few*. London: Hodder & Stoughton, 2018.

Chambers, Becky. *The Long Way to a Small, Angry Planet*. London: Hodder & Stoughton, 2015.

Chen, Mel Y. *Animacies: Biopolitics, Racial Mattering and Queer Affect*. Durham, NC and London: Duke University Press, 2012.

Chen, Mel Y. 'Unpacking intoxication, racialising disability.' *Medical Humanities* 41 (2015): 25–29.

City of Ghosts. Film. United States: Matthew Heineman, 2017.

Clark, Andy. 'Re-inventing ourselves: the plasticity of embodiment, sensing, and mind.' *The Journal of Medicine and Philosophy* 32, no. 3 (January 2007): 263–282. Reprinted in *The Transhumanist Reader*, edited by Max More and Natasha Vita-More, 113–127. Chichester: Wiley-Blackwell, 2013.

Clarke, Bruce. *Posthuman Metamorphosis: Narrative and Systems*. New York: Fordham University Press, 2008.

Cooper, Melinda. *Life as Surplus: Biotechnology and Capitalism in the Neoliberal Era*. Seattle and London: University of Washington Press, 2008.

Corker, Mariam and Tom Shakespeare, Eds. *Disability/Postmodernity: Embodying Disability Theory*. London and New York: Continuum, 2002.

Coupland, Douglas. *JPod*. London: Bloomsbury, 2007.

Coupland, Douglas. *Microserfs*. London: Harper Perennial, 2004.

Crary, Jonathan. *24/7: Late Capitalism and the Ends of Sleep*. Cambridge: Verso, 2014.

Dakers, Stewart. 'A robot carer? No thanks – we still need the human touch.' *The Guardian*, September 1, 2015. www.theguardian.com/society/2015/sep/01/robot-carer-human-paro-seal.

Davidson, Michael. *Concerto for the Left Hand: Disability and the Defamiliar Body*. Ann Arbor: University of Michigan Press, 2008.

Davidson, Michael. *Invalid Modernism: Disability and the Missing Body of the Aesthetic*. Oxford: Oxford University Press, 2019.

Davies, Tony. *Humanism*. London: Routledge, 2008.

Davis, Lennard J. *Bending Over Backwards: Disability, Dismodernism, and Other Difficult Positions*. New York and London: New York University Press, 2002.

Davis, Lennard J. *Enforcing Normalcy: Disability, Deafness and the Body*. London and New York: Verso, 1995.

Davis, Lennard J. *The End of Normal: Identity in a Biocultural Era*. Ann Arbor: The University of Michigan Press, 2013.

Davis, Richard. 'Magneto, mutation and morality.' In *X-Men and Philosophy: Astonishing Insight and Uncanny Argument in Mutant X-Verse*, edited by Rebecca Housel and J. Jeremy Wisnewski, 125–139. Hoboken, NJ: John Wiley and Sons, 2009.

DeLillo, Don. *Zero K*. London: Picador, 2017.

DelVecchio, Mary-Jo et al., Eds. *Pain as Human Experience: An Anthropological Perspective*. Berkeley: University of California Press, 1994.

Der Derian, James. *Virtuous War: Mapping the Military–Industrial–Media–Entertainment Network*. 2nd ed. New York: Westview, 2009.

Derrida, Jacques. *Spectres of Marx: The State of the Debt, the Work of Mourning and the New International*. New York: Routledge, 1994.

Dillon, Sarah. '"It's a question of words, therefore": becoming-animal in Michael Faber's *Under the Skin*' *Science Fiction Studies* 38, no. 1 (2011): 134–154.

Doane, Mary Anne. *Femmes Fatales: Feminism, Film Theory and Psychoanalysis*. New York: Routledge, 1991.

Eilers, Miriam, Katrin Grüber and Christoph Rahmann-Sutter, Eds. *The Human Enhancement Debate and Disability: New Bodies for a Better Life*. Basingstoke: Palgrave Macmillan, 2014.

Erevelles, Nirmala. *Disability and Difference in Global Contexts: Enabling a Transformative Body Politic*. New York: Palgrave Macmillan, 2011.

Erevelles, Nirmala and Andrea Minear. 'Unspeakable offenses: untangling race and disability in discourses of intersectionality.' *Journal of Literary and Cultural Disability Studies* 4, no. 2 (2010): 127–145.

Eriksen, Thomas Hylland. *Tyranny of the Moment: Fast and Slow Time in the Information Age*. London: Pluto, 2001.

Ex Machina. Film. United Kingdom: Alex Garland, 2014.

Eyler, Joshua R. 'Disability and prosthesis in L. Frank Baum's *The Wonderful Wizard of Oz*.' *Children's Literature Association Quarterly* 38, no. 3 (2013): 319–334.

Faber, Michael. *Under the Skin*. Edinburgh: Canongate, 2014.

Featherstone, Mike and Roger Burrows, Eds. *Cyberspace/CyberBodies/Cyberpunk*. London: Sage, 1995.

Federici, Silvia. *Revolution at Point Zero: Housework, Reproduction and Feminist Struggle*. Oakland, CA: PM Press, 2012.

Ferris, Joshua. *The Unnamed*. London: Penguin, 2010.

Ferris, Joshua. *Then We Came to the End*. London: Viking, 2007.

Ferris, Joshua. *To Rise Again at a Decent Hour*. London: Penguin, 2014.

Ferry, Peter. 'Reading Manhattan. Reading American masculinity. Reintroducing the flaneur with E.B. White's *Here is New York* and Joshua Ferris' *The Unnamed*.' *Culture, Society and Masculinities* 3, no. 1 (2011): 49–61.

Fight Club. Film. United States: David Fincher, 1999.

Filer, Nathan. *The Heartland: Finding and Losing Schizophrenia*. London: Faber & Faber, 2019.

Fixed: The Science/Fiction of Human Enhancement. Film. United States: Regan Brashear, 2013.

Flanagan, Martin, Mike McKenny and Andy Livingston. *The Marvel Studios Phenomenon: Inside a Transmedia Universe*. New York and London: Bloomsbury, 2016.

Ford, Martin. *The Rise of the Robots: Technology and the Threat of Mass Unemployment*. London: Oneworld, 2015.

Foucault, Michel. *The Order of Things*. New York: Random House, 1994.

Fraser, Benjamin. 'Disability studies, world cinema and the cognitive code of reality.' In *Cultures of Representation: Disability in World Cinema Contexts*, edited by Benjamin Fraser, 1–17. New York: Wallflower Press, 2016.

Frost, Samantha. *Biocultural Creatures: Towards a New Theory of the Human*. Durham, NC: Duke University Press, 2016.

Fukuyama, Francis. *Our Posthuman Future: Consequences of the Biotechnology Revolution*. London: Profile, 2002.

Fukuyama, Francis. *The Great Disruption: Human Nature and the Reconstruction of Social Order*. London: Profile, 1999.

Garland-Thomson, Rosemarie. 'Disability gain.' Paper presented at 'Avoidance in/and the Academy: The International Conference on Disability, Culture and Education', Liverpool Hope University, September 11, 2013.

Garland-Thomson, Rosemarie. *Staring: How We Look*. Oxford: Oxford University Press, 2009.

Gattaca. Film. United States: Andrew Niccol, 1997.

Ghost in the Shell. Film. Japan: Mamoru Oshii, 1995.

Ghost in the Shell. Film. United States: Rupert Sanders, 2017.

Ghost in the Shell: The New Movie. Film. Japan: Kazuchika Kise and Kazuya Nomura, 2015.

Gibson, William. *Neuromancer*. London: HarperCollins, 1993.

Goodley, Dan, Rebecca Lawthom and Katherine Runswick Cole. 'Posthuman disability studies.' *Subjectivity* 7, no. 4 (December 2014): 342–361.

Goody, Alex. *Technology, Literature and Culture*. Cambridge: Polity, 2011.

Gordijn, Bert and Ruth Chadwick, Eds. *Medical Enhancement and Posthumanity*. London: Springer, 2008.

Graham, Elaine L. *Representations of the Post/human: Monsters, Aliens and Others in Popular Culture*. Manchester: Manchester University Press, 2002.

Grandin, Temple. *Animals in Translation: Using the Mysteries of Autism to Decode Animal Behavior*. New York: Scribner, 2005.

Grandin, Temple. *Animals Make Us Human: Creating the Best Life for Animals*. Boston, MA: Houghton Mifflin Harcourt, 2009.

Green Zone. Film. United States: Paul Greengrass, 2010.

Gregory, Derek. 'From a view to a kill: drones and late modern war.' *Theory, Culture and Society* 28, nos. 7–8 (2011): 188–215.

Gregory, Derek. 'Seeing red: Baghdad and the event-ful city'. *Political Geography* 29 (2010): 266.

Gregory, Derek. 'The everywhere war.' *The Geographical Journal* 177, no. 3 (2011): 238–250.

Grosz, Elizabeth. *Volatile Bodies: Toward a Corporeal Feminism*. Bloomington and Indianapolis: Indiana University Press, 1994.

Grusin, Richard, Ed. *Anthropocene Feminism*. Minneapolis: University of Minnesota Press, 2017.

Grusin, Richard, Ed. *The Nonhuman Turn*. Minneapolis: Minnesota University Press, 2015.

Guizzo, Eric. 'How Aldebaran Robotics built its friendly humanoid robot, Pepper.' *IEEE Spectrum*, December 26, 2014. https://spectrum.eee.org/robotics/home-robots/how-aldebaran-robotics-built-its-friendly-humanoid-robot-pepper.

Halberstam, Judith and Ira Livingston. 'Introduction: posthuman bodies.' In *Posthuman Bodies*, edited by Halberstam and Livingston, 1–19. Bloomington and Indianapolis: Indiana University Press, 1995.

Harari, Yuval Noah. *Homo Deus: A Brief History of Tomorrow*. London: Vintage, 2017.

Haraway, Donna. *Manifestly Haraway*. Minneapolis: University of Minnesota Press, 2016.

Haraway, Donna J. *Modest_Witness@Second_Millennium. FemaleMan©_Meets_OncoMouse™*. New York and London: Routledge, 1997.

Haraway, Donna. *Simians, Cyborgs and Women: The Reinvention of Nature*. London: Free Association Books, 1991.

Harris, Chad. 'The omniscient eye: satellite imagery, "battlespace awareness," and the structures of the imperial gaze.' *Surveillance & Society* 4, no. 1/2 (2006): 101–122.

Harris, John. 'Robots could solve the social care crisis – but at what price?' *The Guardian*, July 2, 2018. www.theguardian.com/commentisfree/2018/jul/02/robo-carers-human-principles-technology-care-crisis.

Hassan, Robert. *Empires of Speed: Time and the Acceleration of Politics and Society*. Leiden and Boston, MA: Brill, 2009.

Hawking, Stephen. *Brief Answers to the Big Questions*. London: John Murray, 2018.

Hayles, N. Katherine. *How We Became Posthuman: Virtual Bodies in Cybernetics, Literature, and Informatics*. Chicago, IL: The University of Chicago Press, 1999.

Hayles, N. Katherine. *How We Think: Digital Media and Contemporary Technogenesis*. Chicago, IL and London: The University of Chicago Press, 2012.

Hayles, N. Katherine. *My Mother Was A Computer: Digital Subjects and Literary Texts*. Chicago, IL: The University of Chicago Press, 2005.

Her. Film. United States: Spike Jonze, 2013.

Herbrechter, Stefan. *Posthumanism: A Critical Analysis*. London and New York: Bloomsbury, 2013.

Hirschmann, Nancy. 'Disability, feminism, and intersectionability: a critical approach.' *Radical Philosophy Review* 16, no. 2 (2013): 649–662.

Hirschmann, Nancy J. 'Queer/fear: disability, sexuality, and the other.' *Journal of Medical Humanities* 34, no. 2 (2013): 139–147.

Holt, Raymond and Stuart Murray. 'Prosthesis and the engineered imagination: reading augmentation and disability across cultural theory, representation and product design.' *Medical Humanities* 41, no. 2 (2020): 55–62.

Hopkins, Patrick D. 'The lure of the normal: who *wouldn't want* to be a mutant?' In *X-Men and Philosophy: Astonishing Insight and Uncanny Argument in the Mutant X-Verse*, edited by Rebecca Housel and J. Jeremy Wisnewski, 5–16. Hoboken, NJ: John Wiley, 2009.

Huyssen, Andreas. 'The vamp and the machine: technology and sexuality in Fritz Lang's *Metropolis*.' *New German Critique* 24/25 (Autumn 1981–Winter 1982): 221–237.

Hylland Eriksen, Thomas. *Tyranny of the Moment: Fast and Slow Time in the Information Age*. London: Pluto, 2011.

I, Robot. Film. United States: Alex Proyas, 2004.

Ihde, Don. *Bodies in Technology*. Minneapolis and London: University of Minnesota Press, 2002.

Ilea, Ramona. 'The mutant cure or social change: debating disability.' In *X-Men and Philosophy: Astonishing Insight and Uncanny Argument in Mutant X-Verse*, edited by Rebecca Housel and J. Jeremy Wisnewski, 170–182. Hoboken, NY: John Wiley and Sons, 2009.

Insomnia. Film. United States: Christopher Nolan, 2002.

Insyriated. Film. Belgium: Philipe van Leeuw, 2017.

Inversion. Film. Iran: Behnam Behzadi, 2016.

Jackson, Liz. 'We are the original lifehackers.' *New York Times*, May 30, 2018. www.nytimes.com/2018/05/30/opinion/disability-design-lifehacks.html.

Jackson, Shelley. *Patchwork Girl*. 1995. Hypertext.

James, Ian. *Paul Virilio*. London and New York: Routledge, 2007.

Johnson, Merri Lisa and Robert McRuer. 'Crispistemologies: introduction.' *Journal of Literary & Cultural Disability Studies* 8, no. 2 (2014): 127–147.

Jurecic, Ann. *Illness as Narrative*. Pittsburgh, PA: University of Pittsburgh Press, 2012.

Kafer, Alison. *Feminist, Queer, Crip*. Bloomington and Indianapolis: Indiana University Press, 2013.

Kafer, Alison and Eunjung Kim. 'Disability and the edges of intersectionality.' In *The Cambridge Companion to Literature and Disability*, edited by Clare Barker and Stuart Murray, 123–138. Cambridge: Cambridge University Press, 2018.

Kakoudaki, Despina. *Anatomy of a Robot: Literature, Cinema, and the Cultural Work of Artificial People*. New Brunswick, NJ and London: Rutgers University Press, 2014.

Kang, Minsoo. 'Building the sex machine: the subversive potential of the female robot.' *Intertexts* 9, no. 1 (2005): 5–22.

Kang, Minsoo. *Sublime Dreams of Living Machines: The Automaton in the European Imagination*. Cambridge, MA and London: Harvard University Press, 2011.

Karvadlo, Jesse. 'X-istential X-Men: Jews, Superman, and the literature of struggle.' In *X-Men and Philosophy: Astonishing Insight and Uncanny Argument in the Mutant X-Verse*, edited by Rebecca Housel and J. Jeremy Wisnewski, 38–50. Hoboken, NJ: John Wiley, 2009.

Kosofsky Sedgwick, Eve. *Epistemology of the Closet*. Berkeley and Los Angeles: University of California Press, 1990.

Kress, Nancy. *Beggars in Spain*. Rockville, MD: Phoenix Pick/Arc Manor, 1991.

Kroker, Arthur. *Exits to the Posthuman Future*. Cambridge: Polity, 2014.

Kumari Campbell, Fiona. *Contours of Ableism: The Production of Disability and Ableness*. Basingstoke: Palgrave Macmillan, 2009.

Kuppers, Petra. 'The wheelchair's rhetoric: the performance of disability.' *TDR: The Drama Review* 51, no. 4 (2007): 80–88.

Lars and the Real Girl. Film. United States: Craig Gillespie, 2007.

Lillvis, Kirsten. *Postmodern Blackness and the Black Female Imagination*. Athens: University of Georgia Press, 2017.
Livingston, Julie. 'Insights from an African history of disability.' *Radical History Review* 94 (Winter 2006): 111–125.
Logan. Film. United States: James Mangold, 2017.
Lucy. Film. France/United States: Luc Besson, 2014.
Ludwigs, Marina. 'Walking as a metaphor for narrativity.' *Studia Neophilologica* 87 (2015): 116–128.
Lury, Celia. *Prosthetic Culture: Photography, Memory and Identity*. London and New York: Routledge, 1998.
Lury, Karen. 'Children in an open world: mobility as ontology in new Iranian and Turkish cinema.' *Feminist Theory* 11, no. 3 (2010): 283–294
Luttwak, Edward. *Strategy: The Logic of War and Peace*, revised ed. Cambridge, MA: Harvard University Press, 2001.
Lykke, Nina. 'Between monsters, goddesses and cyborgs: feminist confrontations with science.' In *The Gendered Cyborg: A Reader*, edited by Gill Kirkup et al., 74–87. Abingdon and New York: Routledge, 2000.
McCaffery, Anne. *The Ship Who Sang*. London: Corgi, 1982.
MacCormack, Patricia. *Posthuman Ethics: Embodiment and Cultural Theory*. London and New York: Routledge, 2012.
McEwan, Ian. *Machines Like Me*. London: Jonathan Cape, 2019.
McRuer, Robert. 'A "last stand" against cure.' Review of *X-Men 3: The Last Stand*. *Ragged Edge Online*, June 2, 2006. www.raggededgemagazine.com/departments/closerlook/001144.html.
McRuer, Robert. *Crip Theory: Cultural Signs of Queerness and Disability*. New York: New York University Press, 2006.
McRuer, Robert. *Crip Times: Disability, Globalization, and Resistance*. New York: New York University Press, 2018.
Mahon, Peter. *Posthumanism: A Guide for the Perplexed*. London: Bloomsbury, 2017.
Making Mr. Right. Film. United States: Susan Seidelman, 1987.
'March of the machines: what history tells us about the future of artificial intelligence – and how society should respond.' Leader in *The Economist*, June 25, 2016. www.economist.com/leaders/2016/06/25/march-of-the-machines.
Maxey, Ruth. 'National stories and narrative voice in the fiction of Joshua Ferris.' *Critique: Studies in Contemporary Fiction* 57, no. 2 (2016): 208–216.
Meekosha, Helen. 'Decolonising disability: thinking and acting globally.' *Disability and Society* 26, no. 6 (2011): 667–682.
Miah, Andy and Emma Rich. *The Medicalization of Cyberspace*. Abingdon and New York: Routledge, 2008.
Miccoli, Anthony. *Posthuman Suffering and the Technological Embrace*. Lanham, MD: Lexington, 2012.
Mitchell, David T., Susan Antebi and Sharon L. Snyder, Eds. *The Matter of Disability: Materiality, Biopolitics, Crip Affect*. Ann Arbor: University of Michigan Press, 2019.
Mitchell, David T. and Sharon L. Snyder. *Narrative Prosthesis: Disability and the Dependencies of Discourse*. Ann Arbor: University of Michigan Press, 2000.
Mitchell, David T. with Sharon L. Snyder. *The Biopolitics of Disability: Neoliberalism, Ablenationalism and Peripheral Embodiment*. Ann Arbor: University of Michigan Press, 2015.

Mogk, Marja Evelyn, Ed. *Different Bodies: Essays on Disability in Film and Television*. Jefferson, NC: McFarland and Company, 2013.

Moravec, Hans. *Mind Children: The Future of Robot and Human Intelligence*. Cambridge, MA and London: Harvard University Press, 1988.

Moravec, Hans. *Robot: Mere Machine to Transcendent Mind*. Oxford: Oxford University Press, 1999.

Morris, Alex. 'The pill freaks of Silicon Valley.' *New York Magazine,* October 19, 2016. www.scribd.com/article/327687787/The-Pill-Freaks-Of-Silicon-Valley.

Morris, David B. *Illness and Culture in the Postmodern Age*. Berkeley, Los Angeles and London: University of California Press, 1998.

Morris, David B. *The Culture of Pain*. Berkeley and Los Angeles: University of California Press, 1991.

Morris, Jenny, Ed. *Encounters with Strangers: Feminism and Disability*. London: The Women's Press, 1996.

Morrow, Anna. 'Identity politics and disability studies: a critique of recent theory.' *Michigan Quarterly Review* 43, no. 2 (2004): 269–296.

Murakami, Haruki. 'Sleep.' In *The Elephant Vanishes*. London: Vintage, 2003.

Murray, Stuart. 'Autism and the posthuman.' In *Worlds of Autism: Across the Spectrum of Neurological Difference,* edited by Joyce Davidson and Michael Orsini, 53–72. Minneapolis: University of Minnesota Press, 2013.

Murray, Stuart. 'Disability and memory in posthuman(ist) narrative: reading prosthesis and amnesia in Hollywood's re-membering of the "war on terror"'. *Parallax* 23, no. 4 (2017): 439–452.

Murray, Stuart. 'From Virginia's sister to Friday's silence: presence, metaphor and the persistence of disability in contemporary writing.' *Journal of Literary and Cultural Disability Studies* 6, no. 3 (2012): 241–258.

Murray, Stuart. 'The ambiguities of inclusion: disability in contemporary literature.' In *The Cambridge Companion to Literature and Disability,* edited by Clare Barker and Stuart Murray, 90–103. Cambridge: Cambridge University Press, 2018.

Naam, Ramez. *Apex*. Nottingham: Angry Robot, 2015.

Naam, Ramez. *Crux*. Nottingham: Angry Robot, 2013.

Naam, Ramez. *More Than Human: Embracing the Promise of Biological Enhancement*. London: Broadway Books, 2005.

Naam, Ramez. *Nexus*. Nottingham: Angry Robot, 2013.

Nakatami, Hajime. 'Introduction: Komatopia.' *Mechademia* 3 (2008): 65–66.

Nayar, Pramod K. *Posthumanism*. Cambridge: Polity, 2014.

'New films throw light on the Arab world.' *The National,* February 6, 2010. www.thenational.ae/arts-culture/new-films-throw-light-on-the-arab-world-1.632583#full.

Nishime, LeiLani. 'Whitewashing yellow futures in *Ex Machina, Cloud Atlas,* and *Advantageous*: gender, labor, and technology in sci-fi film.' *Journal of Asian American Studies* 20, no. 1 (2017): 29–49.

Nootrobox. 'The Complete Full Stack' and 'The Biohacker's Guide.' https://nootrobox.com.

Norden, Martin F. *The Cinema of Isolation: A History of Physical Disabilities in the Movies*. New Brunswick, NJ: Rutgers University Press, 1994.

Nourbakhsh, Illah Reza. *Robot Futures*. Cambridge, MA: MIT Press, 2013.

Nussbaum, Martha C. *Frontiers of Justice: Disability, Nationality, Species Membership*. Cambridge, MA and London: Belknap/Harvard University Press, 2007.

O'Connell, Mark. *To Be a Machine: Adventures Among Cyborgs, Utopians, Hackers, and the Futurists Solving the Modest Problem of Death*. London: Granta, 2017.

O'Dell, Emily Jane. 'From leprosy to *The Willow Tree*: decoding disability and Islamic spirituality in Iranian film.' *Disability and Society* 30, no. 7 (2015): 1123–1126.

Ott, Katherine, David Serlin and Stephen Mihm, Eds. *Artificial Parts, Practical Lives: Modern Histories of Prosthetics*. New York and London: New York University Press, 2002.

Palahniuk, Chuck. 'Insomnia and me: Chuck Palahniuk.' *The Guardian*, April 19, 2014. www.theguardian.com/lifeandstyle/2014/apr/19/chuck-palahniuk-struggles-insomnia.

Palahniuk, Chuck. *Fight Club*. London: Vintage, 2006.

Palahniuk, Chuck. *Invisible Monsters*. London: Vintage, 2003.

Pepperell, Robert. *The Posthuman Condition: Consciousness Beyond the Brian*. Exeter: Intellect, 1995.

Perkowitz, Sidney. *Hollywood Science: Movies, Science, and the End of the World*. New York: Columbia University Press, 2007.

Perkowitz, Sidney. *Digital People: From Bionic Humans to Androids*. Washington, DC: Joseph Henry Press, 2004.

Porter, James. 'Foreword.' In *The Body and Physical Difference: Discourses of Disability*, edited by David T. Mitchell and Sharon L. Snyder, xiii–xiv. Ann Arbor: University of Michigan Press, 1997.

Price, Margaret. 'The bodymind problem and the possibilities of pain.' *Hypatia*, 30, no. 1 (2015): 268–284.

Prince-Hughes, Dawn. *Songs of the Gorilla Nation: My Journey Through Autism*. London: Souvenir, 2004.

Puar, Jasbir K. 'Prognosis time: towards a geopolitics of affect, debility and capacity.' *Women & Performance: A Journal of Feminist Theory* 19, no. 2 (2009): 161–172.

Puar, Jaskir K. *The Right to Maim: Debility, Capacity, Disability*. Durham, NC and London: Duke University Press, 2017.

Pullin, Graham. *Design Meets Disability*. Cambridge, MA and London: MIT Press, 2009.

Quarmby, Katharine. *Scapegoat: Why We Are Failing Disabled People*. London: Portobello, 2011.

Quayson, Ato. *Aesthetic Nervousness: Disability and the Crisis of Representation*. New York: Columbia University Press, 2007.

Redacted. Film. United States: Brian de Palma, 2007.

Reeve, Donna. 'Cyborgs, cripples and iCrip: reflections of the contribution of Haraway to disability studies.' In *Disability and Social Theory*, edited by Dan Goodley, Beverley Hughes and Lennard J. Davis, 91–111. London: Palgrave Macmillan, 2012.

Restrepo. Film. United States: Tim Hetherington and Sebastian Junger, 2010.

Rid, Thomas. *Rise of the Machines: The Lost History of Cybernetics*. Melbourne and London: Scribe, 2016.

Robertson, Jennifer. 'Gendering humanoid robots: robo-sexism in Japan.' *Body and Society* 16, no. 2 (2010): 1–36.

Robocop. Film. United States: Paul Verhoeven, 1987.

Robot & Frank. Film. United States: Jake Schreier, 2012.

Roden, David. *Posthuman Life: Philosophy at the Edge of the Human*. London and New York: Routledge, 2015.

Roh, David, Betsy Huang and Greta Niu, Eds. *Techno-Orientalism: Imagining Asia in Speculative Fiction, History and Media*. New Brunswick, NJ and London: Rutgers University Press, 2015.

Rose, Nikolas. *The Politics of Life Itself: Biomedicine, Power, and Subjectivity in the Twenty-First Century*. Princeton, NJ and Oxford: Princeton University Press, 2007.

Rose, Sarah F. *No Right to Be Idle: The Invention of Disability, 1840s–1930s*. Chapel Hill: The University of North Carolina Press, 2017.

Rose, Steve. '*Ghost in the Shell*'s whitewashing: does Hollywood have an Asian problem?' *The Guardian*, March 31, 2017. www.theguardian.com/film/2017/mar/31/ghost-in-the-shells-whitewashing-does-hollywood-have-an-asian-problem.

Rossini, Manuela. 'Bodies.' In *The Cambridge Companion to Literature and the Posthuman*, edited by Bruce Clarke and Manuela Rossini, 135–169. Cambridge: Cambridge University Press, 2017.

Royakkers, Lambèr and Rinie van Est. 'The cubicle warrior: the marionette of digitalized warfare.' *Ethics and Information Technology* 12 (2010): 289–296.

Royal Academy of Engineering. 'Creating systems that work: principles of engineering systems for the 21st century.' www.raeng.org.uk/publications/reports/rae-systems-report.

Rushing, Janice Hocker and Thomas S. Frentz. *Projecting the Shadow: The Cyborg Hero in American Film*. Chicago, IL and London: The University of Chicago Press, 1995.

Russell, Karen. *Sleep Donation*. Atavist Books, 2014. Kindle.

Ryan, Frances. *Crippled: Austerity and the Demonisation of Disabled People*. London: Verso, 2019.

Samuels, Ellen. *Fantasies of Identification: Disability, Gender, Race*. New York and London: New York University Press, 2014.

Sandberg, Anders. 'Morphological freedom: why we not just want it, but need it.' In *The Transhumanist Reader*, edited by Max More and Natasha Vita-More, 56–64. Chichester: Wiley-Blackwell, 2013.

Sandel, Michael J. *The Case Against Perfection: Ethics in the Age of Genetic Engineering*. Cambridge, MA: Harvard University Press, 2007.

Sandler, Ronald L., Ed. *Ethics and Emerging Technologies*. London: Palgrave Macmillan, 2008: 218–234.

Savulescu, Julian and Nick Bostrom, Eds. *Human Enhancement*. Oxford: Oxford University Press, 2009.

Scarry, Elaine. *The Body in Pain: The Making and Unmaking of the World*. Oxford: Oxford University Press, 1988.

Schleifer, Ronald. *Pain and Suffering*. New York and London: Routledge, 2014.

Schmeink, Lars. *Biopunk Dystopias: Genetic Engineering, Society, and Science Fiction*. Liverpool: Liverpool University Press, 2016.

Schultz, Robert T. 'White guys who prefer not to: from passive resistance ("Bartleby") to terrorist acts (*Fight Club*).' *The Journal of Popular Culture* 44, no. 3 (2011): 593–594.

Shildrick, Margrit. *Dangerous Discourses of Disability, Subjectivity and Sexuality.* Basingstoke: Palgrave Macmillan, 2009.

Shildrick, Margrit. *Embodying the Monster: Encounters with the Vulnerable Self.* London: Sage, 2002.

Shildrick, Margrit. *Leaky Bodies and Boundaries: Feminism, Postmodernism and (Bio)ethics.* London and New York: Routledge, 1997.

Shildrick, Margrit. 'Prosthetic performativity: Deleuzian connections and queer corporealities.' In *Deleuze and Queer Theory,* edited by Chrysanthi Nigianni and Merl Storr, 115–133. Edinburgh: Edinburgh University Press, 2009.

Shildrick, Margrit. 'Re-imagining embodiment: prostheses, supplements and boundaries.' *Somatechnics* 3, no. 2 (2013): 270–286.

Shildrick, Margrit. '"Why should our bodies end at the skin": embodiment, boundaries and somatechnics.' *Hypatia* 30, no. 1 (2015): 13–29.

Short, Sue. *Cyborg Cinema.* Basingstoke: Palgrave Macmillan, 2011.

Shriver, Lionel. *The Mandibles: A Family, 2029–2047.* London: Borough Press, 2017.

Siebers, Tobin. *Disability Aesthetics.* Ann Arbor: University of Michigan Press, 2010.

Siebers, Tobin. *Disability Theory.* Ann Arbor: University of Michigan Press, 2008.

Singer, Peter W. *Wired for War: The Robotics Revolution and Conflict in the Twenty-First Century.* New York: Penguin, 2009.

Smelik, Anneke. 'Film.' In *The Cambridge Companion to Literature and the Posthuman,* edited by Bruce Clarke and Manuela Rossini, 109–120. Cambridge: Cambridge University Press, 2017.

Smith, Marquand and Joanna Morra. 'Introduction.' In *The Prosthetic Impulse: From a Posthuman Present to a Biocultural Future,* edited by Smith and Morra, 1–14. Cambridge, MA and London: MIT Press, 2006.

Smith, Susan. '"Limbitless solutions": the prosthetic arm, *Iron Man* and the science fiction of technoscience.' *Medical Humanities* 42, no. 4 (2016): 259–264.

Sobchack, Vivian. 'A leg to stand on: prosthetics, metaphor and materiality.' In *The Prosthetic Impulse: From a Posthuman Present to a Biocultural Future,* edited by Marquand Smith and Joanna Morra, 17–41. Cambridge, MA: MIT Press, 2006.

Son of Babylon. Film. Iraq: Mohamed Al-Daradji, 2009.

Source Code. Film. United States: Duncan Jones, 2011.

Springer, Claudia. *Electronic Eros: Bodies and Desire in the Postindustrial Age.* London: Athlone, 1996.

Squier, Susan Merrill. *Liminal Lives: Imagining the Human at the Frontiers of Biomedicine.* Durham, NC and London: Duke University Press, 2004.

Squires, Judith. 'Fabulous feminist futures and the lure of cyberculture.' In *Fractal Dreams: New Media in Social Context,* edited by Jon Dovey, 194–216. London: Lawrence and Wishart, 1996.

Srnicek, Nick and Alex Williams. *Inventing the Future: Postcapitalism and a World Without Work,* revised ed. London: Verso, 2016.

Sterling, Bruce. *Schismatrix.* New York: Ace, 1986.

Stock, Gregory. *Redesigning Humans: Choosing Our Genes, Changing Our Future.* Boston, MA: Houghton Mifflin, 2003.

Sunder Rajan, Kaushik. *Biocapital: The Constitution of Postgenomic Life.* Durham, NC and London: Duke University Press, 2006.

Tarnoff, Ben. 'Robots won't just take our jobs – they'll make the rich even richer.' *The Guardian,* March 2, 2017. www.theguardian.com/technology/2017/mar/02/robot-tax-job-elimination-livable-wage.

Tate, Andrew. *Apocalyptic Fiction*. London: Bloomsbury, 2017.
Taylor, Matthew. *Universes Without Us: Posthuman Cosmologies in American Literature*. Minneapolis: University of Minneapolis Press, 2013.
The Dreams of Sparrows. Film. Iraq: Hayder Mousa Daffar, 2005.
'The Guardian view on robots and humanity: passing Go.' *The Guardian*, March 9, 2016. www.theguardian.com/commentisfree/2016/mar/09/the-guardian-view-on-robots-and-humanity-passing-go.
The Hurt Locker. Film. United States: Kathryn Bigelow, 2008.
The Matrix. Film. United States: Larry and Andy Wachowski, 1999.
Toffoletti, Kim. *Cyborgs and Barbie Dolls: Feminism, Popular Culture and the Posthuman Body*. London and New York: I.B. Tauris, 2007.
Tomlinson, John. *The Culture of Speed: The Coming of Immediacy*. London: Sage, 2007.
Tramontane. Film. Lebanon: Vatche Boulghourgian, 2016.
'Transhumanist Declaration.' Various. In *The Transhumanist Reader*, edited by Max More and Natasha Vita-More, 54–55. Chichester: Wiley-Blackwell, 2013.
Turtles Can Fly. Film. Iraq/Kurdistan: Bahman Ghobadi, 2004.
Under the Skin. Film. United Kingdom: Jonathan Glazer, 2013.
Vidali, Amy. 'Seeing what we know: disability and theories of metaphor.' *Journal of Literary and Cultural Disability Studies* 4, no. 1 (2010): 33–54.
Vint, Sherryl. *Bodies of Tomorrow: Technology, Subjectivity, Science Fiction*. Toronto: University of Toronto Press, 2007.
Virilio, Paul. *The Administration of Fear*. With Bertrand Richard. Translated by Ames Hodges. Los Angeles, CA: Semiotext(e), 2012.
Virilio, Paul. *The Lost Dimension*. Translated by D. Moshenburg. New York: Semiotext(e), 1991.
Virilio, Paul. *The Vision Machine*. Translated by J. Rose. London: British Film Institute, 1994.
Vonnegut, Kurt. *Player Piano*. New York: Doubleday, 1999.
Waldby, Catherine. *The Visible Human Project: Informatic Bodies and Posthuman Medicine*. London and New York: Routledge, 2000.
Walker, Matthew. *Why We Sleep: The New Science of Sleep and Dreams*. London: Penguin, 2017.
Weeks, Kathi. *The Problem with Work: Feminism, Marxism, Antiwork Politics, and Postwork Imaginaries*. Durham, NC and London, 2011.
Weheliye, Alexander G. *Habeus Viscus*. Durham, NC: Duke University Press, 2014.
Wendell, Susan. *The Rejected Body*. New York: Routledge, 1996.
Wendell, Susan. 'Unhealthy disabled: treating chronic illnesses as disabilities.' *Hypatia* 16, no. 4 (2001): 17–33.
Wennemann, Daryl J. *Posthuman Personhood*. Lanham, MD: University Press of America, 2013.
Whitehead, Neil and Michael Wesch, Eds. *Human No More: Digital Subjectivities, Unhuman Subjects, and the End of Anthropology*. Boulder: University Press of Colorado, 2012.
Williams, Daniel H. *Robopocalypse*. London: Simon & Schuster, 2011.
Wolfe, Cary. *Animal Rites: American Culture, the Discourse of Species, and Posthumanist Theory*. Chicago, IL: University of Chicago Press, 2013.
Wolfe, Cary. *Before the Law: Humans and Other Animals in a Biopolitical Frame*. Chicago, IL and London: The University of Chicago Press, 2013.

Wolfe, Cary. 'Introduction.' In *Manifestly Haraway,* by Donna Harraway, vii–xiii. Minneapolis: University of Minnesota Press, 2016.
Wolfe, Cary. *What is Posthumanism?.* Minneapolis and London: University of Minnesota Press, 2010.
Womack, Ytasha. *Afrofuturism: The World of Black Sci-Fi and Fantasy Culture.* Chicago, IL: Chicago Review Press, 2013.
Wong, Danielle. 'Dismembered Asian/American android parts in *Ex Machina* as "inorganic" critique.' *Transformations* 29 (2017): 35–51.
World Health Organisation. *World Report on Disability.* WHO, 2011.
Wosk, Julie. *My Fair Ladies: Female Robots, Androids and Other Artificial Eves.* New Brunswick, NJ and London: Rutgers University Press, 2015.
X-Men. Film. United States: Bryan Singer, 2000.
X-Men: The Last Stand. Film. United States: Brett Ratner, 2006.
X2/X-Men 2. Film. United States: Bryan Singer, 2003.
Yuknavitch, Lidia. *The Book of Joan.* Edinburgh: Canongate, 2018.
Zoe. Film. United States: Drake Doremus, 2018.

Index